D0078352

Dispensing Justice Locally

Dispensing Justice Locally

The Implementation and Effects of the Midtown Community Court

Michele Sviridoff
Center for Court Innovation
New York, NY, USA

David B. Rottman
Brian Ostrom
National Center for State Courts
Williamsburg, Virginia, USA

and

Richard Curtis
John Jay College of Criminal Justice
New York, NY, USA

harwood academic publishers

Australia • Canada • France • Germany • India
Japan • Luxembourg • Malaysia • The Netherlands
Russia • Singapore • Switzerland

Amsteldijk 166
1st Floor
1079 LH Amsterdam
The Netherlands

This research project was supported under award 93-IJ-CX-0082 from the National Institute of Justice, Office of Justice Programs, U.S. Department of Justice and under awards SJI-93-12A-E-194 and SJI-93-12A-E-P93-1 from the State Justice Institute. Points of view in this document are those of the authors and do not necessarily represent the official position of the U.S. Department of Justice or of the State Justice Institute.

British Library Cataloguing in Publication Data

Dispensing justice locally : the implementation and effects of the midtown community court
1. New York (N.Y.) . Midtown Community Court
2. Criminology–New York (State)–New York
I. Sviridoff, Michele
345.7′47′01

ISBN 90-5702-614-7

CONTENTS

FIGURES

FOREWORD

Since opening in October 1993, New York City's Midtown Community Court has become a well-established local institution serving the neighborhoods of Times Square, Chelsea and Clinton (formerly known as Hell's Kitchen). The Court does far more than process its caseload of misdemeanor arraignments. It produces more meaningful outcomes—both for the defendants and the neighborhood that has been victimized by crime. This means sentencing offenders to a variety of community service projects that have a palpable effect on the quality of life in Midtown neighborhoods. It means bringing health care professionals, addiction specialists, educators and other social service providers into the courthouse to help solve the problems that often bring defendants to court. And it means reaching into the broader community to identify and respond to problems that don't traditionally enter a court. As a result, individual lives are transformed, streets look better, a neighborhood becomes more of a community. However the Court's contribution may be measured, understanding it depends on human stories.

A Judge's Question

"I like myself," says Midtown defendant, Billy Robertson. "That's the difference." And it's a big difference. At the age of 48, Robertson finally appears to have escaped the destructive routine, based on addiction and petty crime, that he had followed for years. He rightfully claims credit for that himself, but he is the first to acknowledge that he had a lot of help.

Arrested yet again for the shoplifting he committed to support his drug habit, Robertson assumed he faced the usual day or two in a holding cell, suffering the sickness of withdrawal, until he'd be allowed to plead guilty. At that point, he would be sentenced to the time he'd already been held, then released to resume his habit. That was the familiar ritual at the central criminal court Downtown.

But at the Midtown Community Court, the judge paused over his record: some 40 arrests and 30 convictions, all for misdemeanors like criminal trespass and possession of stolen property. "Mr. Robertson," she asked him. "Do you have a problem?"

"Yeah, I do," Robertson responded. It was the first time he'd ever been asked such a thing by a judge.

"Do you need any help?"

When Robertson said he figured he did, the judge referred him to a caseworker who began asking a lot of questions about his background, his previous attempts at drug treatment, his willingness to try again. Impressed that he didn't attempt to lie about his record, the caseworker said he would argue for treatment rather than jail.

If Robertson were to agree, however, he would go right into detox from court—no chance to return home for a final binge. The judge would receive regular reports about his progress in the program, including drug test results. If he didn't get with it in a serious way, she could send him to jail. No court had ever offered Robertson terms like this. He decided he was ready for them. He had a son approaching his teens; it was time to get control of his life.

With the judge's approval, the caseworkers hustled Robertson off to upstate New York for a couple of weeks in a detox center, followed by immediate enrollment in a treatment program based at a Catholic mission in Albany. All went well for several weeks until Fathers' Day arrived and Robertson decided to celebrate by inviting a woman he knew from the city to come up for a visit. They wound up spending the day at a nearby hotel.

When Robertson returned to the mission, he got into an argument with the priests, who told him sternly that they disapproved of his absence. Angry, Robertson took off for New York City, going AWOL though he was only a week or two from a successful graduation.

Back in town, he might have tried to disappear, but he felt bad about checking out on a caseworker who had taken an interest in him. A few days after his return to the city, Robertson went up to the Court and turned himself in.

"I was scared," he recalls, since the judge retained the power to send him to jail. As it turned out, however, the caseworkers were not surprised by his early departure from treatment. "Relapse is part of recovery," one explains, recalling Robertson's case.

But they weren't about to cut him much slack. To avoid jail now, they told him, he would have to re-enter another treatment program and stick it out for the next year. Still committed to getting better, Robertson agreed and went willingly when court-based case managers found him a place in a program run by Project Renewal on the Lower East Side of Manhattan.

There he would stay for eighteen months, with no relapses; eventually the decision to stay became his more than the program's as he began to understand how much his own addiction had depended on the company of other addicts. He didn't want to leave until he knew he could establish himself in a new life. "I wanted to stay clean," he says. "I wasn't leaving until I had all I needed."

The program helped him prepare. Project Renewal found him a job washing dishes at the restaurant atop the Times Square Hotel, a midtown residence for the homeless that also operates a number of businesses. And the program's counselors encouraged him to enroll at Audrey Cohen College, where he obtained a high school GED and completed 50 hours of course work towards a degree.

While all this went on, Robertson was required to remain in close contact with the Midtown Community Court, showing up for meetings with caseworkers and going before the judge once a month. He began to look forward to these appearances. "She'd smile," he says of the judge, "and say, 'Billy, you're doing good. Keep up the good work.'" Then one day, she said, "Mr. Robertson, I'm proud of you. You don't need to come back."

As his recovery strengthened, Project Renewal decided to put Robertson to work at the shelter, running therapy groups. When the agency opened a similar program at the Fort Washington Armory in Washington Heights, it offered Robertson a job there. The jobs, not to mention the newfound self esteem, enabled Robertson to start a new life in a new neighborhood, creating a home for himself and his son. Though they remained a part of his recent past, the years of total immersion in petty theft, alcohol and drug abuse now seemed remote.

"I think Billy stopped seeing drug use as fun, as acceptable," a Midtown caseworker observes. "He became more of an adult; he got back to the people in his life who are important to him, like his son.... To make that kind of transition is nothing short of awesome. Drug use permeated every aspect of his life."

Robertson himself understands the process in simpler terms. During all the years of addiction, he had contemplated treatment a number of times, but never felt pressured into doing anything about it beyond a few abortive attempts at detox. The Court combined a judge willing to apply the necessary pressure with attentive caseworkers and the resources to follow up. "It all started with the Court," Robertson says. "None of this would have happened if that judge had not asked me if I needed help."

Painting 101

Walking up Tenth Avenue, you can spot the wall from more than a block away: a 30-foot expanse of storefront, a full story high, painted powder blue. The color, startling as it is among the urban browns and grays, isn't that remarkable in itself, but it astonishes for another reason: on this day, on this block, it is totally free of graffiti.

The blue wall ought to be an easy, juicy target for crews of young graffiti writers who roam the Hell's Kitchen neighborhood in the middle of the night, armed with spray paint. But it remains free of "tags" like FORT and SHILO because of another crew that goes to work during the day.

This group, led by a work supervisor from the Midtown Community Court, assembles each morning on the sixth floor of the court building. People convicted of low level crimes—shoplifting, turnstile jumping, prostitution and, yes, graffiti writing—show up to complete their community service sentences. For the past five years since the Court opened for business in 1993, the court-ordered anti-graffiti painters have gone into the neighborhood, to paint over the illegal scrawls that appear by night.

They have visited the blue wall about five times, making clear to anyone who writes on it that their work won't last for long. That persistence sends a message. After it was painted over for the fifth time, the midnight writers gave up, deciding to leave the wall alone.

"Initially when they were painting it, the graffiti would come back within a week," says Sarah Desmond, head of the non-profit Housing Conservation Coordinators, the community housing agency that uses the storefront as its headquarters. "Now it doesn't."

On a given day, the painting crew numbers as many as five, as few as one, depending on the flow of sentenced offenders. No experience is necessary: the work supervisor gives sidewalk lessons in brush and roller technique, along with basic neatness.

On a recent morning, he stood before the heavily defaced side wall of an Indian restaurant. With him were two blonde young women named Ruby and Lisa, arrested on a low-level prostitution charge the day before. Though both claimed to be 21, they looked younger, giggling and wisecracking as they pulled on disposable jumpsuits, then struggled into blue vests marked with the Court's logo.

They were childhood friends, they said, who had grown up in a rural part of Maine and come down to New York seeking fast times and fast money in the city's sex industry. Normally, they said, they worked in Queens, where they were rarely bothered by police. Their venture into Manhattan had resulted in their first arrest. "It was dumb, just stupid and greedy" to come into town, Ruby said. In addition to the day of painting, the judge had ordered them to attend a "sex class" that brought experienced and naive women together to focus on the dangers of prostitution.

What they would learn there remained to be seen, but this morning they were learning how to paint a wall with a roller. The supervisor helped them pour paint in an aluminum tray, transfer it to the roller with a few strokes, then apply it to the wall. The women took over, tentatively at first, then getting into it.

"You find people that don't know how to paint," the supervisor said. "I have to give them a quick class in painting 101. Afterwards, they say, 'This is not bad. Maybe I should go home and paint my room.' I say, 'Why don't you stop what you're doing for a living and try to get a couple of painting jobs?'"

After a time, however, the work began to bore Lisa and Ruby. The weather was quite warm, and they started begging for a break. The supervisor made them paint for another half hour before he relented, allowing them fifteen minutes.

Has he had any more serious problems with recalcitrant workers? Some complain more vigorously, he said, or they plead back trouble or other ailments. The most resistant of all are youngsters who have written graffiti themselves and consider it a major breach of peer etiquette, if not a fighting offense, to paint over someone else's work.

"I put it to them simply," the supervisor said. "I tell them, 'Listen, one day of community service could be worth as much as fifteen days on Rikers Island. You choose.' Before I even finish, they're saying, 'OK, where do I start?'"

Despite more griping, Ruby and Lisa wound up putting in a good morning of work on the large wall. When they finished, they were able to stand back in their spattered jumpsuits and regard it with a sense of satisfaction, soon reinforced by words of praise and gratitude from the restaurant's manager.

And if they were not yet ready to acknowledge the virtues of decent employment, they at least felt the burden of pursuing their trade in a place where courts extract punishments in terms of useful sweat. "I think I've learned my lesson," Lisa said wearily.

Whatever it meant to them, the value of their work was hardly lost on the community. At one point during the morning, a woman approached the scene outside the Indian restaurant and introduced herself as a member of a Ninth Avenue tenants' association. Could the crew paint out graffiti on pull-down gates along her block? The supervisor promised to go by and take pictures of the gates, then schedule a day to do the work.

In her office behind the blue wall on Tenth Avenue, meanwhile, Rita Rodriguez of the Housing Conservation Coordinators credits the graffiti program with lifting the neighborhood's spirits. "It makes such a difference," she said. "It feels so much better now when you walk down the street. Graffiti depreciates everything, and your own self-esteem as well."

"The Only Way We Can Talk"

About a dozen people are crowded into the small conference room. The atmosphere is thick with conflict. At one end of the table sit the owner of a music bar, a couple of his managers and his sound man. At the other sit a number of tenants who live above the bar.

Their dispute has been going on for many months. On weekend nights, bands and disc jockeys turn up the volume for the bar's customers; the tenants are losing sleep.

Between them sits a mediator from the Midtown Community Court. After the ritual going around the room with names, the mediator asks who wants to speak first.

The bar owner responds. He recounts all he's done in response to noise complaints. He's had an engineer go over his premises and suggest ways to insulate, and he's permanently disabled the heaviest bass speakers—the ones that shook the whole building when they pounded out certain notes.

A couple of the residents acknowledge some improvement, but others remain unmoved. They refer to an ailing tenant who can't sleep when the music starts. The noise is surely threatening his health.

So the bar owner plays his next card. He's prepared to let technology take over, he says. He'll install decibel meters on all the sound systems and instruct all his people not to let the noise exceed a level disturbing to the tenants. The problem will be to determine that level. Will the tenants agree to give his people access to their apartments one night when the music is on so that they can determine when it gets too loud and set the meters accordingly?

This looks like a breakthrough. The tenants are skeptical but they don't really have a good argument against the idea; the proof will remain in what it's like when they try to sleep. In the meantime, why not give the meters a try?

At this point the mediator steps in. He reviews the proposal from the bar owner and makes sure the tenants understand exactly what they are expected to do in order to test for noise levels. The meeting ends with both sides agreeing to work together on the practical solution.

The meeting has brought everyone together for a fair discussion that avoids the red tape of more formal bureaucratic and legal process. And it might eventually end the dispute.

The Court offers the mediation service for practical reasons of its own. In a number of cases, the meetings have resolved disputes headed for violence, arrests and a place on the Court's calendar.

For example, a chronically angry man failed to clean up after his dog and assaulted an elderly neighbor who complained. In a mediated solution, the assaulter's sisters agreed to take responsibility for cleaning up after his dog. In another case, conflicts over parked cars and signage threatened violence between the owner of an art gallery and workers at the taxi-repair lot next door. A mediator helped the two sides resolve some immediate practical questions and secured a basic agreement to talk out future problems before they could escalate.

The mediators also lend their skills for negotiations that involve the whole community. One brings together representatives of the police, residents, businesses, social service providers and other interested groups to discuss areas, identified by local police and community members as disorderly "hot spots." Mediators facilitate discussions aimed at developing effective ways to deal with the problems associated with each "hot spot."

"Mediation has two purposes," explains a leader of the mediation team. "One is to respond directly to disputes. The other is to identify issues of common concern and encourage partnership, getting people with divergent interests to work with each other on difficult issues. I believe that's a good thing to be doing in a community."

Constructive communication solves problems. That's a point people tend to understand, even when the process bogs down. At the end of one frustrating session—one party to the dispute failed to show, angering those who did—the mediator asks if it's worth trying to convene another meeting.

"Yes it is," a young woman responds immediately. "This is the only way we can talk to each other."

David Anderson

ACKNOWLEDGMENTS

It is a daunting task to acknowledge the many people and organizations who assisted in this research effort. Our research on the Midtown Community Court benefited greatly from the contributions of criminal justice professionals, community members, Midtown Community Court staff, as well as staff from the National Center for State Courts (NCSC) and the Center for Court Innovation (CCI), a project of the Fund for the City of New York. Members of these groups helped explain the intricacies of the New York City criminal justice system; assemble research databases; identify respondents for focus groups; explain procedures at the Court; interpret the stories behind quantitative analyses; and assemble and review preliminary drafts. In addition, many confidential respondents from the community and the criminal justice system contributed time and effort in individual and group interviews.

The project owes a major debt to members of the New York State Judiciary—Judith S. Kaye, Chief Judge of the New York State Courts; Jonathan Lippman, Chief Administrative Judge of the New York State Courts; Robert G.M. Keating, the Administrative Judge of the New York City Criminal Courts during the planning and early operations of the Midtown Community Court; and Judy Harris Kluger, the current Administrative Judge of the New York City Criminal Courts, who was the presiding judge at the Court throughout the research period. It owes a similar debt to Mayor Rudolph Giuliani and members of the New York City government who provided support for the Court throughout the demonstration period, including Katherine Lapp, then the Mayor's Criminal Justice Coordinator; Michael Jacobson, then the Commissioner of the Department of Correction; and Martin P. Murphy, now a Criminal Court judge, who was the Deputy Coordinator for Criminal Justice Services during the research period. Under their leadership, the Court was established as a demonstration project that required rigorous assessment of its impacts on court operations, community conditions and community attitudes. Their fundamental commitment to the Midtown project helped open doors to the research.

The research owes a similar debt to those who conceived and planned the Midtown Community Court. Both Herb Sturz, who pushed the planning of the Court into motion, and John Feinblatt, who coordinated all aspects of planning, developing and operating the Court, recognized the need for evaluative research from the earliest stages. This recognition bred an "open door" policy, ensuring that research staff had immediate, direct access to information about all aspects of the project. Their deep understanding of the importance of integrating research and operations in developing demonstration projects enriched both the process of developing the Midtown Community Court and the research about it.

In addition, we are indebted to the many organizations and individuals that provided support for the development of the Court. The product of a unique public-private partnership, the demonstration project received support from 32 foundations and corporations, many with roots in the Midtown community. The project's Community Advisory Board was a core support for both the project and the research. And, from the very first, Gerald Schoenfeld of the Shubert Organization, Gretchen Dykstra of the Times Square Business Improvement District and Peter Goldmark of the Rockefeller Foundation, served as part of the engine that made both the project and the research happen.

The research also benefited from the support of Dr. Sally T. Hillsman in various guises. First, as Director of the Research Division of the National Center for State Courts, Dr. Hillsman helped engineer the productive collaboration between research staff at the National Center and the Fund for the City of New York. Later, as Deputy Director of the National Institute of Justice, she continued to be a welcome source of enthusiastic support and sage advice.

The project is also indebted to David Tevelin, Director of the State Justice Institute and Jeremy Travis, Director of the National Institute of Justice, for providing the financial support and encouragement needed to carry out the evaluation. The project's monitors at these agencies—Mary DeCarlo at the State Justice Institute and Laurie Bright at the National Institute of Justice—provided welcome guidance and warm support throughout. The project also owes thanks to Nick Demos of the Center for Substance Abuse Treatment, which supported a demonstration project providing substance abuse treatment initiatives at the Court; there was substantial synergy between this research and CSAT-funded research on court-based treatment initiatives.

The project also received strong support from members of separate NIJ and SJI research advisory committees, as well as from members of the Institutional Review Boards convened by NCSC. Formal advisors included a fertile mix of criminal justice researchers and professionals—including John Goldkamp, George Cole, Hon. Bruce Beaudin, Kelly Bacon, Steve Belenko, Steve

Mollica and William Carbone—who reviewed the initial research design and made constructive recommendations about how it might be modified.

Assistance in obtaining data for the research The research could not have been carried out without the assistance of organizations and individuals who helped provide data for both quantitative and qualitative analysis. Staff at New York City's Criminal Justice Agency (CJA)—Jerry McElroy, Mary Eckert, Freda Solomon, Frank Sergi and many others—provided major assistance in both designing and carrying out the research. CJA staff were valuable partners in reviewing the data elements needed for the research; ensuring access to and assembling the baseline and follow-up data sets; identifying potential gaps in the data that could be filled by information from other organizations; and providing additional information as needed to help analyze emerging implementation issues. In addition, Freda Solomon provided a valuable final review of the text and sage editorial assistance.

The Office of the District Attorney of New York County cooperated fully with efforts to compile data on community service and treatment sentences imposed at 100 Centre Street. Paul Schechtman and Barbara Jones facilitated our access to databases maintained by the District Attorney's office, subject to appropriate assurances of confidentiality. Joe Enright, Deputy MIS director, Yvonne Dancy and Bill Tsigaras responded with patience and professionalism to several requests that diverted their attention from pressing day-to-day concerns.

The project also relied on data from the New York State Division of Criminal Justice Services (DCJS) to supplement CJA information about prior criminal history for members of the baseline and comparison samples. The research owes thanks to Paul Schechtman, Barry Sample, Richard DeHais, Bruce Frederick, Dean Mauro, Newton Walker and Harry Baxi of DCJS who helped research staff gain access to these data.

Blanka Eckstein who conducted baseline and follow-up focus groups as a sub-contractor to the project was another source of valuable data and insight. Ms. Eckstein transcribed and organized interview data into meaningful categories and drafted rich, detailed reports, documenting the findings of baseline and follow-up focus groups. This report draws extensively on the rich portrait of community attitudes and opinions that Blanka provided.

Research respondents The project also owes thanks to respondents from local criminal justice organizations and the Midtown community who participated in confidential focus groups, panel interviews and on-going informational and background interviews. In-depth interviews with community leaders and activists allowed us to incorporate local voices and insights into our evolving understanding of the implementation of the Midtown Community Court, its reception by the local community and its effects on quality-of-life conditions. Their willingness to be interviewed periodically throughout the research period added depth to the research.

The research is also indebted to a number of people within the New York State Court System who helped explain routine court procedures and how they might differ at the Midtown Community Court. Court representatives provided a patient explanation of misdemeanor arraignment procedures in New York City and access to information about existing alternative sanction programs at the centralized Downtown court. Thanks for this and much more to Hon. Charles Solomon, Bill Daly, Brian Wynne, Mike Magnani, Joann Sarro and Ann Bader.

Staff at the Midtown Community Court provided major assistance to the process evaluation, explaining changes in court operations; permitting researchers to observe all aspects of court operations; and inviting them to sit in on "debriefing" sessions, exploring emerging operational issues. John Williams, Amanda Burden, Eric Lee, John Megaw, Arleen Ramos, Jeff Hobbs and William Figueroa all provided important insights about how the Court functioned, how it related to the Midtown community, how alternative sanctions were monitored and how Court staff interacted with community-based social service providers.

Assistance in carrying out the research Thanks are also due to the dedicated researchers and technology staff at NCSC, CCI and John Jay College who helped gather, analyze, interpret and explain research data.

At the NCSC, evaluation staff relied on Sally Hillsman, Gene Flango, Bill Hewitt and Pam Casey for sage research advice and a deep well of knowledge about the state courts. Neil La Fountain took the primary responsibility for converting numerous and varied data sets into a single, comparable file of information about arraignment outcomes in New York County. His dedication and expertise made the analysis in Chapter Six possible. Ken Smith served as a research assistant during the evaluation's formative months. Mary Hogan administered the various contracts between NCSC and FCNY. Interest in the Midtown experiment prompted the NCSC to provide services and staffing for the research above and beyond contractual obligations.

Thanks are also due to FCNY staff. Mary McCormick, the President of FCNY, provided an early home for the project so it could leap into action. Michael Rosen, the Director of Fiscal and Administrative Services, helped clarify fiscal and administrative issues that might otherwise have been roadblocks. Amy Barnett, Director of Incubator Programs, provided a steady stream of advice and support. Miriam Ortiz made sure that fiscal procedures ran smoothly.

Midtown research staff were responsible for assembling and analyzing research databases, producing charts, reviewing and editing multiple drafts of the report and assembling the document. Many thanks for the tireless and upbeat support of Rob Weidner, Amy Walter, Greg Steinberg, Jennie Uleman, Caitlin Featherstone and Tamara Dumanovsky, for the major-league editorial assistance provided by Greg Berman and for the assistance of student interns, particularly Liz Wells, Linnea Basu and Laura Hamady.

Assembling the research database on defendant characteristics, case outcomes and alternative sanction compliance at the Court was greatly facilitated by the developers of the Court's technology. Thanks are owed to Richard Zorza, John Williams, Artur Rubenstein and Elena Volenskaya who ensured that research staff would have early access to the Midtown database.

The project was also enriched by graduate student assistants who helped Richard Curtis monitor street conditions in the Midtown area. Particular thanks are owed to Edwina Richardson who assisted Mr. Curtis in interviewing defendants at the Midtown and Downtown courts.

Finally, the project owes an additional debt to William Figueroa and the participants of the Times Square Ink, the Midtown Community Court's copy shop/job training project, for their assistance in producing multiple drafts of this document.

It also owes a deep debt to Amy Walter at Midtown, for her extensive work in helping to turn the original research report into a book.

To all of these individuals and organizations, we offer our deep appreciation and a heartfelt recognition that we could not have done it without you.

CHAPTER ONE

INTRODUCTION

In October 1993, the Midtown Community Court opened as a three-year demonstration project, designed to test the ability of criminal courts to forge links with the community in developing a problem-solving approach to quality-of-life offenses. The product of a two-year-long planning effort, the project brought together planning staff from the New York State Unified Court System (UCS); the City of New York; and the Fund for the City of New York (FCNY), a private non-profit organization. The purpose was to design a community-based courthouse that would provide effective and accessible justice for quality-of-life crimes—low-level offenses like prostitution, shoplifting, minor drug possession, turnstile jumping and disorderly conduct—that often arise in the Times Square area and the surrounding residential neighborhoods of Clinton and Chelsea.

The decision to establish the Midtown Community Court grew out of a belief that the traditional court response to low-level offenses was neither constructive nor meaningful to victims, defendants or the community. This belief was grounded in several propositions, including the following:

- that centralized courts, which focus the lion's share of their resources on serious crimes, devote insufficient attention to quality-of-life offenses;
- that both communities and criminal justice officials share a deep frustration about the criminal court processing of low-level offenses, which is widely viewed as producing "revolving door justice;"
- that community members feel shut off and isolated from large-scale centralized courts;
- that low-level offenses like prostitution, street-level drug possession and vandalism, although often labeled as "victimless," in fact erode the quality of life in communities and create an atmosphere in which serious crime flourishes; and
- that when communities are victimized by quality-of-life crimes, they have a stake in the production of justice and a role to play at the courthouse.

The Midtown Community Court was designed to do substantially more than replicate the routine case processing of low-level crimes in a neighborhood-based setting. It was established to help solve problems that were specific to the Court's Midtown location: high concentrations of quality-of-life crimes; broad community dissatisfaction with court outcomes; visible signs of disorder; and clusters of persistent high-rate offenders with serious problems, including addiction and homelessness. The goal, as the planning team put it, was "to make justice constructive, visible and efficient—and, above all, to make it responsive and meaningful to victims, defendants and the community" (Midtown Community Court, 1994: p. 4).

In developing the Court, project planners collaborated with community groups, criminal justice officials and representatives of local government to identify ways in which a community court could achieve these goals. This collaborative process produced an approach to low-level crime that was designed to "pay back" the victimized community, while providing help for the underlying problems of defendants. As the Court's coordinating team described it:

> *After engaging in dialogue with the community, social service providers, criminal justice experts, the police, victims and former defendants, the Midtown Community Court adopted a new agenda—one that both punishes and helps defendants.... This new agenda is based on simple ideas and common sense: If a defendant pays back the harmed community and at the same time receives help solving problems that can lead to crime, justice in low-level cases can be both restorative to the community and constructive to the defendant (Midtown Community Court, 1994: p. 5).*

The implementation of this new agenda required a fundamental re-thinking of the nature of the courthouse, the information available to the Court and the role that might be played by community-based organizations:

> *(T)his problem-solving approach demands new information, new tools and new partnerships. The Court has to have information about defendants at its fingertips—facts, for example, about substance abuse, homelessness and prior compliance with court sanctions—in order to craft individualized sentences. Community-based organizations must be ready to supervise community service work projects. Non-profit agencies must have staff in place to provide substance abuse treatment, heath care, education and other social services to defendants in the courthouse itself. The community and the*

Court must be ready—and willing—to work together every day (Midtown Community Court, 1994: p. 5).

The process of re-thinking how a community-based court might promote a community-focused, problem-solving agenda led planners to introduce a number of features that depart substantially from "business as usual" in New York City criminal courts. These include:

- a coordinating team, working in partnership with court administrators, to foster collaboration with the community and other criminal justice agencies; oversee the planning, development and operations of court-based programs; and develop ideas for new court-based programs;
- an assessment team, operating between arrest and arraignment, to determine whether a defendant has a substance abuse problem, a place to sleep, a history of mental illness, etc.;
- a resource coordinator to match defendants with drug treatment, community service and other sanctions;
- innovative technology, to provide immediate access to information needed to inform judicial decision-making;
- space for court-based social service providers to address underlying problems of defendants that can contribute to continuing criminal involvement;
- community service projects specifically designed to "pay back" the community harmed by crime;
- a Community Advisory Board to keep the Court abreast of quality-of-life problems in the community, identify new community service projects to address these problems, help plan new projects and provide feedback about the Court;
- court-based mediation to address community-level conflicts, rather than individual disputes; and
- a court-based research unit, to feed back information on case processing and case outcomes, defendant compliance with court conditions and the quality of life in the community, and to suggest adjustments to the experiment as it proceeds.

Need for research As a demonstration project, the Midtown Community Court required rigorous evaluation to document its evolution, identify the characteristics that distinguish the Court from the centralized court and examine its impacts on case outcomes, compliance with community-based sanctions, local quality-of-life problems and community attitudes toward the Court. The primary questions to be explored in examining the Midtown Community Court concern the effects of the effort to dispense justice locally. Although it was designed to change misdemeanor case processing in a variety of ways, the defining characteristic of the Midtown Community Court is the fact that it is a *community* court. A primary focus of the research, therefore, was to examine what it means to *be* a community court—how the concept was defined during the planning period, how it was operationalized during the Court's start-up period, how potential impacts were envisioned by project planners and the extent to which those impacts were realized.

Beginning in 1993, with funds from the State Justice Institute, the National Institute of Justice and the Center for Substance Abuse Treatment (CSAT), research staff at the National Center for State Courts (NCSC), in collaboration with research staff at the Midtown Community Court, have been conducting the first phase of a multi-method research project, designed to examine the implementation and effects of the Court during the first eighteen months. This report presents the findings of that research.

PROJECT ORIGINS

Underlying Problems

The lack of constructive responses to low-level offenses has taken a toll on urban neighborhoods. In some communities, high concentrations of low-level crimes like prostitution, low-level drug possession and sales, shoplifting, vandalism, graffiti and turnstile jumping have substantially eroded the quality of life. In recent years, there has been a growing recognition that high concentrations of low-level crime in urban neighborhoods not only breed fear but also attract more serious crime (Wilson and Kelling, 1982). Residents cite quality-of-life problems as a central factor in decisions about moving out of the city.[1] Large and small-scale businesses pay close attention to levels of crime and disorder in deciding where to locate. Economic development efforts run aground because of concerns about low-level crime and disorder. Yet, the criminal court's response to low-level crimes has rarely impressed the community, the victim or the defendant that such crimes are taken seriously.

Frustration with "business as usual" in low-level courts is widespread among judges, police and community residents alike.

In New York City each day, judges, prosecutors, defense attorneys and court administrators confront hundreds of misdemeanants, many of whom have appeared before the court multiple times for similar offenses.[2] In large cities around the country, the routine processing of low-level offenses has been widely recognized as providing little satisfaction to court personnel or community members. Community surveys consistently point to public dissatisfaction with the outcomes provided by lower courts as well as public support for an expanded use of alternative sanctions (Supreme Judicial Court, Commonwealth of Massachusetts, 1992; Yankelovich, Skelly and White, 1978).

Without suitable alternative punishments at the centralized court or available jail space, many judges have come to believe that the range of available sentences for low-level offenses is too limited. Policy analysts report that, in some urban courts, the criminal justice process itself (arrest, time served before arraignment, bail forfeiture) has, in itself, taken the place of punishment for low-level offenses (Feeley, 1979). Community members complain that courts provide little remedy for the problems that bother them most. Yet intermediate sanction programs (community service, substance abuse treatment), which have the capacity to provide more constructive responses to low-level offenses, have not been used extensively and have not been closely linked to either the courthouse or the communities where crimes occurred.

Although quality-of-life offenses have been traditionally viewed as victimless crimes, policy makers and community groups have increasingly recognized that communities themselves are victimized by these offenses (Wilson and Kelling, 1982). Neighborhood organizations, working in partnership with community police officers, have lobbied to insert Community Impact Statements into defendant case files. Court watch groups have monitored the performance of individual judges and scrutinized judicial response to specific offenses. Yet, centralized criminal courts have rarely responded to these initiatives by providing a forum for the community to have a voice. In fact, courts have traditionally attempted to insulate themselves from community influence.

Police officers feel just as disenfranchised from the court process as the community. In New York City, they frequently complain that they receive little feedback about court outcomes and that the "courts don't back them up." Both police and community members blame the courts for turning the criminal justice system into a "revolving door."

Centralized criminal courts are also plagued by other problems, including inefficiency and a lack of coordination with other criminal justice agencies. Many urban courts are crowded, chaotic and overwhelmed. Defendants face lengthy waits between arrest and arraignment. Police officers are kept off the streets as they deliver arrested offenders to distant centralized courts and wait for complaints to be drawn. Court administrators, pressuring judges to move their calendars quickly, send a message, however unwittingly, that rewards quantity over quality.

Purpose

The Midtown Community Court was created in response to multiple problems, including high concentrations of quality-of-life crimes, community dissatisfaction with the court system's response and an insufficient range of sentence alternatives for these offenses. A fundamental goal of the Court was to build a bridge between courts and communities, based on a common recognition of the need for a more constructive response to misdemeanor crime and crimes of lesser severity.

Before the Court opened, planning staff delineated five ways in which a community-based court could improve justice:

1) *Justice would be swifter.* Mindful that "justice delayed is justice denied," the Court would design sentences that stress immediacy and certainty. Immediate sentencing to perform community-based work projects and/or participate in treatment would enforce the message that crime has consequences and allow service providers to engage defendants promptly in education, treatment or prevention.
2) *Justice would be more visible to the community.* The Court would be accessible to the public, and a Community Advisory Board would help guide the experiment. Offenders would pay back the community through visible work projects carried out in the Midtown area.
3) *Police enforcement efforts for low-level offenses would be encouraged.* The Court would augment the NYPD's community policing program by providing an array of problem-solving tools—community work projects; services for addicts, prostitutes and the homeless. By making the Court's sentences more constructive, the Court would encourage enforcement efforts for these minor offenses.

4) *The Court would marshal the energy of local residents and businesses.* The Court would work with local residents, businesses, social service organizations and law enforcement to forge creative, cooperative solutions to quality-of-life problems that each group now contends with alone. This would broaden the scope of remedies available to the Court in low-level cases.
5) *The Court would understand that communities are victims too.* In a centralized court low-level crimes tend to be seen as isolated incidents, rather than as ongoing quality-of-life conditions. By understanding the magnitude, scope and nature of local quality-of-life crimes, the Court would be able to address the neighborhood's problems.

Research and Policy Influences

The planning for the Court was influenced by emerging criminal justice research and policy literature. As discussed above, the project was grounded in research on criminal courts, indicating that, in some urban settings, the criminal justice process had taken the place of punishment for low-level offenses (Feeley, 1979). Planners were also influenced by the increasing interest in community-oriented policing, the growing effort to promote alternative sanctions and the development of treatment-focused drug courts. Other influences included literature on the role of victims in the criminal justice process, the restorative justice movement and initiatives that specifically promote neighborhood-based justice. Together, these influences helped shape planners' vision of what a community-based courthouse could be.

Community policing: solving community problems In part, the development of the Midtown Community Court represents an extension of the principles of community policing. Criminal justice professionals in recent years have grown increasingly conscious of the complex interrelationships among quality-of-life offenses, perceptions of disorder, levels of fear in urban neighborhoods and the incidence of more serious crime (Kelling and Coles, 1996; Skogan, 1990; Wilson and Kelling, 1982). Based on the belief that community-based disorder poses a serious threat to public safety, neighborhood-oriented policing programs in New York and elsewhere have attempted to reduce disorder, combat fear and involve community members in the solution of the problems that bother them most (McElroy, Cosgrove and Sadd, 1992; Goldstein,

1990; Greene and Mastrofski, 1988; Trojanowicz and Carter, 1988; Pate et al, 1986).

Many neighborhood-oriented policing programs rely on a collaborative problem-solving approach that analyzes neighborhood problems, implements tactics designed to address those problems and reviews the effects of attempted solutions (Goldstein, 1990). Court planners proposed that courts, like community policing initiatives, could provide constructive solutions to community-based conditions of disorder. By designing community service projects that help clean up local "hot spots" and "eyesores," the Court was designed to become a partner in the community's overall problem-solving effort.

The Court's link to community policing goes beyond its effort to build community partnerships and to promote community problem-solving. It also builds on the *imagery* of the community policing movement. Like community policing, the concept of the community court is supported by images from an idealized past, drawn upon to support a vision of a better future (Mastrofski, 1991; Moore and Kelling, 1983). As some commentators on community policing have acknowledged, part of the function of community focused reform is symbolic—an effort to tap "a nostalgia for the U.S. democratic grass-roots tradition of citizen initiative and (meld) it with impatience with an unresponsive law and cumbersome government bureaucracy" (Mastrofski, 1991: p. 47).

Just as community policing looks back to a quieter time, when neighborhood cops maintained order on a well-known beat, community courts evoke images of a time when the courthouse stood at the center of the village green as the local embodiment of justice. Both community policing and community courts represent reactions to an era of centralization, bureaucratization and professionalism. Community policing stands in contrast to an age of police in radio patrol cars, cut off from the community, responding to calls for service issued by a central dispatcher. Similarly, community courts represent a step beyond centralized, high-volume criminal courts, dominated by the need to manage caseloads and dispensing "revolving door justice." Both are haunted by early twentieth century images of local corruption: beat cops and judges on the "take," political favors, cronyism and preferential treatment to favored community groups.

Both of these community-focused criminal justice initiatives attempt to combine a small scale, community focus and intimate local knowledge with the virtues of centralization:

administrative oversight, advanced technology and a capacity for sophisticated analysis. In addition, they introduce a new concern for incorporating the community's voice in identifying local problems and working to develop collaborative solutions to those problems.

Alternative Sanctions In the effort to develop appropriate tools for solving local problems, project planners were also influenced by research literature on alternative sanctions and the effort to develop non-incarcerative sentences to provide proportionate punishment for jail-bound offenders. In recent years, a wide variety of alternatives to incarceration have been designed for jail- and prison-bound populations—intensive supervision programs, shock incarceration, drug treatment as an alternative to incarceration and electronic monitoring, to name a few (Von Hirsch and Ashworth, 1992; Morris and Tonry, 1990; Clear and Hardyman, 1990; Petersilia, 1987; MacKenzie, 1990).

Over the past two decades, the Community Service Sentencing Project (CSSP) in New York City has targeted high-rate misdemeanants, approximately half of whom are assessed as being "jail bound" (McDonald, 1982). Like the Court, this program was designed both as an alternative to jail and an alternative to a "walk." In the early stages of program development, CSSP planners were explicit about the value of developing *both* alternatives to jail and alternatives to nothing:

> *The conventional view, these days, is that programs should be avoided to the extent that they increase either the number of people who are under the net of social control or the intensity of that control (its burdensomeness, for example)... But this by no means disposes of the issue. There is another view, which might be stated as follows: the net of social control is presently inadequate—society does not even attempt to control the great bulk of offenders who are brought before the courts, but releases them after dismissal of the cases, or upon illusory sentences such as probation or conditional discharge.... (T)he formal process is not equipped with effective sanctions short of incarceration with which to signify to offenders that violation of laws will not be tolerated. (McDonald, 1986: p. 39).*

In fact, a substantial body of research literature has demonstrated that many programs, designed primarily as an alternative to costly incarceration, have served instead as alternatives to probation—that the programs have often failed in their efforts to reduce jail time:

> *The major reason why these new punishments fail to save prison beds or money is that they are too often applied to the wrong offender. This is because nowhere have they been built into a comprehensive, graduated and principled punishment system based on defined sentencing policies. They have been scattered and isolated experiments, mostly sailing under the banner of 'alternatives' to imprisonment (Morris and Tonry, 1992: p. 365).*

The Court emphasized both alternatives to "nothing" and alternatives to jail. Planners sought to develop a graduated set of short-term punishments that would be meaningful to the Court's primary stakeholders: the community, victims and defendants. When the planning period began, no alternative sanction programs—even the existing community service model in New York City—had specifically targeted the lowest level offenders, particularly those arrested for quality-of-life offenses. There had been little consistent effort to develop a graduated range of responses for low-level offenders that took into account differences in charge and criminal history, as well as compliance with previous intermediate sanctions. Project planners sought to develop a graduated, proportional array of intermediate punishments that increased in severity as defendants returned to court on new charges.

Drug Courts The recent movement to establish specialized drug courts to link substance-abusing offenders to treatment was also an influence. Drug courts have been pioneers in the effort to develop a problem-solving approach to case processing and to establish a new role for judges, who have long-term assignments to a specialized court part. In their efforts to use the coercive power of the court to link substance-abusing offenders to treatment, drug courts have demonstrated new ways for courts to collaborate with non-traditional partners to achieve desired outcomes.

The need for linkages between the courts and the treatment community had become increasingly apparent with growing knowledge about the numbers of defendants who are dependent on drugs or alcohol, homeless, mentally ill and infected with HIV or tuberculosis. Drug courts have demonstrated the capacity to serve as a gateway to treatment and related services for defendants with multiple problems. Introducing close monitoring of treatment participation and structured, graduated responses to participant non-compliance, drug courts have drawn upon their coercive power to engage defendants in treatment and used the authority of a new type of judge to support and sustain continuing treatment involvement (Deschenes et al, 1995; General Accounting Office, 1995; Deschenes and Greenwood, 1994; Mahoney, 1994; Goldkamp and Weiland, 1993).

Although early drug courts targeted defendants charged with felony offenses, planners recognized that the need for treatment and related services was just as great among low-level offenders. Treatment strategies at the Midtown Community Court were developed with an awareness that misdemeanor courts had limited coercive power to mandate long-term treatment and that past court-based service referrals had led to high rates of "no show" and program drop-out. It was thought that a misdemeanor court, with admittedly little coercive power, would have greater capacity to link defendants to services if they were co-located and co-delivered at the courthouse itself. Planners recognized that, in a low-level court, the effort to engage defendants in a service continuum might require "carrots" as well as "sticks." In adapting elements of the drug court model to a new context, planners explored ways to promote *voluntary* service engagement among defendants whose crimes were minor but whose needs were great.

Community-based justice centers In the seventies, the concept of returning to community-based courts surfaced in discussions of neighborhood-based justice centers that would provide dispute resolution as an alternative to formal adjudication. Interest in neighborhood-based conflict resolution was sparked by a belief that community needs were not being met by courts and that justice had become too remote from communities and the people living in them. Proponents argued that many low-level cases did not require the full weight of court processing, but could be disposed through less formal mechanisms, like mediation. Feeley, however, suggested that "substantive" justice—formal adjudication—was needed for many cases that proved inappropriate for informal resolution.

Restorative justice Recent efforts to promote a restorative community justice model, grounded in the victim movement, envision a broader role for communities, victimized by quality-of-life crimes, in the production of public safety and formal justice (Bazemore and Umbreit, 1994). Proponents of restorative community justice contend that the "community," like the "state" and the victim, has a stake in the course of justice that should be acknowledged and nurtured (Young, 1995). The restorative justice model calls for both individual and community restitution, to pay back the victims of crime; victim impact panels, to educate offenders about the effects of their actions on victims; and rehabilitation programs, to help offenders reconstruct their lives.

Decentralized courts Citizens' displeasure with courts can be traced, in part, to a process of court centralization that New York and other cities undertook in the second half of this century. Centralized courts were increasingly perceived as distant from urban neighborhoods and unresponsive to their problems (Johnson, 1978). As caseloads have expanded, large centralized courts have not been flexible enough to respond effectively. Conditions for both defendants and communities have deteriorated.

The Court springs in part from a renewed interest in bringing court services for high-volume, short-duration cases back to communities through satellite and branch courts. Satellite and branch courts are courts of limited or special jurisdiction that hear traffic, small claims and preliminary or minor criminal matters (National Clearinghouse for Criminal Justice Planning and Architecture, 1976: p. 92–3). Intense interest in their effective development is evident in judicial planning efforts and guides (e.g., Carter Goble Associates, 1985; Hardenbergh, 1991) and the recommendations emerging from the recent wave of state commissions to chart the future course for their judicial branches (e.g., Massachusetts and Colorado).

DEVELOPING THE COURT

Local Influences

In New York State, the concept of community courts surfaced in the nineties, infused with a new concern about developing more appropriate court responses to quality-of-life crime. In 1990, New York State Court administrators proposed establishing community-based courts in the hope that "by speeding justice, bringing it closer to neighborhoods and attending more carefully to crimes like petty larceny, noise violations, prostitution and loitering for the purpose of using drugs, the courts could help restore a sense of order in the city" (Glaberson, 1990). In early discussions, community courts were seen as a means of relieving strain on overtaxed criminal courts; speeding case processing; demonstrating to young defendants that low-level crime was taken seriously; improving community access to and confidence in the criminal justice system; matching defendants to needed social services; and promoting rapid, constructive community-based justice (Crosson, 1990; DeStefano, 1990).

Early discussions of community courts in New York City quickly became polarized around the issue of who would preside. Initial plans called for lay magistrates to respond to low-level quality-of-life crime in New York City, as described by DeStefano:

> *Criminal prosecution… often leads to 'turnstile justice' and ties up a great deal of police, prosecutorial and judicial resources that could instead be handled by administrative tribunals… (H)andling some crimes administratively (does) not mean decriminalizing the underlying offenses, but rather dealing with them in a way that was faster and less costly (DeStefano, 1990: p. 3).*

Yet, there was concern that lay magistrates, unlike criminal court judges, would not have the power to impose jail sentences, thereby eliminating an incentive for rapid plea bargains (DeStefano, 1990; *New York Newsday*, 1990). It was said that the proposal to create community courts "offers more uncertainty than a midnight stroll down a dark Manhattan alley" (*New York Newsday,* 1990: p. 30). The debate about lay judges effectively scuttled the first effort to introduce the community court concept locally and stifled debate about the merits of community-based courts.

Quality-of-life problems in Midtown Subsequent plans to develop a community court project in the Times Square area of Manhattan began to take shape in 1991. These plans were driven less by the need to relieve strain on the courts than by the desire to promote more constructive response to quality-of-life offenses. For decades, the neighborhood surrounding Times Square, with its bustling shops, hotels, entertainment centers and transportation hubs had been a magnet for illegitimate enterprise. The area had developed a reputation as New York City's red light district. Its peep shows, triple-X theaters, video arcades, tawdry storefronts and pulsing neon lights attracted hustlers and runaways, drawn to the glitz and the excitement. Until very recently, the public image of the Times Square area was a cartoon of urban decay: streets crowded with three-card monte players, hawkers of counterfeit goods, hookers, ticket scalpers, pickpockets and shoplifters. By the early nineties, this image, combined with the economic slowdown affecting the city's real estate markets, had increasingly served to keep tourists away and to discourage commercial investment.

Since the mid-seventies, the area had also spawned a series of efforts to "clean up Times Square" (Daly, 1995). By 1993, a number of efforts had begun to change the face of Midtown, such as the transformation of Bryant Park from a haven for drug dealers and drug users to an orderly, bucolic oasis; the establishment of Business Improvement Districts throughout Midtown, to provide enhanced security, street cleanliness and other services to neighborhood businesses; and the planned, ambitious redevelopment of 42nd Street, spearheaded by New York State's Urban Development Corporation.

Yet, at the start of planning, in 1991, the cornerstone of the "clean up" effort (the 42nd Street development project, with its images of lofty office towers) seemed to be stalled by a slowed-down real estate market and skittish economy (Newmark, 1995; Dykstra, 1995). A series of prior clean-up efforts had not substantially affected the highly concentrated quality-of-life problems in Midtown.

Developing the Court

Project planners trace the genesis of the Court to a meeting between a former Deputy Mayor for Criminal Justice and an official of the Shubert Theater organization, held to discuss the negative impact of quality-of-life crimes in the Times Square area on tourism. Business at New York theaters had been slow for some time and many theaters were empty. The meeting produced the idea of transforming an empty theater into a community-based court to deal with quality-of-life offenses in the Times Square area.

Planning for New York's first community court began in October 1991, coordinated by staff from the Fund for the City of New York (FCNY), working in partnership with the Administrative Judge of the New York City Criminal Courts and the Deputy Mayor for Public Safety. During this period, the planning team solicited input from community groups, criminal justice professionals and social service providers; reviewed data about the characteristics of defendants arrested for misdemeanor and lesser offenses; examined caseload patterns at the centralized Manhattan criminal court; documented each step of case processing, from arrest through arraignment and case disposition; identified appropriate social service providers to work at the Court to respond to defendants' underlying problems; developed a variety of community service projects and identified local partners to supervise defendants assigned to work in the target community; and worked to generate political and financial support.

The public-private partnership between the Unified Court System (UCS), the City of New York and FCNY coordinating staff was a central element in the development and operation of the new Court. This central partnership served to foster additional partnerships with city and community-based agencies that collaborated in the development and operations of community service and social service programming. Together, the core planning team assembled a court-based FCNY coordinating team that would be responsible for coordinating day-to-day operations, community service and social service programs, technology and on-site research. Working in close partnership with UCS, coordinating staff would also be responsible for fostering and overseeing Court-community collaborations with a plethora of community groups, city agencies and non-profit organizations.

Although the Times Square business community provided strong impetus for developing the Court, the Court's constituency and target area are broader than the Times Square neighborhood alone. The Court's "community" includes multiple Midtown constituencies, both business and residential. The problems that affected the Times Square area had spread into the surrounding residential neighborhood of Clinton and Chelsea—neighborhoods that include over 100,000 residents. Midtown residential neighborhoods, west of Eighth Avenue, were heavily burdened by concentrations of visible street prostitution and low-level drug trafficking. Potential customers, drawn to the area from New Jersey and outer boroughs, circled the residential neighborhood in the forties, west of Times Square, in search of street prostitutes. Residents of Clinton and Chelsea complained that prostitution and low-level drug offenses were far too visible and that the neighborhood was marred by the proliferation of graffiti and other signs of disorder. Local block watch groups vigorously petitioned the courts for a more intensive response:

> *Every night and day we have to deal with 'sex for sale': Street prostitutes expose themselves on our sidewalks, streets and doorways. They yell out their services to cars, and their johns*

> *harass female residents of all ages.... Prostitution is not a victimless crime (Abrams, 1993: p. 69).*

These common problems helped planners forge an unusual coalition between the Midtown business and residential communities—two communities that represent decidedly different worlds. Midtown Manhattan houses some of the nation's most powerful business organizations, including major hotels, theaters, law firms, the *New York Times*, flagship department stores and other large-scale organizations. It also houses large numbers of store-front mom-and-pop businesses, serving the residential community.

As shown in the Attachment, the residential community within the Court's target area (the 10th, 14th and 18th precincts) is not affluent, particularly when compared to Greenwich Village, just south of the target area; to the neighborhood just east of the Midtown Community Court's target precincts; and to Manhattan's upper east side. Clinton, an area formerly known as "Hell's Kitchen," which stretches west of Eighth Avenue from roughly 34th Street to 57th Street, had been relatively untouched by the gentrification that affected much of Manhattan in the eighties. Although it contains both pockets of poverty and pockets of affluence,[3] the Midtown residential neighborhood is Manhattan's closest approximation to a middle-class/working-class neighborhood.

The neighborhood was seen as an appropriate testing ground for a community court for several reasons. Midtown precincts had the highest volume of misdemeanor crime in the city, accounting for 43% of all low-level arrests in Manhattan. Midtown had a substantial degree of existing community organization—block associations, community improvement groups—within both the residential and the business communities. A Times Square Business Improvement District (BID), to be established in 1992, was expected to bring new resources, enhanced security and an intensive focus on quality-of-life problems to the area; the concurrent and complementary development of the BID and the Court were seen as a means of promoting a new, collaborative approach to public safety in Midtown. And, perhaps most important, there was a potential site available, potential financial resources to support the project and the demonstrated will to make a change.

The planning effort generated strong community involvement; financial support from 32 foundations and corporations, many of them located within the target area; and commitments from city, state and Federal agencies to support the project. When the initial site fell through late in the first year of planning, local community leaders, already deeply committed to the project, proved instrumental in identifying the current site for the Court—a former magistrate's court on 54th Street, directly adjacent to the Midtown North Precinct house.

With joint funding from New York City and corporate and foundation supporters, the former courthouse was refurbished to house a new courtroom on the ground floor and administration offices and service delivery areas on the top two floors. The renovation also created an opportunity for the use of the latest computer technology, linking a network of courthouse computers to a mainframe computer with all court records at the Office of Court Administration in Albany, New York. The re-design of the building reflected the project's commitment to a new style of urban courthouse, including brightly lit, bar-free holding cells, encased in shatter-proof glass; dedicated interview space for attorneys and their clients; and an entire floor set aside for on-site community service projects, treatment readiness groups, health testing, health education and other court-based social services. This design was based on a recognition that trials were not the business of the day in courts of limited jurisdiction. Instead, the courthouse provides dedicated space, designed to support alternative court responses to low-level crime, tailored to the realities of an urban misdemeanor court.

Early Challenges

The project was not without its critics. Although the central planning team included key leadership within the Unified Court System, the Mayor's Office, the New York City Police Department and the community, there was early opposition from both the prosecutor's office and New York City's Legal Aid Society. The prosecutor's office questioned the fairness of devoting resources to a single community and argued that any new resources should be used to improve conditions at the Downtown court. In early interviews with the press, the prosecutor predicted that the Court would cost an additional three million dollars annually and create inefficiencies: "There are just a huge number of court files to be passed back and forth." (Bennet, 1992). The prosecutor's office reported that "only about twenty arrests per day" would be processed at the Court and argued that, from a fiscal perspective, "a community court should be located in Washington Heights or Harlem... where it is time-consuming to transport prisoners

Downtown" (Adams, 1992).[4] The prosecutor saw little value in the proposed focus on "community" and contended that creating the new Court would be "fiscally irresponsible" (Levitt, 1992: p. 33). Critics dubbed the project the "rich man's court."

Although the defense bar was drawn by the project's efforts to link defendants to court-based services, there was concern that developing intermediate sanctions for convicted offenders who might otherwise have been released would constitute inappropriate "net widening." Some defense attorneys predicted that widespread use of intermediate sanctions might serve to "set up" large numbers of defendants to fail, thereby increasing secondary jail sentences in response to non-compliance. They also voiced concern that the availability of on-site social services might unfairly encourage rapid guilty pleas among defendants seeking access to treatment or other assistance. In addition, the local defense bar was concerned that the Court would be excessively influenced by a community hunger for a harsher response to low-level crime, thereby promoting a form of "vigilante" justice.

Cost was also a central part of the debate. The planning team had generated sufficient funding to support the building renovation, the Court's technology (including both software development and hardware) and staff salaries over the course of the three-year demonstration period. Yet, criminal justice agencies that planned to devote staff members to the new Court argued that decentralization would strain their existing resources.

The planning process also stimulated discussion about the appropriate role for the private sector within the city's criminal courts. The prosecutor's office maintained that, "The privatization of criminal justice, if that is what is proposed, can lead only to unequal treatment and widespread resentment" (Abrams, 1993: p. 54). Some critics were concerned that the project's effort to include a community voice would threaten the independence of judicial decision-making.

The process of planning the Court focused broad attention on sentencing patterns and generated a fertile conversation about "going rates" for low-level crime. Local judges were particularly concerned about the limited range of responses for low-level offenses: "Right now, we have a choice between band-aids and brain surgery," one judge commented. "We'd rather have sentences that mean something," another judge remarked (Abrams, 1993: p. 57). The Manhattan prosecutor, however, was skeptical about the appropriateness of alternative sanctions for specific types of offenders: "Does anyone seriously believe that career prostitutes are likely candidates for community service sentences?" (Abrams, 1993: p. 63). Other Manhattan prosecutors questioned the Midtown Community Court's ability to implement immediate assignment to alternative sanctions. Others raised questions about the Court's ability to process cases efficiently enough to meet a court ruling that mandated penalties when arrest-to-arraignment time exceeded 24 hours. They predicted that, because the Midtown Community Court would operate for only one shift per day, it would be forced to transport large numbers of cases to the Downtown court, which operates 24 hours per day.

Further, a number of questions surfaced during the planning period about the Court's ability to influence court outcomes. Some criminal justice personnel argued that the Court would not be able to affect "going rates" for misdemeanors. They contended that defendants, offered intermediate sanctions in Midtown, would simply adjourn their case to "judge shop" at the Downtown court. Instead of an increased use of intermediate sanctions, they predicted an increase in adjournment rates.

There were other questions raised during the planning period as well. Community groups and local police predicted that many defendants would fail to complete alternative sentences. This prediction, along with a corollary—that defendants would resist community service sentences—supported a further hypothesis: that the project would not improve either community conditions (graffiti, street cleanliness) or community attitudes toward the Court. Even the most optimistic members of the community were aware of the difficulty of affecting entrenched street-level quality-of-life conditions like prostitution and unlicensed vending and of reducing arrest frequency among high-rate low-level offenders.

In response to all this, Court planners demonstrated that Midtown precincts produce the highest volume of misdemeanor arrests in Manhattan and, therefore, could produce a sufficient caseload to support transferring the staff of a misdemeanor arraignment part to a new location. They also argued that concerns about equity were not applicable to demonstration projects, which provide a small-scale pilot test of new ideas; that court-based services would be equally available to all defendants, whether or not they accepted a plea at arraignment and that efforts to promote immediacy and accountability could substantially improve compliance with alternative sanctions.

Emphasis was placed on the unique ability of a community-based court to focus on the specific problems of a particular neighborhood which were generally overlooked in a centralized court setting. In addition, it was argued that community groups did not seek "vigilante justice" but had expressed broad support for intermediate sanctions as an alternative to jail.

In spite of these controversies and criticisms, the project generated sufficient support from community organizations, community leaders, local government and the criminal justice system to begin operations exactly two years after planning began. The duration of the planning period for the Court, which included the time spent on building renovation, is seen as extremely brief in the context of New York City and its politics.

RESEARCH ON THE MIDTOWN COMMUNITY COURT

Such a broad agenda poses a substantial challenge for research. Instead of introducing a single program into an existing court, the project established a new neighborhood-based courthouse, designed to change "business as usual" in a variety of ways. Coordinating staff frequently refer to the Court as a laboratory for testing ideas about how a community-based court might operate. The Court was expected to foster multiple initiatives—providing new information in the courtroom; building integrated court technology; establishing neighborhood-based community service programs; introducing an array of court-based social services; promoting community outreach, dialogue and collaboration; and introducing a court-based research capacity. The project was also designed to produce new programmatic components in response to emerging needs.

Given the multi-faceted nature of the project, it was important that research on the Court follow this evolution closely: how the project evolved; issues that surfaced during project implementation; the case disposition process; the various components of the Court; the role played by the community; changes in community attitudes and conditions of disorder; and preliminary impacts on case processing, sentence outcomes, community service compliance rates, community attitudes and community conditions.

A variety of potential impacts were envisioned. It was anticipated that the project would:

- promote efficiency by enabling local police officers to return to their beats more quickly, using court technology to speed case processing and facilitating immediate assignment of defendants to alternative sanction programs;
- make justice both constructive and visible by developing an expanded array of community-based service projects, increasing the Court's use of community service sentencing, improving community service compliance rates and providing systematic feedback to the community;
- encourage police enforcement of low-level offenses by demonstrating that the Court takes these offenses seriously and by using community service projects and court-based social services as part of community problem solving; and
- develop new roles for the community at the courthouse, opening new avenues for dialogue and collaboration.

If the Midtown Community Court achieved these objectives, the following results were expected: reduced arrest-to-arraignment time; increased use of intermediate sanctions; reduced reliance on short-term jail sentences; improved community service compliance rates; improved community conditions; and improved community attitudes toward the Court.

These potential impacts were closely interconnected. It was expected, for example, that increased community service sentencing and improved compliance rates would produce substantial benefits for the community: cleaner streets, reduced graffiti and visible "payback." It was also hoped that the combination of punishment and help would serve to reduce the frequency and extent of quality-of-life crimes. These achievements, in turn, would affect the attitudes of community leaders, residents, local police and other criminal justice personnel.

In its entirety, the project provided fertile ground for both quantitative and qualitative research. To examine the various questions discussed above, research was needed to examine the Court's impacts on the use of community service and social service sentences, alternative sanction compliance rates, community attitudes and community conditions. Yet, before conducting a full examination of these potential impacts, it was also essential to examine the evolution and implementation of the project and to identify whether there were unanticipated factors that limited its ability to achieve its primary objectives.

The research included the following:

Documentation of court activities

- Observations of court process and interviews with Court personnel, including both courtroom and coordinating staff;
- A quantitative analysis of Court caseloads and case processing and how they change over time;
- Interviews and observations, documenting the role of community partnerships in developing and operating the Court; and
- Interviews and observations, documenting the developing role of technology at the Court.

Community impacts

- Baseline and follow-up focus group interviews with community members and criminal justice personnel about their perceptions of, experiences with and expectations for the Downtown criminal court and the Midtown Community Court;[5]
- In-depth interviews with community leaders, service providers, community service supervisors and Court personnel about perceived impacts on the community and their participation in court-related activities;
- Ethnographic street interviews, defendant interviews and structured observations of local quality-of-life conditions;
- Analysis of arrest patterns for quality-of-life offenses; and
- The accomplishments of community service projects and assessment of street and sidewalk cleanliness.

Caseloads and case processing

- Baseline comparison of misdemeanor caseloads from and case outcomes for Midtown and the rest of Manhattan (offense type, adjournment rates, case dispositions and sentences, etc.);
- A quasi-experimental comparison of misdemeanor case outcomes for Midtown cases processed at the Midtown Community Court and in the Downtown criminal court;
- Pre-post analysis of misdemeanor case outcomes for Midtown cases;
- Pre-post analysis of misdemeanor case outcomes in the rest of Manhattan to document criminal justice trends;

- Analysis of the frequency of defendants with multiple cases at the Court for different charges and the effect of their recidivism on sentence outcomes; and
- Comparison of community service compliance at the Midtown Community Court and the Downtown court.

In summary, this work describes the workings of the Midtown Community Court and reviews its preliminary impacts. Early chapters present a detailed description of the various activities—case processing, community service projects, mandatory and voluntary social services, community engagement, technology development—carried out at the Court during its start-up period. They also review key issues that arose during the implementation period, including the effort to schedule a larger caseload; issues associated with the introduction and expansion of new technology; the effect of new information on the courtroom workgroup; and the effort to ensure strict accountability through close monitoring of alternative sanction compliance. Later chapters present the results of the comparison of case outcomes at the Court and the Downtown court; review the Court's effects on community conditions; analyze the project's impacts on community expectations and attitudes; and examine the implications of the project for jurisdictions throughout the country that seek to build stronger bridges between courts and communities.

Notes

1. Studies by the Commonwealth Fund and the Manhattan Institute showed that 59 percent of people who left New York in the early nineties did so to improve their quality of life (Horowitz, 1993).
2. In 1993, the year the Midtown Community Court opened, the New York City criminal courts handled over 260,000 arrest cases in addition to over 200,000 summons cases. This volume exceeds that of any other court in the State of New York, and makes the Criminal Court of the City of New York the busiest court of limited jurisdiction in the nation.
3. In 1990, residents of one Midtown census tract, with a high concentration of welfare hotels, had a median income of roughly $5,200. In another census tract, along Manhattan's plush Central Park South, median income was over $150,000. The vast majority of census tracts (74%) in the target area, however, had median incomes below $40,000—close to the median income in the five boroughs of New York City as a whole.
4. The prosecutor's office generally supported the value of intermediate sanctions programs. Some members of the prosecutor's office, in fact, conceded that planning for the Court helped spur the expansion of alternative sentencing programs Downtown. The planning period for the new

Court coincided with early stirrings of change towards the increased use of community service sentencing at the Downtown court, spearheaded by the prosecutor's office. This expansion extended throughout the research period.

5. Research staff also recruited community members and college students to employ observational measures from the National Center for State Court's Trial Court Performance Standards to compare the Midtown Community Court with the Downtown criminal court in terms of accessibility, audibility and treatment of defendants. Because these instruments proved less appropriate than anticipated for an arraignment court setting, TCPS data proved more valuable in bolstering qualitative assessments of differences between the two courts than as a tool for conducting quantitative analysis of differences.

CHAPTER TWO

THE COURTHOUSE

The courthouse was envisioned as a multi-purpose building, capable of accommodating a mix of court and community functions. When visitors come to the Midtown Community Court, they enter a neo-classical, hundred year-old building, originally designated as a magistrate's court. A large green and white banner, clearly labeled "Midtown Community Court," announces its presence. An accompanying banner indicates the presence of off-off-Broadway theaters that share the mixed-use building.

The Court's location places it just outside the dense and bustling heart of the theater district, close to the quieter residential neighborhood once known as Hell's Kitchen. Tourists visiting New York City are unlikely to stumble across the Court unless they circle the block looking for a parking space. Foot traffic on the block is moderate as sidewalks are often blocked by police cars. This location differs substantially from the idealized image of a courthouse at the heart of the village green, but its community focus has more to do with the way that the courthouse is used and the way that the Court interacts with the community than with the centrality of its location.

The Court has pulled together a variety of agencies capable of providing health care, education, counseling and substance abuse programs within the court building itself. Project planners have consciously attempted to redefine the role of the courthouse as both a community resource, a site for community service projects and a place where defendants can get help. Planners were aware that criminal justice, social service, education and health care organizations have often let bureaucratic divisions hamper or delay access to services. In response, the Court forged new coalitions and brought multiple service providers—the Department of Health, the Board of Education, the Human Resources Agency, substance abuse treatment providers—together under one roof.

On a typical day, the Midtown Community Court is a beehive of activity. There is much for visitors to observe on a routine tour. It soon becomes evident that the courthouse differs substantially from large-scale, centralized urban courts. The difference in size is apparent immediately with a single courtroom and a small lobby area. In contrast to the Downtown court, where long lines of people wait to pass through magnetometers, lines at the Court security desk are small and move quickly. Because few people enter the courthouse at any given time, there are more court officers attending to each entrant than there would be in a larger one and consequently some visitors to the Court are surprised by the high visibility of security and the number of court officers. Although some basic security procedures—for example, screening by magnetometers—do not differ from those in use at the centralized court, the ratio of court officers to visitors—and the level of scrutiny afforded each visitor—is higher. Visitors at the Court wear guest passes and are required to sign in and out at a security desk.

As they wait for security clearance, visitors might observe community service crews, cleaning the hallways of the building or moving out to paint over graffiti on nearby Ninth Avenue. Defendants, arriving at the Court with Desk Appearance Tickets, check in with court officers who enter information about their arrival directly into the court computer and electronically assign a defense attorney to new cases. A directory in the lobby helps guide visitors to specific destinations within the building. Information about the day's caseload is displayed on a scrolling video-screen at the security desk that shows the defendant's name, the top charge for each case, the attorney's name, case status (awaiting information, ready for arraignment) and disposition outcome.

The Court occupies over half of the six story building. In addition to the courtroom, the first floor provides space for holding cells and attorney-client interviews. Defendants are first brought next door to the Midtown North precinct house and subsequently escorted to the holding area to await arraignment. Those who are arrested at night are lodged at the precinct house until the Court opens for business at nine a.m. The holding cell area is brightly lit, well-ventilated and freshly painted and group holding cells, closed in by shatterproof glass, are bar-free and roomy. Video monitors, like those in the lobby, display scrolling information about the status of each case, providing feedback to defendants about case dispositions, as they are entered.

THE COURTROOM

In keeping with its community focus, the courtroom was designed to provide an inviting, accessible space for community observers and for other community uses. The judge, attorneys, the court reporter and clerks occupy their traditional positions in the courtroom but technology plays a far more substantial role than in traditional New York City courtrooms. A large-screen video monitor provides information on both the daily caseload and the current case before the Court. Computers are stationed at key points throughout the courtroom—the judge's bench, attorneys' tables, the clerk's station—so that Court staff can easily review detailed information about each case. Mezzanine space has been set aside for clerical functions (paying bail, posting fines) and for attorney-client interviews, reducing the hubbub caused by side conversations in the courtroom.

The primary business at the Court is the arraignment of defendants charged with low-level crime. Although it is an official misdemeanor arraignment part of the New York City Criminal Court, like arraignment parts at the centralized Downtown court, it does not conduct trials but disposes of a substantial proportion of its cases (roughly 75%) at first appearance.[1] Defendants who are required to participate in community service and/or social service programs at arraignment are escorted by court officers in small groups from the courtroom directly to the Court's alternative sanction floor for scheduling.

The courtroom is staffed by a traditional complement of court personnel who have been transferred from the centralized Downtown court. These include a Criminal Court judge, defense attorneys, an assistant district attorney, court clerks, court officers, a court stenographer, translators and interviewers from the pretrial service organization, the New York City Criminal Justice Agency, Inc. (CJA).

Both court clerks and court officers at the Court play an expanded role that reflects the Court's agenda. Clerks have become active partners in the development of an expanded version of the state court information system which incorporates new information to facilitate the scheduling and monitoring of intermediate sanctions. They enter information about case dispositions and sentences directly on-line, providing immediate, visible information about case outcomes. Court officers shoulder increased responsibilities, including electronically checking in defendants in the lobby; providing information to community members in a mixed-use court building; serving as defendant escorts to ensure immediate scheduling of alternative sanctions; and monitoring defendants as they serve sentences inside the building.

The role of pretrial interviewers at the Court has also been expanded. In the Downtown criminal court, the primary purpose of pretrial interviewing is to make recommendations about pretrial release while at Midtown it also provides an inventory of defendants' underlying problems. Staff from CJA use an expanded version of the standard pretrial interview to determine whether a defendant has a substance abuse problem, a place to sleep, access to public entitlements, a history of mental illness, etc. Information from this interview is displayed immediately on court computer screens visible to Court personnel,[2] color-coded to highlight problems (substance abuse, homelessness, illiteracy), thereby providing an early signal to the judge, defense attorneys and prosecutor that a defendant has self-identified as a substance abuser, homeless, etc. CJA staff also record summary information about defendants' prior criminal histories. The results of this interview, combined with information about charges and the defendant's criminal history, are used regularly by Court personnel to shape individualized sanctions.

In addition to traditional court staff, a resource coordinator, affiliated with neither the prosecution nor the defense, is charged with making recommendations in each case about appropriate intermediate sanction programs available at the Court. These include community service, an array of short-term and long-term substance abuse treatment initiatives, job readiness training sessions and a variety of on-site motivational groups designed to engage particular types of defendants (e.g., prostitutes, their customers, the homeless) in treatment and health services. For each case, the resource coordinator reviews electronic information about the defendant's problems and criminal history, using search tools to scan "rap sheet" information about prior warrants, assesses the risk of non-compliance, and then enters a recommendation about appropriate alternative sanctions. The resource coordinator maintains close contact with court-based case managers and treatment staff, who can be summoned to the courtroom to conduct detailed assessments of candidates eligible for long-term substance abuse treatment programs and determine the likelihood of immediate placement in local detox or treatment facilities.

The role of technology The Court's technology affects the way that the judge and the attorneys do their job. Information gathered through the CJA assessment interview and the sentence recommendation made by the resource coordinator are immediately visible to the judge and attorneys on a single color-coded court computer screen. This screen incorporates traditional case file information from multiple sources: arrest information, electronically transmitted from the Police Department; complaint information, which is either faxed and scanned or electronically transmitted by the District Attorney's office; and criminal history information, electronically transmitted by the Division of Criminal Justice Services in Albany.

For defendants who reappear at the Court on a subsequent case, the record of their compliance with alternative sanctions is immediately accessible at arraignment. A "prior court" button flashes to alert court actors that there are previous cases to review, reducing the need for postponements to determine whether prior court conditions have been met. The judge, prosecutor and defense attorneys can review information on these cases by clicking to a screen which shows prior case dispositions, sentences and the extent of compliance with community service and/or social service requirements. The judge refers to this information regularly before sentencing repeat offenders.

For a small number of defendants, the Midtown judge, like judges in drug courts throughout the nation, serves to monitor and encourage the defendant's progress in treatment. Defendants sentenced to long-term drug treatment as an alternative to jail reappear regularly; although familiar in drug courts throughout the country, this repeated monitoring is a new role for an arraignment court judge. For these defendants, information about treatment participation is also immediately accessible on the court computer. Court-based case managers monitor participation in detox and treatment programs, conduct urinalysis tests and provide electronic updates to the judge.

THE ALTERNATIVE SANCTIONS/SOCIAL SERVICE FLOOR

The Court has devoted an entire floor for the scheduling and monitoring of alternative sanctions and the provision of court-based social services. Separate space has been allocated to service providers from city and community-based agencies to respond to defendants' problems with substance abuse, housing, health, education and employment. Defendants sentenced to alternative sanctions meet first with representatives of the city's Department of Health (DOH), stationed at the Court, who conduct health education interviews; offer referrals to substance abuse treatment, health services and other assistance; and provide on-site testing for HIV, TB and STDs, along with pre- and post-test counseling. After meeting with DOH, defendants move on to an intake counselor who reviews pre-arraignment assessment data, gathered before clients appear on the Court's social service floor. The intake counselor updates contact information; describes the services available on-site; encourages voluntary participation in a variety of services; and schedules both mandatory and voluntary sessions with counseling staff.

In the sixth floor reception area, a prominently displayed sign in English and Spanish asks whether defendants "need help" with housing, health, education, substance abuse and other problems and lets them know whom to ask for assistance. Below the sign, a table is stocked with hot soup and tea, to which defendants help themselves. Educational videos warn about the risks of substance abuse and HIV infection.

A variety of activities takes place in group and individual meeting rooms. The community service coordinator might be meeting in one room with a group of sentenced offenders to review the terms of their community service contract. In another room, a health education group for "johns" could be reviewing the risks associated with patronizing prostitutes. In still another room, a group of substance abusing offenders might be receiving acupuncture or learning about the long-term costs of addiction. In other rooms, a court-based case manager could be helping a former defendant enter a long-term treatment program or battered women's shelter voluntarily or be on the phone with treatment providers, getting updated information about a defendant's court-ordered participation in a residential drug treatment program and entering that information directly into the Court's computer. Elsewhere, staff from the city's welfare agency might be meeting with a defendant in need of emergency housing.

At night, new groups move into the space—a mediation session about a community dispute in one room; an AA meeting in another; ESL and GED classes in a third. Literacy volunteers work one-on-one with students in ESL and GED classes. Both classes and AA groups are open to defendants and members of the community. Some observers have commented that the atmosphere of the sixth floor changes subtly in the evening as the flow of cases from the downstairs courtroom diminishes and the courthouse opens itself to broader community uses.

OTHER USES OF THE COURTHOUSE

The fifth floor houses the judge's chambers, administrative offices and offices for attorneys, CJA interviewers, the chief clerk and technology staff. A visitor to this floor might observe a Community Advisory Board meeting, bringing together community members, coordinating staff and judges to review new developments at the Court. The Board might hear from a defendant who has successfully participated in long-term treatment or learn about plans for building a geo-mapping capacity, to show community members how offense patterns in the target area have shifted over time. Later in the day, coordinating staff might meet with a touring group of judges from an upstate county, interested in the Court's use of on-site social services. Elsewhere on the floor, technology staff might be developing the capacity to provide an electronic display of how different groups of defendants fared in court-based alternative sanction programs.

In the basement, where court officers have their locker rooms, space has been set aside for a court-based community service project—Times Square Express—which provides free bulk-mail services (copying, stuffing, labeling, sorting and affixing postage) to non-profit organizations in the Court's target area. Other work crews pass through as they pick up cleaning supplies, painting equipment and gardening tools for various work projects. Clearly, the courthouse serves as a site for much more than the routine adjudication of low-level offenses.

Notes

1. A baseline review of case outcomes suggested that the vast majority of Midtown cases would be disposed at arraignment. Cases that are not disposed at first appearance are calendared for a subsequent appearance at the Downtown court.
2. The development of the expanded assessment instrument was the subject of considerable debate during the planning period. Although defense attorneys recognized that information about defendants' self-reported substance abuse would help the Court shape appropriate alternative sentences, they were concerned that this information might have negative consequences on defendants whose cases moved beyond the Court. The following terms were established: information from assessment interviews could be subpoenaed for purposes of impeachment only; information would be limited to reports about *prior* substance abuse, but not current substance abuse; and information from the pre-arraignment assessment would not be included in the permanent case file.

CHAPTER THREE

THE COURTROOM: CASELOADS, CASE PROCESSING AND CASE OUTCOMES

This chapter describes the day-to-day business of the Midtown Community Court: the kinds of cases that come in; the frequency of warrants, adjournments, guilty pleas, dismissals and sentences of various types; and the relationships among defendant characteristics, case characteristics and court outcomes. It delineates points in the case flow where cases fall away from the movement toward rapid disposition at the Court, either because defendants fail to appear at arraignment or because they adjourn the case for a subsequent hearing at the Downtown court. It also reviews how various measures of court performance—caseloads, sentence outcomes, adjournment rates—changed as the new Court evolved over the first eighteen months.

This chapter also provides responses to some of the questions that were raised about the new Court during the planning period, including the following:

- Would substantial numbers of defendants need to be transported Downtown because the Court was unable to arraign them in a single shift per day?
- Would the Midtown area produce a sufficient number of cases to meet caseload projections?
- Would defendants routinely adjourn their cases to the Downtown court to avoid intermediate sanctions at Midtown?
- Would judges make use of the expanded array of sentencing options available at the new Court?

ARREST-TO-ARRAIGNMENT PROCESS

Target Zone Cases

Cases are sent to the Court if the arrest occurred in the Court's target area which covers three Midtown precincts—Midtown North, Midtown South and the 10th Precinct.[1] In 1992, the year before the Court opened, these three precincts alone accounted for 43 percent of the misdemeanor arrests made in Manhattan's 21 precincts—the highest volume of low-level crime in the city.

The Court operates Monday through Friday, from nine a.m. until the last defendant is arraigned and handles both summary arrests, in which defendants are detained before arraignment, and Desk Appearance Tickets (DATs), in which defendants with identification and without open warrants are scheduled to appear at arraignment on a specified future date, roughly three weeks after the instant arrest.[2] Detained defendants who have been lodged overnight at the Midtown North precinct house are escorted to the Court's holding cells to await arraignment.

All DATs issued in the three target area precincts are sent to the Court. Because the Court is not open on weekends, it does not accept summary arrests made between nine a.m. on Friday and noon on Sunday. These cases are arraigned at the Downtown court.

Arrest-to-Arraignment Procedures

The Court's arrest-to-arraignment procedures were designed to speed case processing. Before the Court opened, police officers had to escort defendants Downtown and, in some instances, wait until they had been interviewed by an Assistant District Attorney (ADA), responsible for preparing the complaint. In other cases, for example, prostitution and shoplifting, police officers could file an expedited affidavit that eliminated the need for a face-to-face interview. Court clerks had to assemble a full set of paper records before defendants could proceed to arraignment.

The burden of processing misdemeanor cases in New York City has, in recent years, led to chronic, recurring crises in the criminal justice system. Between 1980 and 1989, the volume of misdemeanor arrests in the five boroughs that comprise New York City escalated steadily, increasing from 68,000 to over 133,000. The mounting volume has given rise to heightened concerns about the costs associated with arrest-related processing time for police officers, overcrowding in pre-arraignment holding facilities and the length of time between arrest and arraignment (Cosgrove, 1993). At the peak of this escalation, the average time between arrest and arraignment hovered close to 72 hours, leading to a Federal court order that imposes penalties when arrest-to-arraignment time exceeds 24 hours.

The Court instituted several changes designed to reduce processing time. Due to its location, police officers do not have to escort defendants Downtown, but can bring them directly to the Court, close to the arrest point, saving travel time.[3] In follow-up focus group interviews, some police officers reported that this practice had substantially reduced overtime expenditures. In addition, the sophisticated technology helps clerks identify the oldest cases in the system to reduce the risk of exceeding the 24 hour limit on arrest-to-arraignment time.

CALENDARED CASELOADS

Caseload Volume

Planners anticipated a sufficient case volume to produce 58 arraignments a day, a number that is roughly equal to the average caseload in a Downtown arraignment part. They also estimated that close to half of these arraignments would involve defendants held on summary arrests and the remainder would involve defendants appearing on DATs. By the end of the first eighteen months, the Court's daily caseload had reached this number and, as anticipated, the arraigned caseload was split almost evenly between DATs and summary arrests. Throughout, project staff monitored the size and composition of the caseload to identify target area cases that had not yet been transferred to the Court.

The goal was to build a caseload incrementally, permitting the new Court to develop and refine operating procedures. In early weeks, the Court accepted a narrowly defined band of summary arrest cases from two precincts only. Other cases were added incrementally, as follows: November 1993, DATs; January 1994, the third Midtown Precinct (10th Precinct); and March 1994, summary arrests made by the Transit Police.

Some target area cases, over and above weekend summary arrest cases, were not arraigned at the Court.[4] This was because, for selected summary arrest cases, the District Attorney's office required arresting officers to be interviewed by an ADA at the central courthouse until technology, permitting a video-conference interview, was available in local precincts. A substantial proportion of these cases involve drug charges.

Because defendants in drug-possession cases were seen as particularly in need of the Court's court-based treatment capacity,[5] coordinating staff, in August 1994, reached an agreement with the District Attorney's office to permit defendants held on misdemeanor drug charges to be delivered to the Court before the arresting officer met with the ADA. This increased the number of drug cases entering the Court from an average of 54 per month (March, 1994–September, 1994) to an average of 96 per month (October, 1994–March, 1995).[6]

Other cases from beyond the original target area were selectively added to the Court and by October 1994, all Manhattan prostitution cases were transferred to the Court. This decision was influenced by continuing concerns about crowding at the Downtown court. As a Court clerk described it, "We weren't getting enough cases and 100 Centre Street was flooded." The selection of Manhattan-wide prostitution cases was influenced by early indications that sentencing practices at the Court had reduced the concentration of prostitution in Midtown and by concerns about the threat of displacement. In the Court's second year, 27 percent of the prostitution cases entering the Court were from non-target area precincts.[7]

As new groups of cases were added, the volume of cases scheduled for arraignment at the Court increased gradually, as shown below.

Relieving Pressure on the Downtown Court

Some proponents of community courts have argued that decentralization of low-level cases might relieve overcrowding in the centralized court. In fact, almost 24,000 cases which otherwise would have been calendared Downtown were calendared at the Court. These cases would otherwise have been sent Downtown. By March 1995, roughly 25 percent of Manhattan misdemeanor cases were calendared at the Court. As a police officer put it during the second focus group interview, "When you take out the people who are only misdemeanors..., you're physically removing these bodies from the feeding line Downtown."

The transfer to Midtown, however, did not reduce Downtown caseloads as much as anticipated. This was because a city-wide increase in the level of police enforcement of "quality-of-life" crimes increased the overall volume of misdemeanor

Figure 3.1 Caseload Volume by Quarter

Quarter	Number
Fourth quarter 1993	2,134
First quarter 1994	3,584
Second quarter 1994	4,284
Third quarter 1994	4,100
Fourth quarter 1994	4,790
First quarter 1995	5,058
Total	**23,950**

cases entering Manhattan courts. In 1994, misdemeanor arrests in Manhattan increased by 20 percent, from 62,122 to 74,626. Most of this growth took place outside of the Court's target area where arrests increased by 32 percent; arrests in Midtown precincts increased by only 2 percent.[8] Consequently, although over 16,000 cases were transferred to the Court in 1994, the total number of Downtown misdemeanor cases dropped by less than 4,000 cases (from roughly 62,000 to 58,400).

While the relief was not as great as anticipated, the Court helped avert unprecedented overcrowding at the Downtown court. Without this release valve, the calendared misdemeanor case volume Downtown would have equaled nearly 75,000 cases.

Even though the creation of the Court siphoned a substantial number of cases from the Downtown caseload, the Downtown court faced a continuing struggle in its effort to process cases quickly. By December 1994, arrest-to-arraignment time in the Downtown court had increased from an average of 28 hours in 1993 to over 33 hours, well above the statutory limit. In contrast, the Court averaged roughly seventeen hours for this period.

The difference between the two courts in average arrest-to-arraignment time is particularly striking because the Court operates only one eight-hour shift per day. In contrast, the Downtown court runs multiple arraignment parts and holds arraignments for at least sixteen hours per day shifts; moreover, three days a week arraignments Downtown are held around the clock.

Caseload Composition

In New York City, charge type has traditionally been one of the primary determinants of case outcomes for low-level offenses. Changes in caseload composition, therefore, can have a strong influence on outcomes in the aggregate.

The Court's calendared caseload was composed primarily of five types of cases: turnstile jumping (42%), unlicensed vending (18%), petit larceny (16%), prostitution (7%) and low-level drug offenses (4%). "Other" cases included a diverse mix of offenses—assault, disorderly conduct, panhandling, soliciting a prostitute, criminal trespass, etc. The caseload mix at the Court changed substantially over time, as new cases were added and enforcement priorities changed. The change in composition of the Court's caseload is shown in Figure 3.2.

Although the caseload grew overall in the second nine months of court operations, some types of cases increased far more than others.[9] Due to increased enforcement, the number

Figure 3.2 Caseload Volume

	First Nine Months % of Total	Second Nine Months % of Total	Total
Turnstile jumping	38% (3,826)	45% (6,252)	42% (10,078)
Unlicensed vending	23% (2,255)	15% (2,077)	18% (4,332)
Petit larceny	18% (1,767)	14% (1,950)	16% (3,717)
Prostitution	7% (700)	7% (989)	7% (1,689)
Low-level drugs	3% (293)	5% (752)	4% (1,045)
Other	11% (1,092)	13% (1,861)	12% (2,953)
Total	100% (9,933)	99% (13,881)	99% (23,814)

and proportion of turnstile jumping cases grew substantially. The number and proportion of cases classified as "other" rose following increased enforcement for panhandling and "john" arrests (soliciting prostitution). The number and percent of drug cases also increased following the transfer of additional defendants arrested on drug charges directly to the Court but the percent of prostitution cases held steady. This reflects two countervailing trends: a decreased concentration of prostitution in the Midtown area and the subsequent transfer of prostitution cases from other precincts, in recognition of the fact that the Court had already had an effect on the volume of local prostitution. Vending cases dropped from 23 percent to 15 percent, a change that reflects decreased vending activity in the target area (see Chapter 7).

DESK APPEARANCE TICKETS: FAILURE-TO-APPEAR AT ARRAIGNMENT

Not all cases calendared at the Court are arraigned at the first scheduled appearance. This is because a substantial proportion of defendants are issued DATs. When these defendants fail to appear at arraignment, a warrant is issued for their arrest. They are not arraigned until they return to the Court, either voluntarily or involuntarily, in response to a warrant or for a new offense.[10]

Issues Related to DATs at the Court

In recent years, faced with the court ruling mandating penalties when arrest-to-arraignment time exceeds 24 hours, the criminal justice system in New York City has attempted to reduce arrest-to-arraignment time by increasing the number of DATs. Between 1989 and 1992, the percent of misdemeanor arrests in which DATs were issued doubled (from 21% to 42%) (Cosgrove, 1993). Although this helped reduce concerns about arrest-to-arraignment time, it gave rise to new concerns about DAT arrests, which became known as "disappearance" tickets, because of the high failure-to-appear (FTA) rate at arraignment.

A number of questions were raised early about DAT appearances at the Court. Would non-appearance rates be unusually high in the beginning because of confusion about the Court's location? Would appearance rates suffer early on, before the city's pretrial agency had sufficient information to remind Midtown defendants with DATs about calendared appearances?

Calendared DATs in the Court Caseload

In the first eighteen months, DATs constituted 68 percent of the Court's calendared caseload (16,135 cases). In Midtown, as in the rest of Manhattan, prostitutes are almost never issued DATs (there are rare exceptions to this practice, involving the need to release defendants held more than 24 hours before arraignment). Assault cases at the Court involved DATs almost exclusively. Figure 3.3 shows the percent of various charge types that involved DATs at the Court.

DAT Appearance Rates

Before the Court opened, over half (55%) of the defendants who received DATs in Midtown precincts failed to appear at arraignment. The FTA rate for defendants arrested in Midtown precincts was substantially higher than the rate for defendants arrested in other Manhattan precincts (48%). This baseline difference was evident for all charges except illegal vending (Midtown vendors had a *lower* FTA rate than others: 54% compared to 65%).

Over the first eighteen months, 53 percent of DATs (36% of calendared cases) at the Court failed to appear at arraignment and had a warrant issued for their arrest. The DAT FTA rates varied substantially by charge, as shown in Figure 3.4. FTA rates were particularly high among some relatively infrequent offenses that were classified as "other": panhandling, 77 percent; criminal trespass, 70 percent; and criminal possession of stolen property, 60 percent.

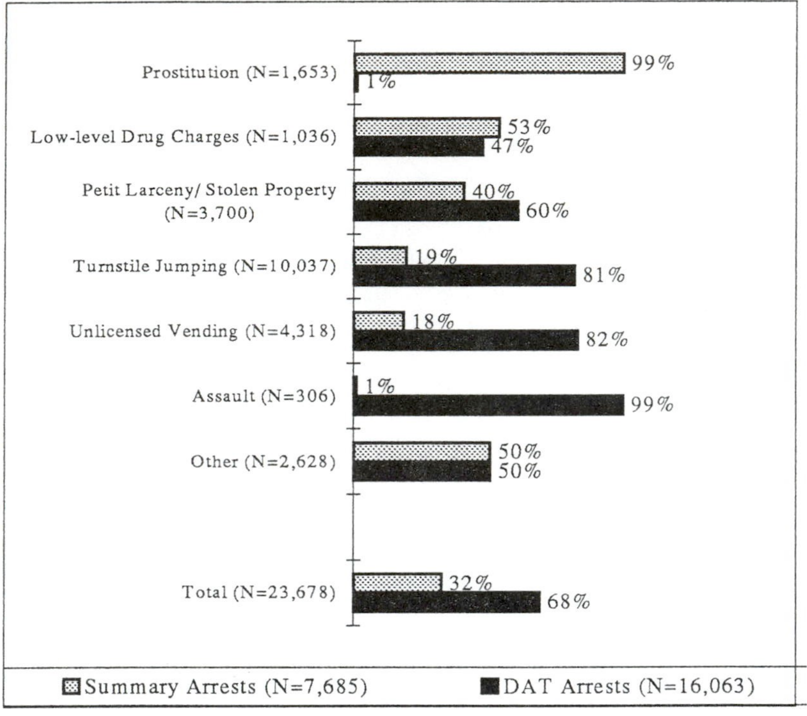

Figure 3.3 Percent of Summary and DAT Arrests for Calendared Cases by Charge

During the research period, three offenses accounted for the vast majority of DATs at the Court: turnstile jumping, 51 percent (8,183); unlicensed vending, 22 percent (3,553); and petit larceny, 14 percent (2,226). No other single charge accounted for more than 5 percent of DATs. Because FTA rates vary by charge, changes in the mix of cases entering the Court have a direct effect on DAT appearance rates.

Because of the widespread concern with DAT non-appearance, the Court conducted an experiment with DAT scheduling. In February 1994, to test the hypothesis that more rapid scheduling might increase appearance rates, Midtown DAT cases were scheduled for arraignment within a week of arrest. Analysis showed that appearance rates for these cases did not differ from cases with a three-week lag between arrest and arraignment.

Roughly a year after the Court opened, the NYPD, in an effort to reduce the FTA rate, revised procedures to exclude defendants classified as "misdemeanor recidivists" from DAT

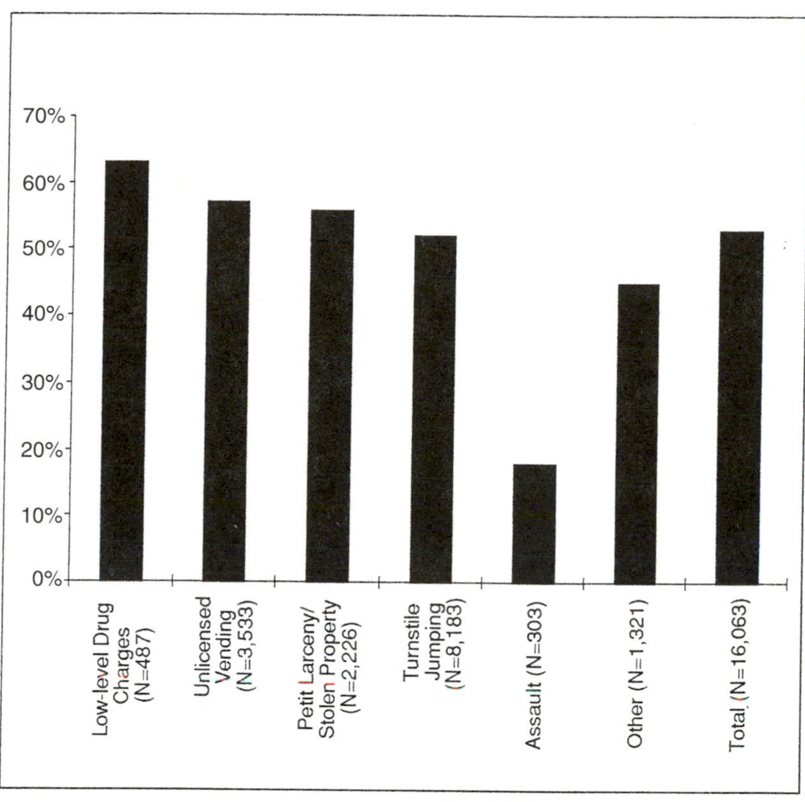

Figure 3.4 DAT Failure-to-Appear by Charge

eligibility. This may have had some influence on FTA rates at the Court; they declined from 56 percent in the first nine months to 50 percent in the second nine months. Additional analysis suggests that the drop also reflects a combination of: (1) an increase in the number and proportion of DATs for turnstile jumping (first nine months, 47%; second nine months, 54%) and (2) a decline in FTA rates for turnstile jumping (first nine months, 56%; second nine months, 49%).

ARRAIGNMENT OUTCOMES

The Characteristics of Arraigned Defendants

In contrast to the Downtown court where CJA staff do not interview defendants receiving DATs and defendants charged with prostitution, CJA staff at Midtown interview all arraigned defendants. The expanded CJA interview, conducted at Midtown, was designed to provide information—whether defendants have a substance abuse problem, a place to sleep, access to public entitlements, a history of mental illness, etc.—to help judges shape appropriate sentences. This information permits a detailed description of the defendant population at the Court.

In most criminal courts, sentencing decisions are driven primarily by information about charge and criminal history. Planners were convinced that routine access to additional information about defendants would help the Court shape appropriate, proportionate sentences.

As Figure 3.5 illustrates, like most criminal justice populations, the defendant population at the Court is predominantly male (74%) and comprised of racial/ethnic minorities (84%).[11] The defendant population is substantially disadvantaged: nearly three-quarters (73%) were not working at the time of arrest; nearly a fifth were either currently homeless (9%) or had been homeless (9%). Although less than half (40%) have a record of prior convictions, prior records tend to be either extensive or serious: over three quarters (77%) of defendants with priors have either five or more misdemeanor convictions (32%) or at least one prior felony conviction (45%) (see Figure 3.5).

Overall, defendants whose cases are arraigned at the Court bring multiple problems into the Court. Distinct sub-populations of defendants brought different sets of problems into the courtroom: a need for English as a Second Language classes for the unlicensed Senegalese vendors who live and work in Midtown; a need for education about HIV and other sexually transmitted diseases among the customers of Midtown prostitutes; and a need for referrals to battered women's shelters among prostitutes, beaten up by their pimps.

Adjournments at Arraignment

In Manhattan, the majority of low-level cases that reach arraignment are disposed at first appearance (61%). Some early critics argued that adjournment rates at the Court would be high. They contended that defendants who did not like the disposition or sentence offered at Court arraignment would try to get a better offer by adjourning their cases to the Downtown court or "forum shopping." They predicted that the Court's effort to increase the use of intermediate sentences might serve instead to increase adjournments and, thereby, multiply the number of court appearances and increase system costs.

Figure 3.5 Demographic Characteristics of Defendants Arraigned at the Midtown Community Court, October 12, 1993—March 31, 1995[12]

Total N = 15,203

Charge	**Percent**	**Number**
Turnstile jumping	38	5,771
Petit larceny/stolen property	16	2,441
Unlicensed vending	15	2,314
Prostitution	11	1,651
Drugs	5	728
Assault	2	251
Other	13	2,030
Totals	**100**	**15,191**
Missing:	...	12
Prior Convictions	**Percent**	**Number**
No	60	8,309
Yes	40	5,441
Conviction type and number		
Misdemeanor only, 1–4	9	1,207
Misdemeanor only, 5+	13	1,788
Felony conviction(s)	18	2,446
Totals	**100**	**13,750**
Missing:	...	1,453
Borough of Residence	**Percent**	**Number**
Manhattan	35	4,118
Brooklyn	13	1,482
Bronx	16	1,931
Staten Island	1	99
Outside New York City	12	1,411
Totals	**100**	**11,783**
Missing:	...	3,420
Age	**Percent**	**Number**
16–18	11	1,425
19–25	25	3,190
26–40	48	6,104
41–60	15	1,879
61–79	1	107
Median Age = 29		
Totals	**100**	**12,705**
Missing:	...	2,498
Race/Ethnicity	**Percent**	**Number**
White	17	2,208
Black	50	6,652
Asian	2	322
Native American	<1	13
Latino	26	3,446
Other	5	685
Totals	**100**	**13,326**
Missing:	...	1,877

Figure 3.5 *Continued*

Gender	**Percent**	**Number**
Female	26	3,609
Male	74	10,074
Totals	**100**	**13,683**
Missing:	...	1,520
Self-Reported Prior Drug Use	**Percent**	**Number**
Heroin, Crack, Cocaine	18	2,399
Marijuana, Alcohol	11	1,479
No Use	71	9,605
Totals	**100**	**13,483**
Missing:	...	1,720
Employment Status	**Percent**	**Number**
Working Full-Time	19	2,490
Working Part-Time	7	863
Doing Odd Jobs	1	129
Not Working	73	9,292
Totals	**100**	**12,774**
Missing:	...	2,429
Educational Attainment	**Percent**	**Number**
Less than high school	44	5,584
High School Diploma or GED	34	4,356
More than high school	22	2,815
Totals	**100**	**12,755**
Missing:	...	2,448
Homelessness[13]	**Percent**	**Number**
Homeless at arraignment	9	1,121
Previously homeless	9	1,108
Never homeless	82	10,514
Totals	**100**	**12,743**
Missing:	...	2,460

In the first eighteen months, 73 percent of the Court's cases were disposed at arraignment; over a quarter of Midtown cases (4,123) were adjourned for disposition at the Downtown court. There are a variety of reasons, other than "forum shopping" why defendants might adjourn cases at arraignment. Some offenses, like assault, require an interview with the complainant before they can be disposed; they are almost invariably continued at arraignment. Other cases are continued because defendants have additional matters before local courts that may be affected by the instant case.

As shown in Figure 3.6, the frequency of adjournments at arraignment at the Court varied substantially by arrest type (summary or DAT) and by charge. Defendants with DATs were more likely to adjourn their case (33%) than defendants who were held before arraignment (21%). The difference in the rate of adjournment for summary arrests and DATs is evident for all offenses. Adjournment rates for assault, unlicensed vending and prostitution were higher than for other offenses.

"Forum shopping" Adjournment rates for two offenses—prostitution and unlicensed vending—exceeded preliminary estimates. Attorneys and other courtroom staff were convinced that defendants arrested on these charges were "forum shopping"—searching for more lenient sentence offers at the Downtown court:

> *Unlicensed general vendors now don't plead guilty, so their cases will be heard Downtown.*
> *I know of two girls who work in the -th Precinct. These girls get locked up, what? ... three times a week? They had ... between them, over $4,000 in bail. And they're still out in the street every day, working.*

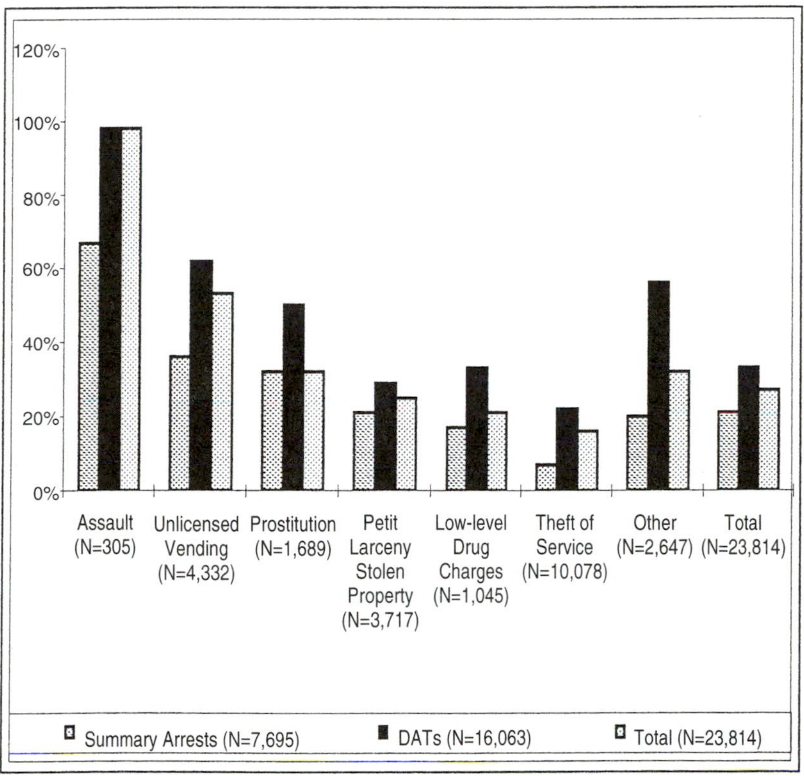

Figure 3.6 Adjournment Rates by Charge and Arrest Type

Several believed that "forum shopping" was particularly prevalent among Senegalese vendors who worked Midtown streets:

> *With the vendors, all these people who come from Africa, they never or hardly ever plead guilty to anything. I don't know if it's a national trait or if they've gotten together and formed a coalition that decided, 'we're not going to plead guilty.'*

"Going rates" and disposition patterns for these offenses at the Downtown court were fairly well established before the Court opened. The most common outcomes included sentences of "time served" for prostitutes, conditional discharge for vendors who were held before arraignment and fines for vendors with DATs. In the year before the Court opened, the vast majority of prostitution cases were disposed at Downtown arraignment; adjournments were infrequent (8%). Adjournments at the Downtown court in the baseline year were far more frequent for vendors (33%), and even more frequent among vendors arrested in Midtown precincts (44%).

Unlicensed vending Some criminal justice personnel interpreted the relatively high adjournment rates for unlicensed vending at the Court as a response to the Court's effort to impose intermediate sanctions as an alternative to "walks"—sentences with no conditions imposed. Adjournment rates for vendors remained high—roughly 50 percent—throughout the first eighteen months. According to several criminal justice officials interviewed in the course of the research, unlicensed vendors in New York City face few consequences if they adjourn their cases repeatedly or if they fail to appear at court. Although unlicensed vending in New York City is a misdemeanor, the vast majority of illegal vending cases do not involve penal law charges: most are Administrative Code offenses. Although FTA rates are high both at arraignment and subsequent to arraignment, the absence of a fingerprint record for vendors to link new arrests to prior criminal history reduces the chances that a warrant will "drop" if defendants are arrested on new charges. It also reduces the court's leverage, since vendors appear before the court with no prior record of arrests. Because the vast majority of cases involve DATs, when defendants adjourn their cases, they are generally released on their own recognizance.

Prostitution Adjournment rates for prostitution increased gradually over the first eighteen months, from 27 percent in the first quarter to 38 percent in the sixth quarter. Additional analysis showed, however, that adjournment rates for prostitution charges dropped substantially thereafter. In fact, adjournment rates for prostitution were heavily influenced by two defendants, sisters, who first appeared at the Court early in 1994. Between them, they adjourned nearly 90 cases over fifteen months. They rarely took a plea at the Court and always posted bail immediately. Together they were responsible for over 20 percent of the prostitution adjournments that year and singlehandedly accounted for most of the increase in adjournments over the first six quarters.

Yet, the sisters were unable to keep "playing the system" indefinitely. Eventually, they were sentenced to jail at the Downtown court for a multitude of open cases. The next time arrest brought them to the Court, they agreed to enter a new program run by a community group that works with prostitutes. The sentence involved a six-day structured curriculum that focuses on setting personal priorities and reviewing patterns of behavior. They completed the curriculum and came back voluntarily to work with counseling staff. Within weeks, they called to let staff know that they had accepted jobs working as exotic dancers in Queens; one has since begun waiting tables. After the sisters entered the program, the adjournment rate for prostitution cases at the Court fell so dramatically that from June to October 1995, almost 90 percent of prostitution cases were disposed at first appearance.

Bail setting and detention Critics who predicted high rates of adjournment also predicted increased system costs resulting from an expansion of pretrial detention. In fact, very few defendants at the Court were detained after arraignment. Most defendants (77%) whose cases were adjourned at arraignment were released on their own recognizance. Bail was set in 18 percent (736) of adjourned cases at Midtown, a lower rate than Downtown (35% in the year before the Court opened).[13] Bail was more likely to be imposed for defendants with adjourned cases who were arrested on charges of prostitution (51% of adjourned cases), petit larceny (45%) and low-level drug charges (42%), than for other combined charges (illegal vending, turnstile jumping and "other": 4%).[14] Defendants arrested for unlicensed vending, the category with the highest rates of adjournment at the Court, rarely had bail conditions imposed due to the absence of a record of prior criminal involvement.

Disposition Rates

There are two points at which Manhattan misdemeanor cases fall away from the movement toward disposition at arraignment:

when defendants issued DATs fail to appear at arraignment and when arraigned defendants choose to continue or adjourn their case for a subsequent hearing. Figure 3.7 shows the joint effect of these two points of attrition on the proportion of the overall caseload disposed at the Court, broken down by charge.

As shown, approximately half of all cases calendared at the Court are disposed at arraignment: roughly a quarter of all cases fail to appear at arraignment and another quarter are adjourned for a subsequent hearing. The pattern of case attrition differs substantially by charge. For example, defendants charged with unlicensed vending have high rates of both non-appearance and adjournment. Few prostitution cases are lost because of failure-to-appear at arraignment as DATs are rarely issued for this charge; yet defendants charged with prostitution have relatively high adjournment rates at the Court. Although few defendants charged with assault failed to appear at arraignment, the vast majority of these

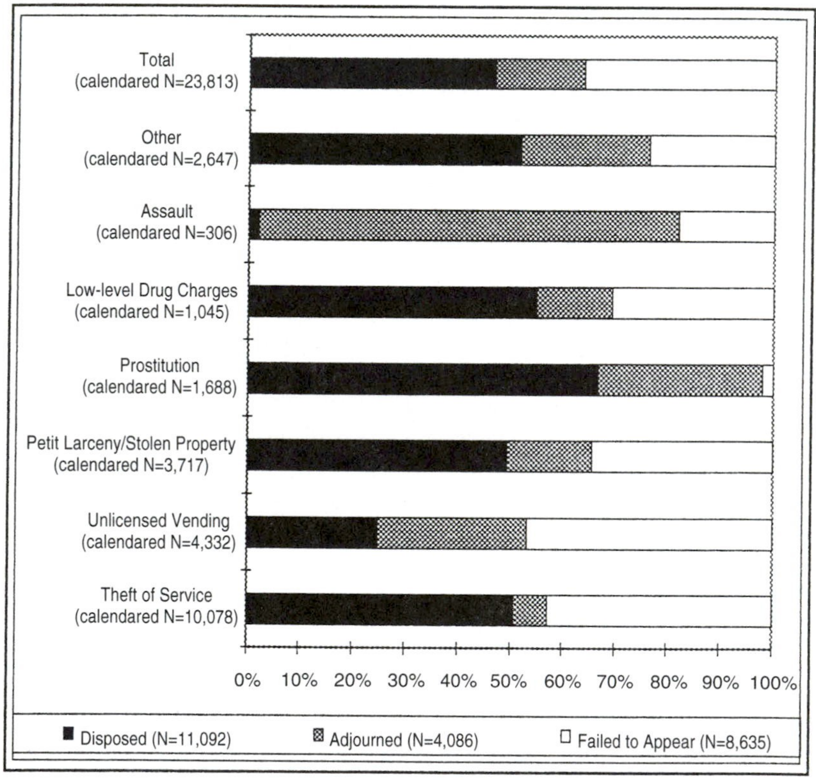

Figure 3.7 Rates of Arraignment and Disposition by Charge

cases were adjourned because of the need for an interview with the complaining witness; these cases are rarely disposed at arraignment, either at the Court or the Downtown court.

Case Dispositions

In New York City, there are two types of conviction—following trial and through guilty plea—and three types of "non-conviction"—acquittal, dismissal and adjournment in contemplation of dismissal (ACD). Less than 1 percent of misdemeanors and lesser offenses in New York City are disposed through trial. The vast majority of low-level offenses are disposed either through a guilty plea, an ACD or a dismissal.

ACDs are generally reserved for defendants with little prior involvement in the criminal justice system. Defendants who receive an ACD have their cases dismissed and sealed six months after disposition if certain conditions are satisfied. The Court typically requires that defendants receiving ACDs have no new arrests over the six-month post-disposition period. In recent years, Manhattan courts have imposed specific conditions upon defendants receiving ACDs increasingly, including short-term community service or social service sanctions.[15]

Disposition outcomes at the court Over the first eighteen months, 69 percent of dispositions (7,683) involved a guilty plea. The rest were either ACDs (28%) or dismissals (3%). The likelihood of conviction for cases disposed at arraignment varied according to defendants' criminal history, arrest type and charge. Those with prior convictions were far more likely to be convicted (98%) than those who had none (31%). Similarly, defendants who were detained after arrest were far more likely to be convicted (69%) than defendants who received DATs (30%). Conviction was also more common among defendants arrested for prostitution, unlicensed vending and drug charges than for defendants charged with turnstile jumping or petit larceny, as shown in Figure 3.8.

SENTENCES AND SANCTIONS

For many years, criminal court judges in New York City have been frustrated by the limited range of sanctions between nothing and jail for low-level offenders. A central priority of the Court was to expand the middle range of sentencing for low-level offenses. To do this, an array of intermediate sanctions, including community

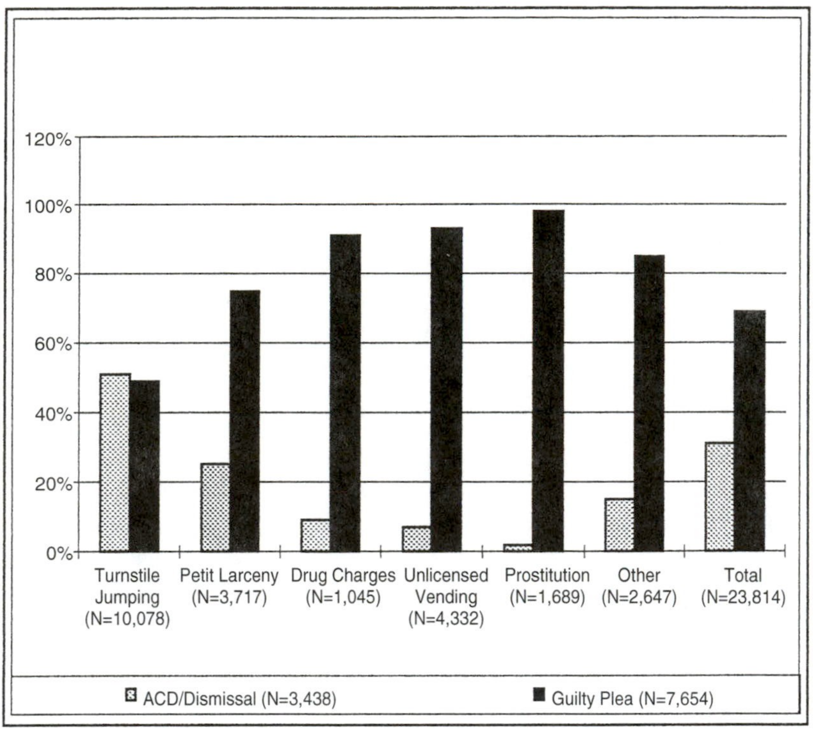

Figure 3.8 Conviction Rates by Charge

service and social service sentences—health education groups for prostitutes and their customers; treatment readiness programs for defendants with substance abuse problems; and counseling/case management sessions for individuals with special needs, such as street youth, homeless defendants and the mentally ill—was established. These intermediate sanctions were used extensively and consistently. A large majority of cases disposed at arraignment (77%) received sentences of community service, social service or both.[16]

Developing Graduated Responses

The Court planning team recognized the importance of designing intermediate sanctions that were proportional to the "weight" of the case. They were aware that defendants were likely to adjourn their cases to the Downtown court if sentences were substantially more severe than "going rates" Downtown. Therefore, both community service and social service programs were designed to "graduate" in length and intensity in response to the extensiveness of the defendant's criminal history.[17] A central objective was to encourage judges and attorneys to "buy into" alternatives to traditional case outcomes.

The Court established three tiers of substance abuse interventions to provide judges with sanctions of slowly ascending seriousness—sanctions that are typically unavailable to misdemeanants in the city's criminal courts. These include:

- A one-session introduction to treatment designed to convey basic information about addiction, drug treatment options and drug-related health risks such as HIV;
- A short-term treatment readiness program, composed of acupuncture and a series of stand-alone, cognitive and experiential sessions that expose participants to the basics of drug treatment and move them toward accepting treatment;
- An alternative-to-incarceration/treatment program that requires offenders to: (1) attend the treatment readiness program described above; (2) provide urine samples; (3) move on to court-based case management and community-based out- or in-patient treatment as needed; and (4) reappear before the Court to report on their progress.

The Correlates of Sentence Outcomes

Although the traditional determinants of case outcomes are criminal history and charge, the Court was designed to add other influences: information about problems that might be addressed through mandatory social services and information about prior compliance with Midtown sanctions to help determine the risk of failure for subsequent alternative sanctions. All this information would be used to decide the nature of a particular sentence ("pay back" or help), to determine sentence duration and the degree of supervision (high or low community service supervision; alternative sanction or jail).

Relationships among criminal history, substance abuse and homelessness At the Court, charge, prior criminal history and the extent of reported substance abuse all influence sentence outcomes and all are strongly correlated. The criminal histories of Midtown defendants vary substantially by charge: those charged with prostitution had the highest frequency of prior conviction records (69%), followed by defendants charged with drug possession (61%); prior records of conviction were relatively infrequent among defendants charged with assault (14%) and unlicensed vending (12%). The extent of self-reported substance abuse is also closely linked to charge type: reported substance abuse was relatively frequent among defendants charged with either drug possession (45%) or petit larceny (29%) and infrequent among defendants charged with unlicensed vending (6%) and assault (5%).[18] The extent of self-reported substance abuse, in turn, is closely associated with prior convictions: defendants reporting prior use of heroin, crack or cocaine were far more likely to have prior convictions (69%) than defendants who denied prior use of all substances, including marijuana and alcohol (31%).

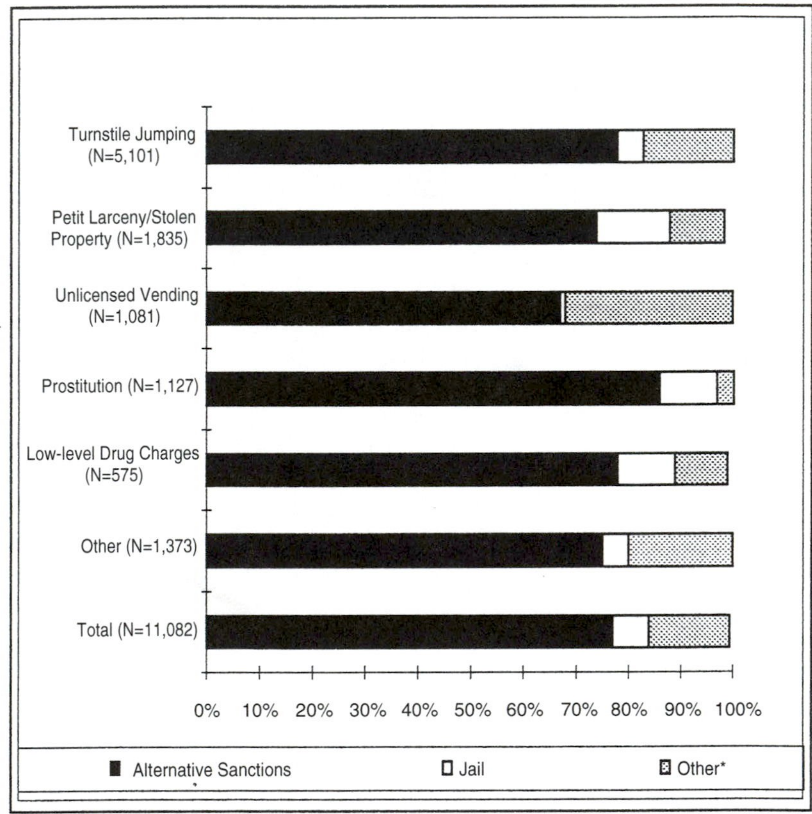

* Includes conditional discharges without conditions, adjournments in contemplation of dismissal without conditions, fines, license suspensions and time served.

Figure 3.9 Case Outcomes by Charge

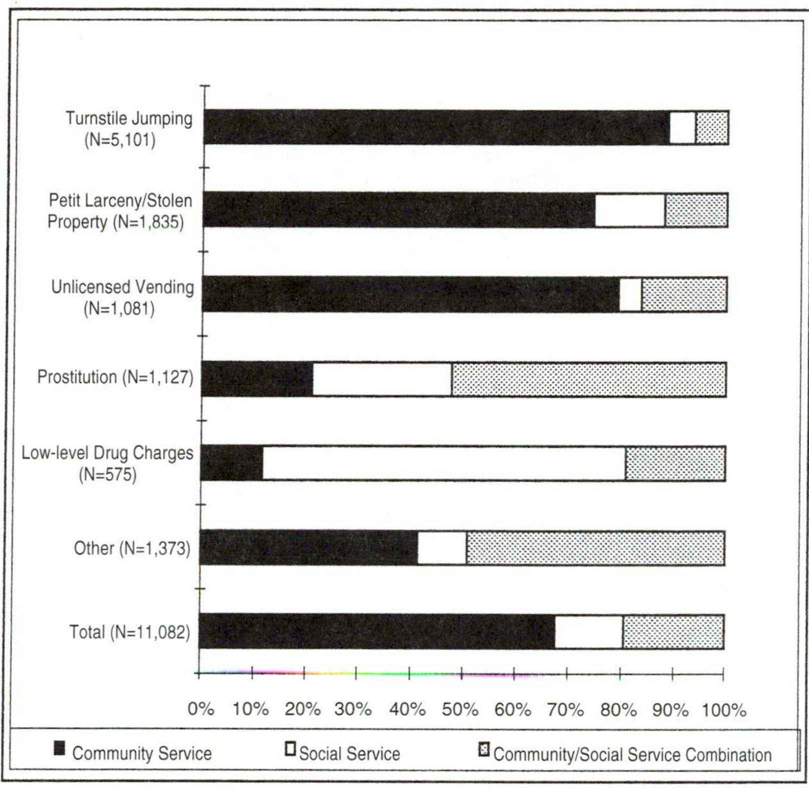

Figure 3.10 Alternative Sanctions by Charge

Sentence outcomes and charge type Outcomes for cases disposed at arraignment varied substantially according to charge type. As shown in Figures 3.9 and 3.10, the frequency of alternative sanctions (community service and/or social service) was highest among defendants arrested for prostitution (87%) and lowest among defendants arrested for unlicensed vending (67%). Jail sentences were imposed most often on defendants arrested on charges of petit larceny (14%),[19] drugs (11%) and prostitution (11%). As discussed, defendants arrested for these charges were more likely to have prior convictions (prostitution, 69%; drugs, 61%; and petit larceny, 48%) than defendants arrested on other charges (31%).

Social service sanctions alone were most often handed out to defendants arrested for low-level drug charges (54%) and prostitution (53%)—charges often associated with a need for either substance abuse treatment, health education or both. Community

Figure 3.11 Sentence Outcomes by Conviction History

	No Prior Convictions	Prior Convictions	TOTAL
Community service	60% (3,726)	40% (1,683)	52% (5,409)
Social service	8 (483)	13 (557)	10 (1,040)
Community service/ social service	13 (807)	19 (804)	15 (1,611)
Jail	1 (75)	17 (707)	7 (782)
Time served	>1 (33)	2 (100)	1 (133)
Other	17 (1,055)	9 (377)	14 (1,432)
TOTAL	100% (6,179)	100% (4,228)	99%* (10,407)

Missing: 725
*Does not equal 100% because of rounding.

service sanctions alone were most frequent for defendants arrested for turnstile jumping (69%), petit larceny (55%) and illegal vending (53%). Combined community service and social service sanctions were most likely among defendants arrested for prostitution (45%) and "other" charges (37%), including soliciting prostitution and panhandling in the subway.

Sentence outcomes and prior convictions Sentence outcomes were also related to defendants' prior criminal record, as shown in Figure 3.11. Defendants with no prior convictions were far more likely to receive community service sanctions (60%) and less likely to receive jail sentences (1%) than those with prior convictions (40% community service; 17% jail). Social service sanctions, either with or without community service, were more common among those with prior convictions (32%) than among those with no prior convictions (21%).

Additional analysis shows that, among defendants who had prior convictions, the number and type (misdemeanor/felony) of prior conviction was related to the likelihood of getting a jail sentence.

Sentencing and reported substance abuse As anticipated, self-reported prior substance abuse at the Court was related to

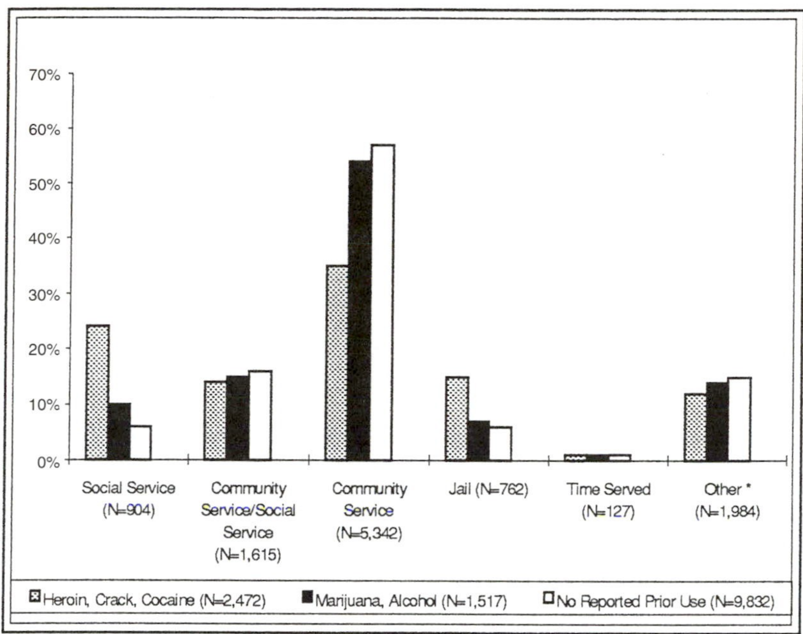

* Includes conditional discharges without conditions, adjournments in contemplation of dismissal without conditions, fines and license suspensions.

Figure 3.12 Self-Reported Prior Substance Abuse by Sentence Outcome

the likelihood of a social service sanction. Defendants who reported prior use of serious drugs (heroin, crack or cocaine) during the intake interview were more likely to receive a social service sanction, with or without community service, than others (Figure 3.12).

Defendants who reported prior use of serious drugs were also more likely to receive a jail sentence than other defendants (15% compared to 6%). This is largely explained by differences in prior criminal history among those who report prior use of serious drugs: 69 percent of defendants reporting prior use of serious drugs have prior convictions, compared to 31 percent of those who report no prior substance abuse.

Sentence Length

Community service sanctions Community service sanctions at the Midtown Community Court ranged from one day to fifteen days, although the vast majority were brief. The average length of community service sanctions varied by charge, ranging from 1.3 days for unlicensed vending to 3.4 days for prostitution. The number of days also varied according to prior criminal history, ranging from 1.3 days for those with no prior convictions to 3.8 days for those with five or more misdemeanor convictions.

Social service sanctions Like community service sanctions, the majority of social service sanctions were brief. Over half of the defendants sentenced to court-based social services (58%) were required to attend single-session engagement groups. Another 17 percent were sentenced to programs of intermediate duration, like the treatment readiness program or a group addressing issues related to prostitution—sanctions that typically ranged from two to six days. The length of *short-term* social service sanctions at the Court varied according to the arraignment charge, defendants' prior criminal histories and their self-reported history of substance abuse.

A small proportion of defendants sentenced to social services at the Court (6%) were ordered to participate in long-term treatment/case management, a sentence that is generally imposed as an alternative to jail for defendants with histories of addiction.

Escalating Short-term Sanctions

By establishing a graduated range of intermediate sanctions, the Court expanded that capacity to promote proportionality. Given this capacity, planners anticipated that the length of short-term sanctions—both community service and social service—would increase gradually for defendants who had multiple appearances at the Court.

During the research period, the vast majority of defendants appeared at the Court only once; only 8 percent of *all* arraigned defendants had more than one case at the Court. However, this figure varied substantially by charge. For example, defendants charged with prostitution were the most frequently arrested in Midtown and one quarter of defendants charged with prostitution at their first Midtown appearance had multiple cases.[21]

Analysis shows that intermediate sanction lengths did increase for "repeaters" (Figures 3.13a and 3.13b).

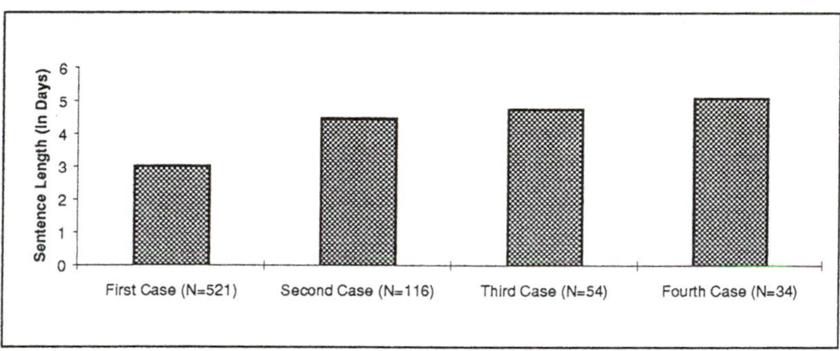

Figure 3.13a Average Alternative Sanction Length for Defendants with One or More Midtown Community Court Cases: Defendants First Arraigned on Prostitution Charges

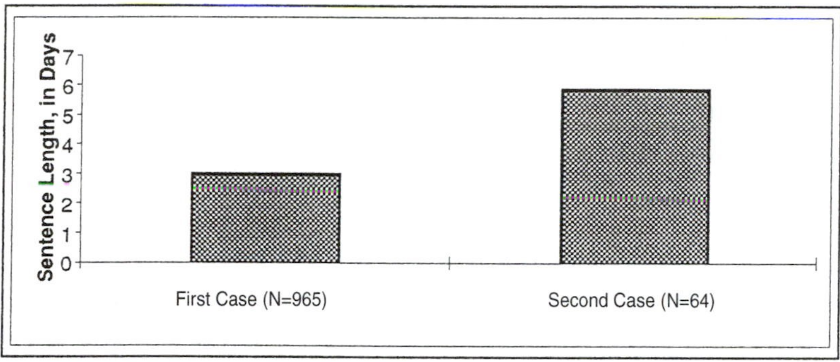

Figure 3.13b Average Alternative Sanction Length For Defendants with One or More Midtown Community Court Cases: Defendants First Arraigned on Petit Larceny Charges

According to Court personnel, the increasing length of community service sentences was a visible burden to repeat offenders charged with prostitution:

> *Some of the ladies of the evening are very annoyed, 'cause they have to work their regular job until seven, eight a.m. and then they have to come to our jobs and work six or seven hours there—work community service. I've heard some of them talking about leaving. I heard one say, 'I just can't do this.' Because after a while they have so many days .... The first few times you get a day or two. That's o.k. But then they get ten days ... I've heard them talking about leaving the city.*

Long-term treatment/case management as an alternative to jail The long-term treatment/case management program at the Court represents the final stage of escalated sanctions at the Court, short of jail. The target population for the program includes substance-abusing defendants with extensive criminal histories who would be facing jail sentences at the Downtown court.[22]

Over the first eighteen months, 184 defendants assessed as having serious substance abuse problems were sentenced to the Court's long-term treatment/case management program. Most defendants entering treatment/case management were assessed as being jailbound for over 120 days. The majority of participants (67%) had a charge of petit larceny, the charge most often associated with lengthy jail sentences in Manhattan. The typical participant had a lengthy record of prior misdemeanor convictions (fourteen on average) and a history of prior incarceration (79%).

Although the program originally required six to twelve months of treatment participation, over time it became evident that for some groups of defendants who faced relatively brief jail sentences, a lengthy treatment mandate would not be a proportionate response to charge and criminal history. Therefore, some defendants facing brief jail terms for turnstile jumping or low-level drug charges were sentenced to participate in treatment/case management for briefer periods (e.g., 30 days). These cases represent an attempt to use limited coercive power as far as it could stretch, in an attempt to promote recovery.

Figure 3.14 Prior Misdemeanor Convictions for Selected Charges: Social Service Sanctions and Jail Sentences

	Petit Larceny	**Low-level Drug Charges**
One to three days, social service sentence	Median = 0 Mean = 2.1 (N = 152)	Median = 0 Mean = 1.4 (N = 182)
Four+ days, social service sentence	Median = 5 Mean = 5.2 (N = 103)	Median = 4 Mean = 7.8 (N = 202)
Long-term treatment/ case management	Median = 9 Mean = 16.7 (N = 119)	Median = 5 Mean = 9.0 (N = 200)
Jail	Median = 15 Mean = 19.5 (N = 259)	Median = 9 Mean = 13.7 (N = 65)

Correlates of sentence length For the two charges closely associated with extensive substance abuse—low-level drug charges and petit larceny—the length of social service sentences was strongly linked to the extent of prior misdemeanor convictions. Figure 3.14 demonstrates how the Court used a graduated range of sanctions, ranging from brief engagement groups to jail sentences, in the attempt to shape an appropriate, proportionate response.

Jail sentences Jail sentences for misdemeanor cases disposed at arraignment in Manhattan are typically brief. At the Court during the research period, 26 percent (202) of the jail sentences were for five days or less. Half (388) were for six to 30 days and the remainder (193) were for over 30 days.

In the year before the Court opened, jail sentences of one to five days for Midtown cases were more common (33%, compared to 26% at Midtown). These sentences typically involve little actual time served as inmates in New York City receive credit for one day of "good time" for every two days of incarceration. Because time spent in detention before arraignment is counted in this calculation, such brief jail sentences generally amount to no more than a day or two in jail. One of the goals of the project was to demonstrate that intermediate sanctions could provide a constructive alternative to short-term jail. Alternative sanctions were seen as spurring accountability and provide a more meaningful punishment than short-term jail.

Charge type was linked to sentence length. The longest jail sentences were handed out to defendants charged with petit larceny (mean: 78 days). The average jail sentence for other charges ranged from eight days for defendants charged with unlicensed vending to 20 days for defendants charged with low-level drug charges.

Not surprisingly, defendants with more extensive or more serious criminal histories received longer sentences than others. Jail sentences averaged 14 days for those with less than five prior misdemeanor convictions; 34 days for those with five or more prior misdemeanor convictions, but no felony convictions; and 42 days for those with a prior felony conviction.

Overall, the review of case processing and outcomes provides a preliminary indication of differences between the Midtown and Downtown courts. Sentences at Midtown appear to reflect the Court's emphasis on promoting an intermediate response between nothing and jail for low-level offenses.

Notes

1. The catchment area covered by these precincts stretches from 14th Street to 59th Street, between Seventh Avenue and the Hudson River. Between 29th and 59th Streets, it also includes the area between the west side of Lexington Avenue and Seventh Avenue.

   Arrests in this area can be made by a variety of enforcement agencies. These include the New York City Police Department (NYPD); the New York City Transit Authority Police Department (TAPD); the Port Authority Police Department; the Stores Mutual Protection Agency, which is authorized to arrest shoplifters in Midtown department stores; the New York City Housing Authority Police Department; police agencies serving local railways (e.g., Amtrak, LIRR); and other groups. During the research period, the vast majority of arrests were made by the NYPD and the TAPD. In the spring of 1995, the TAPD was merged with the NYPD.
2. DATs cannot be issued to arrestees who lack identification or are under the influence of drugs or alcohol. Various types of defendants who appear frequently at the Court are also barred from receiving DATs, including those arrested for photographable offenses (prostitution, soliciting prostitution and trademark counterfeiting) or marijuana sales.
3. A video-conference link between the Midtown North precinct house and the District Attorney's office, established in August 1995, was introduced to eliminate the need for a face-to-face interview between arresting officer and an Assistant District Attorney in cases that were not eligible for expedited affidavits.
4. Data gathered by New York City's Criminal Justice Agency show that weekday summary arrests, made in Midtown but docketed Downtown, were composed primarily of low-level drug charges (36%), shoplifting (14%), traffic (8%), assault (6%) and criminal trespass (6%). CJA data also show that a small number of DATs slipped through the cracks and were sent to the Downtown court.
5. Data collected in Manhattan for the federally-funded Drug Use Forecasting project show that 87% of misdemeanants arrested on drug possession charges test positive for drugs at arrest—a higher rate than for any other charge. This finding supports the project's belief that defendants arrested on low-level drug charges are particularly appropriate for court-based treatment interventions.
6. Even after this agreement, however, a substantial number (roughly 80 per month) of weekday misdemeanor drug cases arising in Midtown precincts continued to be sent to the Downtown court. Efforts to have these cases sent to the Court continued beyond the research period. The District Attorney's office has explained that misdemeanor drug cases, associated with felony arrests for drug sales, are kept together. Project staff have continued to explore this matter, pointing out that the large majority of the Midtown misdemeanor drug cases arraigned at the Downtown court are disposed at arraignment and, therefore, have little bearing on the processing of associated felony cases.
7. Over the first eighteen months, 95% of all Court cases arose in the Court's three target precincts. A small percent of Court cases were brought to the Court from other precincts by transit police, whose districts were not precisely coterminous with police precincts. Similarly,

other cases from non-target precincts were brought to the Court by special police units (e.g., Public Morals), conducting "sweeps" in Midtown that were not strictly limited by precinct boundaries.

8. The fact that Midtown experienced little growth in arrest volume is partly explained by a substantial drop in arrests for prostitution and illegal vending in Midtown in 1994. As discussed in Chapter 7, the decrease in arrest volume is related to a decrease in the concentration of quality-of-life offending that springs at least partly from defendants' response to the Court.

   Because arrest volume grew far more outside of Midtown than in Midtown in 1994, the percent of Manhattan misdemeanor cases arising in Midtown declined. Since 1990, this figure ranged from a high of 43 percent in 1992 to a low of 34 percent in 1994.
9. These differences between the first and second nine-month periods may also reflect some seasonal differences in both offense levels and enforcement activity. Enforcement of some offenses, particularly prostitution and unlicensed vending, varies according to season—peaking in summer for prostitution cases and near Christmas for vending cases.
10. In some cases, DATs are issued, cases are calendared, but the complaint is not prepared on the calendared arraignment date. In these cases, defendants are told to call the District Attorney to find out whether the case will proceed. In other instances, court papers are ready but fingerprints and rap sheets are not available. These cases are adjourned for fingerprints.
11. The proportion of female defendants arrested in Midtown (26%) is higher than in the rest of Manhattan (15% in the three Midtown precincts in the year before the Court opened); this is because of the large number of prostitution arrests in Midtown.
12. All data are drawn from a pre-arraignment interview conducted by staff from the city's Criminal Justice Agency. Of the 15,203 defendants arraigned between October 12, 1993 and March 31, 1995, 1,520 were not interviewed, generally because defendants spoke neither English nor Spanish. Some information is unavailable for some variables because defendants did not respond to a particular question.
13. Residence at a shelter is counted as homelessness.
14. In the remaining 5 percent of Midtown cases, either, (1) bail or parole conditions, set on other cases, were continued; (2) defendants were remanded in response to outstanding warrants; or (3) information on release status was missing.
15. Bail amounts were typically low: 32% under \$250; 49% between \$251 and \$500; and 19% over \$500. Among defendants for whom bail was set at arraignment, 30% (224) posted bail at the Court. The remaining 70% were detained after arraignment at the Court. The overwhelming majority of defendants who posted bail (95%) had been charged with prostitution.
16. In practice, ACDs are rarely restored to the calendar in Manhattan following a new arrest. They are more likely to be restored if the defendants has failed to comply with the conditions imposed in conjunction with the ACD.
17. In New York City, conditions can be imposed for both defendants whose cases end in conviction and for cases that are adjourned in con-

templation of dismissal (ACD). Sanctions imposed in conjucntion with an ACD are not "sentences" because defendants have not been convicted of a crime. The discussion of "sentencing" in this report includes both sentences and sanctions imposed along with ACDs.

18. In addition to "graduating" the length of community service, the Court has established graduated supervision levels. Defendants can be assigned to high or low supervision projects, based on the Resource Coordinator's review of risk factors for non-compliance—warrants, homelessness, charge. Defendants assessed as requiring "high supervision" can be assigned to on-site community service projects that begin immediately after arraignment.
19. Charges associated with high rates of substance abuse were also associated with other problems: reported prior homelessness was relatively frequent among defendants charged with drug possession (38%) and petit larceny (21%) and relatively infrequent among defendants charged with unlicensed vending (12%) and assault (3%).
20. Petit larceny cases in New York County have been typically treated as more "serious" than other misdemeanor offenses; as shown in Chapter 6, jail sentences for this offense at the Downtown court are far more common than for other offenses.
21. Among defendants with multiple appearances at the Court, the average number of Midtown arraignments was 2.8 (3.5 for prostitution). Overall, defendants with multiple cases accounted for 19% of Midtown arraignments. This figure is substantially higher for prostitution, where defendants with multiple cases accounted for 54% of all arraignments.
22. Although the Court did not employ formal guidelines to identify jailbound defendants, the population of defendants entering the mandatory treatment/case management program closely resembles the target population of programs that employ criteria for identifying jailbound offenders. For example, when the Court opened, Manhattan's Community Service Sentencing Project targeted a mixed population, half of whom were assessed as facing long-term jail. The "jailbound" population of misdemeanor defendants was defined as: being charged with petit larceny; having been sentenced on a prior conviction within the last thirteen months; and having been sentenced to incarceration on the last conviction or having a record of thirteen or more prior arrests.

CHAPTER FOUR

BUILDING COMMUNITY PARTNERSHIPS

COMMUNITY ROLE

Traditionally, community members have little role to play in courts, particularly low-level criminal courts. As misdemeanor trials are infrequent, these courts have little interaction with community members, in their role as jurors, individual victims or witnesses in criminal trials. The primary role for the community in misdemeanor courts is that of *audience* and that role is quite limited. The day-to-day proceedings of these courts do not produce compelling courtroom theater, particularly when compared to the drama of a hotly contested murder trial or the support group atmosphere of a felony drug court.

One of the primary tasks of the planning period was to examine how courts might best relate to the community. This conversation was conducted in close collaboration with community groups and carried out at community meetings with members of local community boards, neighborhood block associations, precinct-community councils and other neighborhood groups. The goal of these meetings was to determine how courts might improve the handling of quality-of-life offenses. During the planning period, coordinating staff enlisted community members to serve as partners in the development and operations of community service projects and court-based social services.

This process reflected a central premise of the Court: that communities, victimized by low-level crime, have a stake in court outcomes and a broader role to play in the production of justice. This premise led to the creation of a number of new roles for community groups at the courthouse. In the first month, the coordinating team established a Community Advisory Board to provide feedback about community conditions and to assist in the planning of new projects. In the first eighteen months, coordinating staff also provided feedback to the community about Court accomplishments through newsletters, community presentations and articles in community newspapers; established a capacity for the mediation of community-level conflicts; and began to work collaboratively with local police to solve neighborhood problems. In addition, staff hosted frequent tours of the Court for school groups, court watchers and visitors from other jurisdictions; established student internships with local colleges;

participated in public forums to promote dialogue about the role courts could play in neighborhoods; and hosted community meetings at the courthouse itself.

Defining the community The Court defines its "community" in terms of the various stakeholder groups in the Court's target neighborhood. Because Midtown Manhattan, the hub of New York City, is a center for commerce and tourism, the Midtown community is substantially broader than the residential neighborhood. It includes those who live in, work in and visit Midtown, as well as organizations that are dedicated to the improvement of Midtown. The stakeholders of the Court have been broadly defined to include community leaders and residents, representatives of the local business community, community-based social service providers and members of the city's criminal justice community, especially local police.

Defendants are also stakeholders in the Court. Some defendants—particularly those arrested on charges of prostitution and unlicensed vending—are residents of the Midtown area. Others are drawn to Midtown as the base for a variety of illegitimate activities. Defendants, therefore, have a dual role at the Court—as members of the community and as outsiders who, in various ways, prey upon it.[1]

The Court's effort to promote dialogue and collaboration with the community and to address community problems has four distinct components:

> *Paying back the community*: Community courts seek to "pay back" their host neighborhoods by sentencing offenders who have committed low-level crimes to perform community service—cleaning graffiti, maintaining local parks, stuffing envelopes for area non-profits—in the neighborhoods where crimes took place. Most of these sentences are performed in public, making justice more visible. Community groups participate in this process by identifying needed community service projects and by providing supervisors for work crews.
>
> *Using the Court as a gateway to treatment*: Being arrested is often a moment of crisis in the life of a defendant. With their coercive power, community courts can take advantage of this window of opportunity to motivate defendants to seek help for their problems. Community courts can enlist community-based service providers to provide court-based services to both defendants and non-defendants and galvanize

community members to participate in this process. The Court houses a broad array of social services on-site, including drug counseling, education and health care.

Increasing community involvement: Community courts can give residents a voice in the justice system through advisory boards, which offer programmatic input and identify pressing community needs. They can also provide unprecedented feedback to community groups, including local police, about court outcomes and programs.

Solving community problems: Many chronic quality-of-life and interpersonal problems in a community never reach a courtroom. Court-based mediators can address festering problems—for example, how late a noisy auto repair shop should stay open or how a simmering dispute between two neighbors should be resolved—by convening interested parties, facilitating discussions as an objective third party, and arbitrating when necessary.

This chapter describes how these features of the Court were implemented over the first eighteen months.

COMMUNITY SERVICE: PAYING BACK THE COMMUNITY

Community Service Sentences in New York County

Although the Court is not the first court in town to use such sentences, it is unique in the following respects: promoting extensive use of community service as a sentencing option; soliciting information from the community about how to allocate community service crews; and assigning sentenced offenders to complete their community service in the neighborhood where crimes take place. Community service was first introduced in New York City in 1979 by the Vera Institute of Justice. The Community Service Sentencing Project (CSSP) placed representatives in court to recommend that screened, eligible candidates be sentenced to perform constructive labor. The program offered a ten-day community service sentence to defendants with relatively extensive criminal histories, who were arrested on petit larceny charges. It targeted a mix of jailbound and non-jailbound participants and employed a full-time enforcement staff to return noncompliant participants to court.

Careful selection and rigorous enforcement in CSSP produced relatively high compliance rates. In the year before the

Court opened, 543 defendants in Manhattan were sentenced to CSSP. 60 percent of participants completed the program. Manhattan judges reported that CSSP had a great deal of "credibility" with them. As one judge put it, "If CSSP violates them, they're dead." Yet, the program's focus on a jailbound population eliminated the vast majority of misdemeanants; in 1992, CSSP participants represented less than 1 percent of arraigned misdemeanants in Manhattan.

During the Court's planning period, New York City courts began to use shorter-term community service sentences with some frequency. Typically, defendants arrested for fare-beating might be sentenced to help clean subway stations for a day or two under the supervision of the Transit Authority. Other defendants might be sentenced to crews supervised by the city's Parks Department, Human Resources Administration or other city agencies. In 1992, the first full year of operation, over 16,000 defendants in Manhattan—roughly a quarter of arraigned defendants—were sentenced to short-term community service. But "no show" and dropout rates were high: 19 percent failed to show up at the program office to be scheduled to a work site and less than half (41%) completed their sentence. Information on program status was unavailable for over a quarter of sentenced participants (28%), because the agencies to which they were assigned had not reported results back to the program.

Attitudes toward community service programs Given these results, the broadened use of community service sentences, at least in the early months, did not garner much credibility with judges. As one judge put it, "To get the defendants *into* the programs, you have to get them *to* the programs. You lose much of your power over them as soon as they walk out the door" (Abrams, 1993: p. 60). Judges also voiced concern about lengthy delays between sentencing and the first scheduled program date, distant program sites and the difficulty of getting rapid feedback about the compliance of sentenced offenders.

Some community members were also concerned about the ability of community organizations to supervise work crews and the risks of non-compliance with community service sentences.

> *All I've seen is a revolving door… particularly when it comes to community service. A lot of warrants, a lot of community service being imposed, but not getting done.*

The Legal Aid Society questioned whether defendants would be able to perform same-day community service after being held in lock-up for days or hours. Local police officers were particularly skeptical about the likelihood that Midtown offenders would complete community service:

> *They hope they'll pick up a guy for shoplifting, bring him before a judge... and the guy will plead guilty and the judge will say, 'O.K., go sweep 34th Street for six hours... .' But in reality you are going to get people who are mentally disturbed, have no idea who or where they are, homeless people, people with bugs.*

In spite of this skepticism, community members were generally supportive of the community service concept:

> *It's a great idea. It will get some needed work done in the community. Maybe more important, it will make people feel something is being done, set right. That not all these bad guys are getting away with it.*
>
> *I would certainly like to see a guy who I see every other day urinating in a certain spot on the block working in that spot.*
>
> *They'll definitely think twice about spraying the same wall again after spending a few hours cleaning it off.*
>
> *The offenders learn something from this. And you have children living in the neighborhood and they will get to see people working off their punishment. That's an educational process.*

Community Service at the Court

In its first eighteen months, the Court assigned over 7,300 defendants to fifteen community service projects. Some projects take place at the courthouse itself, including a bulk mailhouse, serving Midtown non-profit organizations and crews assigned to clean the courthouse. Other projects assemble at the courthouse and work in the surrounding neighborhood, including a neighborhood clean-up crew that paints over graffiti and "spruces up" a busy commercial strip in residential Clinton and a horticulture crew that clears and maintains local tree beds. A variety of community organizations supervise off-site community service crews—a recycling center, the Times Square Business Improvement District, the Fashion Center Business Improvement District, the Salvation Army and the YMCA. Other work crews work locally under the supervision of city agencies, including the Transit Authority and the Department of Parks and Recreation. A number of work details have been suggested by local citizens. For example, the horticulture crew was developed based on a recommendation made at a community meeting. Similarly, the work done by the neighborhood clean-up crew is largely determined by the community. Based on community recommendations, the crew has focused primarily on an area selected by residents—the Ninth Avenue commercial strip, which houses a substantial number of empty storefronts that were marred by graffiti. Community residents suggested that a clean-up effort would attract merchants and restauranters to fill vacant space. The clean-up crew has also been dispatched to clean out and paint tenements being rehabilitated by a non-profit development group; to clean up a neighborhood pier that permitted access to the public; to move furniture into low-income housing that was sponsored by community organizations; and to paint office space for local non-profit organizations.

Other crews were established to "pay back" organizations that are located in and serve the Midtown community. Times Square Express (TSX), a bulk mailing house, housed in the basement of the courthouse provides bulk mail services for non-profit organizations in the Court's target area. During the research period, TSX put over 1,600 defendants to work, copying, organizing, sorting, folding and labeling large volume mailings.

Increasing visibility Coordinating staff used a number of methods to make community service projects visible to the community. Participants wear clearly marked uniforms on work sites—mesh vests on clean-up crews, jumpsuits for painting crews, smocks in the mailhouse—all stamped with the Court's logo. TSX affixes a special stamp to postmarks on bulk mail sent out by the project to announce that the mailing was carried out as "a community service project of the Court." The neighborhood work crew posts "wet paint" signs at work sites that identify the fresh coat of paint as the work of Court community service crews. The project has also disseminated information about the accomplishments of work crews in newsletters, at community meetings and through the press.

Project staff calculate that on an average day over thirty offenders work off their sentences in Midtown. During the research period, over one thousand tree pits were cleared and maintained, graffiti was removed from nearly three hundred walls and pull-down gates, and over a million pieces of mail were sorted, stuffed and labeled free-of-charge for local non-profit organizations.

Even so, after the first year the community groups reported a need for more "high visibility community service" work. They wanted to see more defendants assigned to highly visible work crews in the community (e.g., graffiti removal and street cleaning crews), rather than to the mailroom or less visible, off-site crews. To address this concern, coordinating staff revised the protocol that sets priorities for assigning defendants to community service sites. This modification was based on the finding that some groups of defendants who had higher compliance rates than originally expected could be assigned to community-based projects without substantial risk of either non-compliance or harm to the community.

Promoting compliance and ensuring accountability Community service programs at the Court were designed to reduce the risk of non-compliance in a number of ways. Court officers escort defendants directly to the alternative sanctions floor, making it difficult for defendants to walk out before scheduling. Community service staff are encouraged to have defendants begin work within a day of sentencing. Rather than wait until the end of a community service sentence, off-site supervisors fax attendance information daily to the Court where staff enter that information directly onto the Court's computer system. Information about community service completion status is immediately available on the computer system and visible in the courtroom for defendants who return to court on new charges.

In the Court's first month, a formal assessment scale was developed to help determine each defendant's risk of non-compliance and appropriate level of supervision.[2] Based on this scale, the resource coordinator makes a recommendation using information about defendants' charge, criminal history, warrant history and homelessness to determine the appropriate supervision level. Defendants with a history of warrants or without a stable address are assigned to the highest level of supervision. These defendants work on crews at the courthouse itself and are expected to begin community service either on the day of arraignment or the first court day following arraignment. Defendants with no criminal history are assigned to the lowest supervision level and can be scheduled to work off-site.

Coordinating staff worked closely with groups supervising community service projects to develop protocols for minimizing risks to public safety. They established formal procedures for addressing problems on the work site, including lateness, non-appearance, substance abuse, theft, persistent idleness, cursing and verbal harassment of supervisors, community members or co-workers. These procedures were formally outlined in a training manual and distributed to all agencies who agree to supervise work crews.

The project staff also take measures to communicate to defendants the importance of maintaining a high standard of conduct when they are doing their community service. Community service staff schedule defendants to specific work sites and review the terms of their sentence. They also explain the program requirements, the dates and times defendants are required to appear, the terms and conditions of participation and procedures for re-contacting Court staff, if necessary. Expectations about defendant behavior are reinforced through written contracts which spell out the length and type of service to be performed. Each defendant who is sentenced to community service must sign this contract, demonstrating their understanding of the Court's requirements. Defendants who fail to appear for scheduled community service sessions, and do not call to re-schedule, are sent letters of delinquency, informing them that a warrant will be issued for their arrest if they do not call within 24 hours.

Promoting immediacy Community service staff are encouraged to schedule defendants to begin community service as soon as possible after arraignment. During the first eighteen months, 40 percent of community service participants were scheduled to begin work within a day of arraignment. However, as the Court's caseload grew, alternative sanctions staff found that they were hard-pressed to schedule large numbers of defendants during rush periods. The frequency of same day/next day sentences varied over the six quarters of the research period, ranging from a high of 62 percent in the first quarter, when case volume was low, to a low of 28 percent in the fifth quarter. The proportion of defendants who rescheduled their start date more than fifteen days after sentencing also expanded, from 3 percent in the first quarter to 10 percent in the fifth quarter.

This increase was associated with a dip in community service compliance, when rates fell from 81 percent in the first quarter to 73 percent in the fifth quarter. Analysis showed that defendants who did not begin community service within fifteen days of sentencing—typically those who rescheduled frequently—were substantially less likely to complete community service (66%) than those who began immediately (85%).

In response to these findings, alternative sanctions staff decided to tighten scheduling procedures; defendants were required to report to Court to re-schedule community service and to re-appear before the judge if they attempted to re-schedule a third time. As a consequence, the frequency of late starts (sixteen or more days) declined substantially—back down to 3 percent by the end of the second year. At the same time, community service compliance rates increased to previous levels indicating that improved scheduling procedures affected compliance rates.

Community Service Compliance

The majority of defendants sentenced to community service at the Court (75%) completed their sentence. Completion rates varied significantly according to the number of community service days assigned, the type of charge and the defendant's prior criminal history. Self-reported prior homelessness and prior substance abuse were also associated with the extent of compliance.

Community service sentences at the Court are typically brief: 61 percent of community service sentences are for one day, 20 percent for two days, and 19 percent for three or more days. Compliance is substantially higher for one day sentences (85%) than for sentences of two days (63%) or more (55%). The drop-off in compliance is related to several factors. First, longer sentences are more demanding and, therefore, harder to complete. Second, longer sentences are handed out to higher risk defendants—those with more extensive criminal histories and other associated risk factors (homelessness, substance abuse, etc). Third, one-day sentences which begin at the courthouse on the day of sentencing reduce the likelihood of failure.

Because sentence length is so strongly linked to completion, it is important to control for differences in sentence length when examining the relationship between community service completion and other factors. It is possible that apparent differences in completion rates for defendants with and without prior convictions, for example, are explained by differences in sentence length. In fact, there are strong associations between the number of community service days assigned and prior convictions, arraignment charge, reported prior substance abuse and prior homelessness.

All of these factors are independently related to community service completion rates. For sentences of equal length, defendants without prior convictions were more likely to complete community service than those who had been previously convicted; defendants who had never been homeless were more likely to complete community service than those who had been homeless; and those who denied prior substance abuse were more likely to complete community service than those who reported prior use.

Charge type also affects the extent of community service compliance after controlling for the length of community service. Those defendants charged with illegal vending and "other" offenses have a relatively high frequency of compliance, whereas defendants arrested on drug charges have a relatively low frequency of compliance, particularly for sentences of more than one day. Defendants charged with prostitution, who are less likely to complete one day sentences than other groups, have an above-average completion rate for longer community service sentences. In contrast with other charge types, differences in sentence length are not associated with substantial differences in the extent of compliance.

Overall, the community service completion rate at the Court was substantially higher than community groups had expected. Although compliance for defendants charged with prostitution was somewhat lower than for other offenses, a substantial number of these defendants completed relatively lengthy community service sentences.[3] This is particularly noteworthy given early predictions that defendants charged with prostitution would almost never complete community service.

Over the first eighteen months, Midtown work crews completed nearly 10,000 days of labor in the Midtown area. By the end of the research period, several groups that had initially been skeptical about the likelihood of compliance—including local police—requested assistance from Midtown community service crews.

USING THE COURT AS A GATEWAY TO SERVICES

As coordinating staff explained:

> *There is substantial evidence that low-level offenders are in need of a wide variety of intensive services to respond to their widespread substance abuse, homelessness, serious mental and physical health problems, educational and vocational deficiencies, family problems, lack of access to entitlements, etc. There is also evidence that this population has relatively little systematic contact with service providers who might address these problems. For many, the criminal justice system constitutes their primary connection with the world of structured services. Yet the crimes they commit are typically not serious enough to connect them with the service provision and referral capacity of correctional supervision (prison, jail, parole or probation).*

The Court has attempted to use the courthouse as a staging-ground for services both for defendants who are sentenced to participate in health education, treatment engagement groups and long-term treatment/case management, and for defendants who take advantage of court-based services voluntarily.

Court-Based Services in New York County

During the planning period, there was little capacity at the centralized court to sentence defendants arraigned on misdemeanor charges to programs that would address underlying health and substance abuse problems. Downtown judges would occasionally mandate that defendants whose rap sheets pointed to a substance abuse problem enter substance abuse treatment. Sometimes, defense attorneys identified a particular program that the defendant would enter. In other instances, defendants were sent to a Drug Treatment Referral Office that had the capacity to screen, refer and place defendants in substance abuse treatment.

But, treatment was ordered in only a small proportion of cases.[4] Reports from the Drug Treatment Referral Office reveal that in 1992, 203 defendants were referred to it and 55 defendants were placed in community-based treatment. The treatment referral office, however, had limited capacity to follow up on defendants' progress in treatment or to provide feedback about participation to the Court. During the Court's first year, funding for staffing the Drug Treatment Referral Office at the Downtown court was withdrawn.

In 1991, the Foundation for Research on Sexually Transmitted Diseases (FROST'D) began accepting defendants arrested on charges of prostitution and low-level drug possession in a two-day treatment readiness program designed to provide health education and an introduction to substance abuse treatment. In the second half of 1992, over 1,300 defendants (4% of arraigned misdemeanants) were sentenced to the program at the Downtown court.

Perceived need for access to services among misdemeanants

During the planning period, coordinating staff held focus groups with defendants at the Downtown court to identify gaps in their access to services. They found that some defendants were unable or unwilling to obtain needed medical treatment, at times for unexpected reasons. For example, prostitutes reported that they wanted greater access to medical care for a variety of conditions, including pregnancy, HIV and other sexually transmitted diseases. Yet, they generally believed that their pimps would punish them if they took "time off" from the streets for treatment. Focus group members—including four prostitutes who had worked the Times Square area—urged that if access to medical treatment were available at the Court, they could receive HIV tests, treatment for STDs or pre-natal care while they were still under the Court's supervision without risk of repercussion.

A group of ex-offenders in the later stages of substance abuse treatment explained that their first exposure to drug treatment had often come too late. Rather than linking them to outpatient drug programs in the early stages of their addiction and criminal careers, offers of treatment by courts and prosecutors came when they were facing substantial jail terms or while serving time in state prisons. By this time, they explained, they had been processed through the criminal justice system multiple times and were considered ineligible for outpatient treatment by the higher courts.

Expectations for court-based services Court personnel and community groups generally acknowledged that courts had a role to play in linking defendants to social services, although their expectations about the rehabilitative capacity of those services were modest. Before the Court opened, community residents were less aware of the Court's plans for housing social services than they were of the community service component. Yet they proved generally supportive of the concept.

> *If five people a year change their lives around and become productive citizens, that's one hell of a lot. What price for a person's life? So from that side, the Court has a lot of room to be successful.*

> *Even the prostitutes who will never stop being prostitutes—doesn't mean you can't do something in that area of behavior that may not benefit somebody. For example, convince them to have safe sex.*

Community groups, however, were convinced that specific subgroups of defendants would prove resistant:

> *I think most of us agree that prostitutes are not going to be rehabilitated. There is nothing you can do with them. In my opinion, a lot of the people who'll be brought there won't be rehabilitated... the three-card monte players.*

Some were generally skeptical of rehabilitative efforts:

> *That's a pretty heavy burden to put on the system, that we can change people's lives and turn them into law-abiding citizens. I think that's too much of a burden.*

Court-Based Services at the Court

The Court was expected to increase capacity to link defendants to needed services in two ways:

- by drawing a variety of service providers into the Court so that case processing and social services would be located under one roof; and
- by establishing sanctions of graduated severity for substance-abusing offenders which are typically unavailable to misdemeanants in the city's Criminal Courts.

Providing on-site services By locating and delivering misdemeanor case processing, substance abuse treatment initiatives and other supportive services at the courthouse itself, the Court tries to link together service providers with a client population that they often fail to reach. The idea was to capitalize on the "moment of arrest" as a motivational force:

> *Given that substance abusers often begin the recovery process when they suffer or come face-to-face with loss—whether it be loss of job, family or spouse or the threat of incarceration—the Court will exploit the court setting by seizing the moment of arrest and immediately engaging offenders in treatment.*

Staff believed that an on-site service capacity would help cut down the high no-show and drop-out rates that undermined programs in the past.

In addition, a number of community-based organizations providing various services placed staff at the Court on a part- or full-time basis. They were drawn to the project by the recognition that it provided easy access to a hard-to-reach target population.

Promoting voluntary use of on-site services Midtown staff have used a variety of tactics to encourage voluntary participation in services. The CJA pre-arraignment assessment interview provides the first indication that services are available and contains items gauging whether defendants want help with treatment, employment or education. The judge regularly encourages defendants to make use of court-based services even if they adjourn their case or receive a jail sentence. A sign in English and Spanish on the alternative sanctions floor asks whether defendants need help with housing, health, education, substance abuse and other problems. Educational videos play in the Court's alternative sanction scheduling area. In addition, defendants are actively encouraged to participate voluntarily in services in the process of scheduling their participation in alternative sanction programs. Furthermore, case managers meet individually with participants assigned to short-term treatment readiness sessions to promote further participation in treatment and related services.

The first stop for defendants after they have checked in on the alternative sanctions floor is the Department of Health (DOH) office. Staff from DOH stationed at the Court conduct health education interviews; offer referrals to substance abuse treatment, health services and other assistance; and provide on-site testing for HIV, TB and other STDs, along with pre- and post-test counseling. Audits of defendant participation in counseling sessions, court-based GED and ESL classes, voluntary health testing and other services reveal that between fifteen and 20 percent of defendants sentenced to intermediate sanctions at the Court take advantage of some court-based service voluntarily.

Voluntary participation: linking short-term program graduates to long-term services The combination of staff from city- and community-based agencies with social service staff has helped the Court place non-jailbound defendants (and an occasional walk-in client) in inpatient and outpatient treatment programs and helped them access other social services. By the end of March 1995, 144 defendants, most of whom had participated in short-term alternative sanctions, began working with case managers voluntarily.[5] For example:

- Esteban Vargas was sentenced to one day of community service after jumping a turnstile. While waiting to be assigned to a job site, he overheard a case manager speaking to a client and asked if he could speak to the case manager as well. He reported a history of cocaine and heroin abuse and said he wanted help getting into treatment. He tested positive for both drugs. Case managers helped him enter a local detox facility that day and continued to monitor him in outpatient treatment. Through the end of the research period, he reported voluntarily to the Midtown Community Court for urine testing and individual counseling. Case managers worked with him to develop an employment plan and helped him maintain residence in transitional housing.

- The intake counselor met with Richard Lewis, who was sentenced to one day of community service. Richard acknowledged having a serious crack problem and requested a referral to detox. A placement was arranged for the next day, but Richard did not show up. He called the next day to report that he had been rearrested and sent to the Downtown court. He faced a jail sentence unless he arranged to enter a treatment program. He told his defense attorney about the referral and placement service available at the Court. Together, the defense attorney and Court case managers helped craft a sentence at the Downtown court that would draw upon Court case management services.

Potential voluntary long-term treatment participants have been identified by a variety of Court personnel whom they come to know as they complete their sentences. Over time, with repeated contact and exposure and sometimes after multiple arrests, they have become familiar and comfortable with Court personnel. In some instances, the social service staff have used a new moment of crisis—a beating by a pimp or a customer, a boyfriend's serious addiction—to draw prostitutes into deeper involvement with appropriate services:

- Beverly, a prostitute who had been sentenced to a short-term social service intervention, asked to speak to a court-based case manager about her boyfriend. She reported that he had a serious problem with crack cocaine and was interested in treatment. The case manager assured her that he could arrange a treatment placement if she brought her boyfriend in, but doubted that she would return. In fact, she and her boyfriend arrived at the Court the next day; he was placed in the Manhattan Bowery Program, a local residential treatment facility. After helping her boyfriend enter treatment, Beverly acknowledged her own substance abuse problem. Case managers helped her enter a residential program for pregnant substance abusers.
- Rhonda, who had already been at the Court four times on prostitution charges, showed up at community service

> badly bruised with her cheekbone protruding. She started to cry when the community service supervisor asked about her injuries, admitted that her pimp had been beating her up and claimed she was ready for a change. She stayed at the Court all day, meeting with social service staff who arranged a placement in a battered women's shelter. By the end of the day, representatives of a residential program for battered women met with her, assessed her and moved her into their out-of-state facility. Over the next few days, her pimp and his other commercial sex workers—known as wife-in-laws—came to the Court several times looking for her. Rhonda spent several months in residential placement before moving back home to Massachusetts. She subsequently moved back to New York and came back to the courthouse for help finding a job. With the help of project staff, she found work at a local florist.

The voluntary use of court-based services represents a new function for the courthouse. These services are not limited to defendants who are sentenced to participate in treatment or health education. Instead, some defendants and community members have begun to see and use the courthouse in a different way, as a place to get help.

Establishing a Graduated Array of Social Service Sanctions

In New York City, over 75 percent of detained offenders, tested under the National Institute of Justice's Drug Use Forecasting (DUF) program, test positive for drugs before arraignment. In February 1995, a special DUF testing project at the Court revealed that 72 percent of Midtown defendants tested positive for drugs. Not surprisingly, the Court focused heavily on substance abuse treatment.

To provide judges with sanctions of ascending severity for substance-abusing offenders, the Court established a graduated array of treatment-based interventions, appropriate for defendants with modest, moderate and extensive criminal histories. Support from the federal Center for Substance Abuse Treatment helped the Court develop three tiers of substance abuse interventions ranging from a single-session treatment engagement group to mandatory long-term treatment/case management.

In the Court's first eighteen months, over 9,500 offenders participated in health education and/or substance abuse interventions at the Court. Over 6,500 defendants sentenced to perform community service took part in court-based health education interviews conducted by DOH; another 1,700 were sentenced to single-session engagement groups targeted at substance abusers, prostitutes and the customers of prostitutes; nearly 1,000 defendants were sentenced to the multi-session treatment readiness program; and over 330 entered long-term treatment/case management on either a mandatory or voluntary basis. Project staff relied upon an expanding network of local detox, outpatient and residential treatment providers to enable an immediate start after arraignment.

Compliance with short-term social service sanctions Short-term social service sentences are handed out to non-jailbound defendants with minimal to moderate criminal histories. The immediate goals are modest:

> *A career prostitute may learn about safe sex, hear of ways out of prostitution or get advice on how to deal with her pimp's escalating physical abuse. A person addicted to drugs may for the first time meet someone who has kicked their own habit. For these defendants, the services offered at the Court can be a stepping stone towards change and a guide to reducing harm in their lives.*

During the first eighteen months, 68 percent of defendants sentenced to short-term social services at the Court completed their sentence. Most social service sentences at the Court (94%) require short-term participation in structured groups. Like those for community service, sanctions range from one day to four or more, with the majority being one day. Similarly, compliance is substantially higher for one day sentences. The number of days assigned varies according to the extent of prior convictions, arraignment charge, reported prior substance abuse and prior homelessness.

As with community service, after controlling for differences in sentence length, completion rates varied according to prior criminal history, reported prior substance abuse and reported prior or current homelessness. There was only one exception to this pattern: defendants who deny prior substance use and who receive social service sentences of four days or more are less likely to complete social service sentences (31%) than defendants who report prior use (heroin/crack/cocaine, 38%; marijuana/alcohol, 44%).

The extent of social service completion also varies according to the defendant's charge at arraignment. Although in the aggregate, the number of days mandated is strongly related to completion, for some charges—petit larceny, "other"—compliance rates decline sharply when sentences are longer than one day. In contrast, for prostitution, the drop in compliance is only apparent for sentences of four days or more.

Toward the end of the research period, coordinating staff began focusing efforts on improving compliance with these sentences. These efforts included establishing pre- and post-counseling procedures for participants in the treatment readiness program; monitoring the rescheduling process closely; changing the program schedule to permit immediate enrollment of more defendants to groups; and establishing formal procedures for judicial review for non-compliant participants.

Mandatory Long-Term Treatment/Case Management

The Court also developed the capacity to case manage defendants sentenced to long-term substance abuse treatment as an alternative to jail. Planning staff were aware that criminal courts generally have very limited coercive power to help link non-jailbound defendants arrested on charges of disorderly conduct, criminal trespass, prostitution, turnstile jumping and panhandling, to long-term treatment. Yet the problems of these defendants—substance abuse, homelessness, health problems, unemployment—are often as serious as those of "jailbound" defendants. Typically, criminal justice and social service professionals have been stymied by the court's lack of coercive power in these cases and few service interventions have been tried.

The long-term mandatory case management program at the Court was originally designed for defendants who faced between four and twelve months in jail. In New York City Criminal Courts, jail sentences of this length generally involve petit larceny (shoplifting) charges in conjunction with extensive criminal histories. In addition, defendants arrested for low-level drug possession charges who have extensive previous convictions are also frequently sentenced to jail, although typically for shorter terms than shoplifters. If a defendant agrees to the terms of the sentence, the judge imposes a conditional discharge, dependent upon successful completion of treatment. An alternative jail sentence is also specified should the defendant fail to comply with the treatment regimen.

The program originally required that defendants remain in treatment under the supervision of the Court for a minimum of six months. Yet, over time, the Court began taking a more flexible approach to defining appropriate terms of court supervision. Some jailbound defendants, facing shorter jail sentences, were placed in mandatory case management/treatment for less than six months to begin exposing them to treatment in the absence of sufficient "teeth" to *mandate* lengthy involvement.

The implementation of the long-term treatment program at the Court began before the full counseling staff had been hired. On the Court's opening day, project staff (the clinical director and visiting staff from Samaritan Village) were called to assess a heroin-using defendant who was seen by the judge and attorneys as an appropriate candidate for a long-term treatment-based program as an alternative to jail:

> *Lisa, a defendant sentenced to the long-term alternative-to-incarceration program on the day the Court opened, reported a 20-year history of heroin addiction. Lisa was clearly "jail-bound," with a criminal history of multiple incarcerations for petit larceny. Project staff placed her in a local detox facility and arranged subsequent placement in long-term residential treatment at Samaritan Village. Shortly after completing detox, Lisa absconded to her sister's house out of state. A warrant for her arrest was issued. A month later, Lisa's sister called program staff to discuss re-admission. It took another month for Lisa to return to court. At that time, she requested a month-long remand to the detox facility at the local jail. After completing her sentence, she returned voluntarily to the case management program. Thereafter, she became an active long-term participant in case management and received assistance in finding housing and health care.*

Demonstrating coercive power Court personnel sought to maximize the opportunity for linking high-risk offenders to treatment through the Court. It soon became clear that, in a misdemeanant population, the very characteristics that are associated with being jailbound—high rates of rearrest, high risk of failure-to-appear—also make program candidates high risk for treatment. It is not surprising, therefore, that many participants failed quickly. During the Court's early months, judges, attorneys and case managers learned that mandatory long-term treatment participants were at high risk for treatment failure. Of the 186 mandatory treatment clients, 79 disappeared within two weeks of their sentence.

Although the mandatory long-term treatment program was designed to be tolerant of the "zig zags" that are characteristic of treatment progress, there was little tolerance for rearrested participants who absconded without entering treatment/case management. By the end of the eighteen-month period, nearly two-thirds of program failures had been rearrested and incarcerated. For these defendants, the jail sentences (averaging five months) were almost invariably imposed. The fact that jail sentences were imposed rigorously for defendants who reappeared at both the Downtown court and the Court demonstrated that, unlike many local programs, the program had "teeth."

In response to this experience, the Court designed procedures to show that it meant business. For mandatory program participants who showed up but were demonstrably resistant to treatment, judges began using short-term detention—a day in the Court's holding cell, short-term remands—to increase compliance. For example:

> *Gary Baum, in his early fifties, had a 20-year history of abusing either heroin or, more recently, a mixture of methadone, crack and benzodiazepine. Over the past 20 years he had amassed a substantial record of arrests for shoplifting. Although he agreed to enter the long-term treatment program, he wanted to stay in his current methadone program, was unwilling to enter alternative treatment placements, showed up at the Court high and repeatedly tested positive for cocaine. Although he attended the Court's treatment readiness program, his participation was minimal. In response to this behavior, at his next scheduled court appearance, he was detained for two weeks with the understanding that the full alternative jail sentence would be imposed if he did not participate in treatment thereafter. On the day of his release, program staff picked him up at the Downtown court. Thereafter, his behavior and demeanor changed markedly. He enrolled in residential treatment and participated successfully in mandatory long-term/treatment case management.*

Social service staff identified the need for a variety of additional court-based services that were useful in addressing the underlying problems of defendants. New court-based services were introduced, including a six-day group for prostitutes with extensive prior arrests. Short-term sanctions were modified—for example, introducing a life skills training component into the four-day treatment readiness program—in an effort to improve the Court's capacity to engage a hard-to-reach population in services. Project staff began planning new initiatives that would help link defendants to expanded employment services, primary health care and an on-site Narcotics Anonymous group, open to both defendants and community members. Throughout the research period, the Court's social service component was continually evolving and growing, as project staff sought to develop new ways to address the underlying problems of low-level offenders.

COMMUNITY INVOLVEMENT

The Court attempted both to enlist community members in an advisory capacity and to increase the feedback provided to the community about its operations. It also sought to become a new type of community resource by developing a capacity for mediating community-level disputes; hosting community meetings to address public safety concerns; and opening some court-based services to community members.

In its first month, the Court established a Community Advisory Board, scheduled to meet bi-monthly to recommend appropriate community service projects and provide feedback to the Court about community problems and perceptions. Advisory Board members include representatives of both the residential and business communities: a former chairperson of Community Board 4, the president of the Times Square Business Improvement District, a partner in a prominent local law firm, the general manager of the Port Authority of New York and New Jersey and community leaders drawn from local Community Boards and civic organizations. As anticipated, the Board helped develop local community service projects and provided feedback about community issues and concerns. The Advisory Board also heard from offenders who had been placed in treatment by the Court to help develop additional procedures for addressing the problems of high risk offenders; reviewed information about court outcomes; and helped develop strategies for finding additional housing or employment for defendants.

By the end of the research period, project staff had also begun to mediate community-level disputes at the Court; experimented with a victim-offender reconciliation panel, bringing together a small group of community leaders and local prostitutes to examine the impact of street prostitution on the neighborhood; and developed a touch-screen electronic suggestion box to permit defendants and community members to send recommendations and complaints to members of the Court staff.

Project staff also conducted a substantial amount of community outreach. Student interns canvassed the commercial strip along Eighth and Ninth Avenues to expand the mailing list for the Court's newsletter. Coordinating staff hosted several police-community council meetings at the courthouse; made presentations at police roll calls and at meetings of local Community Boards and Block Associations; distributed newsletters documenting the accomplishments of community service and social service projects; contributed a monthly column to a community newspaper; and staffed a booth at the Ninth Avenue International Food Festival to disseminate information about the Court. They also hosted a series of tours for criminal justice personnel, social service providers, community members, journalists, student groups, policy makers and visitors from other cities, states and nations. The Court established additional connections to the residential and business communities through the Mayor's Midtown Citizen Committee and local Community Board officials.

The Court's efforts to disseminate information about its accomplishments were supplemented by extensive media coverage. Articles about the Court were prominently featured in international, national and local media, including Australia's *Beyond 2000;* Japanese television news; Court TV's *Instant Justice;* NBC and ABC national news; National Public Radio; *Wired*; *The National Law Journal; New York Magazine*; *The New York Times;* and other local newspapers, television and radio stations.

Community desire for information about the Court Outreach efforts were designed to provide a response to a community desire for information. Before the Court opened, community leaders and residents complained that traditional courts provide little feedback to the community about the Court's accomplishments.

> *There needs to be more news about the courts. I never hear anything unless something goes wrong.... I ought to know what's going on in the courts, what judges are doing, why they are doing it.*
>
> *People don't notice when things are better, not the way they do when things get bad.... Somehow the Court has to make a connection between what they do and the fact that there was some improvement.*

Community members wanted the kind of information provided through local newspapers in smaller communities documenting the outcomes of criminal court cases. Local community leaders, particularly those who had worked with project planners early on, expected aggressive outreach and communications—newsletters, handouts, publicity about community service projects and community impacts—from the new Court.

At the end of the first year, community leaders were disappointed with the amount of feedback they had received. Although they understood that the process of establishing the new Court was quite demanding, they still wanted more information:

> *They've been in operation for a year and there should be that slide talk that goes out to community organizations....*
>
> *There should be a 20-minute presentation of what the Court has accomplished.*
>
> *They do need a newsletter every month, they need inspirational stories, they need statistics... at least quarterly. The Community Court has a responsibility to make itself known and to the extent that it speaks to being a community court, its responsibility is to define who that community is and how to reach them. And in my mind they haven't done that as well as they might have.*

Beginning in the second year, project staff began disseminating information to community leaders and community residents more frequently. A first-year progress report was widely disseminated. Quarterly newsletters were issued. The Community Advisory Board was convened regularly and sub-committees were formed to advise the Court about the development of new initiatives. The hunger for feedback led Court staff to write a monthly column describing Court accomplishments in a neighborhood newspaper, the *Chelsea-Clinton News*. By the end of the research period, community leaders were substantially more satisfied with the amount of feedback provided.

Other roles for the community After the first year, project staff began to call on the Community Advisory Board in new ways: to help plan a pilot employment program for defendants who completed Midtown community service sentences and to help identify potential uses for a geo-mapping capacity at the Court. In the Court's second year, community leaders provided substantial support in designing a not-for-profit copy shop, Times Square Ink, that would serve as a job training center for participants in a proposed employment program. Community partners were instrumental in helping the project leverage resources from the private sector, including office space from the 42nd Street Development Project; securing marketing assistance from an experienced Midtown printing firm; identifying potential corporate customers; and connecting the project with prospective employers for program graduates.

Concerns about the community's role Some Court personnel interviewed before the Court opened were concerned about the possibility that community members would expect too powerful a voice:

> *The name is Community Court, but it will still be a court, and all the rules apply.... Nobody can tell a judge what to do. A judge is independent.... I think that might be a rubbing point.*
>
> *Sometimes communities expect to have a voice in the administration of justice .... or in response to crimes. They might expect a greater say than they're actually going to get. There might be some friction. Don't forget, a lynch mob is one community response to crime.... There is the possibility that they might think, 'We now have our Community Court and we can run it the way we want'... Well, they may have a greater say in some of the ancillary things, programs and things, but they're not going to have a direct say.*

In practice, these concerns about the community expecting too much of a voice at the Court proved unfounded. Although local court watch groups regularly monitored case outcomes for particular types of defendants (prostitutes, "johns"), they proved to be less hungry for "vigilante justice" than the defense bar had predicted. Instead of clamoring for more and lengthier jail sentences, community members became active partners in developing and administering alternative sanctions programs. For example, one local group, Residents Against Street Prostitution (RASP), had lobbied long and hard for a more constructive response to street level prostitution than sentences of time served. Over the first two years, RASP published several community newsletters about the Court, praising its impact on case outcomes and the availability of community service crews to address local eyesores.

Judges working at the Court were careful to define themselves as impartial decision-makers who were not responsive to community pressure. The coordinating team served as a mechanism for interacting with the community and addressing neighborhood problems through court-based programs.

Mediating Community Disputes

In the first year, the Court joined forces with the Office of Court Administration to establish a different type of mediation service dedicated to resolving broad-based community conflicts. According to coordinating staff, this was expected to provide another tool for addressing quality-of-life problems in the target area:

> *Some quality-of-life problems in communities seldom come to the attention of the police or courts. Even though they are chronic and divisive, they may not constitute violations of law. Courts have developed the tools of mediation and arbitration to help solve disputes among members of the community that never actually reach a courthouse. The Court is using these tools to help people living in the Times Square, Clinton and Chelsea area. Mediators working at the Court hear disputes that involve the placement of dog runs, the hours and noise of an auto repair shop, and the conversion of a business to an adult movie house (Midtown Community Court, 1994: p. 10).*

By the end of the first year, community leaders were both well-informed about and appreciative of the Court's mediation services.

> *The Court... has a mediation program which tries to settle disputes between residents and businesses.... They stepped in between that [pornographic video store] they were going to open and the community groups.... Other merchants agreed to pay rent to the landlord until they could find a better tenant.*
>
> *At the Community Board, we've taken advantage of that service a lot. In our role as trying to mediate between various interests in the community, we've used the mediation services regularly. And they've been very responsive.*

Reaching Out to Local Police

The role played by police officers in New York City misdemeanor courts generally ends with the drafting of the criminal complaint. Because less than 1 percent of misdemeanor cases proceed to trial, police officers rarely have a role in the court processing of low-level crimes and typically receive no feedback about the outcomes of their cases. As a consequence, many are skeptical about how courts deal with low-level offenses. They frequently complain that the "courts don't back them up" and produce nothing more than "revolving door justice." As one officer put it:

> *[M]ost police officers don't trust the court system. If the courtroom Downtown worked, there would be no need for [the Court]. No cop I know believes in the system.*

Officers also complained about multiple disincentives to enforcing low-level crime. They pointed out that they were often chastised for accumulating overtime associated with low-level arrests; that both ADAs and judges were uninterested in such cases and "dismissed them with 'time served';" and that the environment—waiting for ADAs, waiting in court—served as a disincentive to aggressive enforcement of low-level offenses. They also contended that the Police Department itself discouraged the enforcement of some quality-of-life offenses: "[M]aking a [low-level] drug collar is like walking on egg shells wearing golf shoes."

Before the Court opened, police officers were clearly its most skeptical constituents. One officer was perplexed by the Court's combined focus on punishing defendants by having them pay back the community, and helping them through Court-based social services: "Who is running the show there? Is it some liberal yuppy or G. Gordon Liddy?"

Convinced that "cutting police out of the process was a disservice to both the officers and the Court," coordinating staff made a series of efforts to reach out to local police. This included meeting with precinct commanders; attending precinct roll calls to describe the Court to patrol officers and rookies; hosting police-community council meetings at the courthouse; and establishing a close working relationship with the Community Affairs Officer at Midtown North. Local precincts have also requested and received assistance from Midtown community service crews for both specific local clean up projects and routine precinct house maintenance.

Concerted efforts were made to provide feedback to local police about case outcomes. Early in the first year, they began sending aggregate data to precinct commanders that provided information about sentence outcomes for specific charges. Later that year, they sent detailed feedback reports to each precinct that showed the arrests made by individual officers; the arraignment disposition and sentence for each case; information about compliance with community service and social service sentences; and information about outstanding warrants. This feedback process generated additional requests from both precinct commanders seeking information about case outcomes for a specific type of offense or a particular precinct and aggressive community police officers eager for information about outstanding warrants as a potential enforcement tool. By the end of the research period, court technology staff were developing procedures for linking local police officers to electronic feedback information, accessible through computer links between the Court and Midtown North.

Local police officers gradually began taking advantage of the Court's local presence. On several occasions, they returned known offenders with outstanding warrants directly to court—a practice that is rare in New York City where misdemeanor warrants have the lowest enforcement priority. In addition, they have drawn upon court-based social services to help them link troubled individuals on their beats to appropriate services, as these examples illustrate:

- A police officer from Midtown North brought a mentally retarded woman who had lost her money to con artists to the Court's social service floor. Counselors helped the woman call her mother in Ohio, who had recently filed a missing person report. They arranged the woman's transportation back to Ohio through Traveler's Aid and made sure that her mother was there to meet the bus.
- A local officer sought help from court-based social service staff for a neighborhood resident who had been arrested many times and who had recently been released from jail. Although this individual had not been rearrested, the officer knew that he had a serious substance abuse problem and believed that substance abuse treatment could help him avoid rearrest. Court-based counselors interviewed him and arranged a placement in a local treatment facility.
- On a weekend night, a local police officer arrested Mandy, a prostitute who had been at the Community Court multiple times and who had already established a relationship with Court-based social service staff. Over the previous month, she had talked to social service staff about leaving her pimp to return home. Although she was brought to 100 Centre Street on the weekend arrest, the officer called Court social service staff to discuss her case. Alerted by the officer's call, counseling staff

reached out to Mandy after her release and provided assistance in her efforts to leave her pimp and return to her home town.

By the end of the research period, Court staff and community police officers had begun collaborating on a new initiative that would build upon existing informal relationships between Court staff and local police. A proposed street outreach program would pair community patrol officers with court-based social service staff, offering immediate assistance—substance abuse treatment, access to battered women's shelters, housing assistance, Traveler's Aid—to street people who loitered or convened at known "hot spots". An outreach team was assembled to target locations frequented by addicts and prostitutes, including a crack den/crash pad that has generated repeated complaints at community meetings. Court-based social service staff will join with the police in helping to link troubled individuals directly to services.

By bringing together multiple partners—both inside and outside the Court—the Court has focused increased attention on the needs of the Midtown community and the defendant population. A team spirit has developed that cuts across institutional boundaries at the courthouse, as representatives of various groups—Court personnel, local police, coordinating staff, social service providers from community-based organizations, staff from city agencies, community service supervisors—work together to address defendant problems. It's not uncommon for community service supervisors or police officers to identify individuals who have serious drug problems or who are the victims of domestic violence and refer them to on-site counselors. Together, the small size of the Court and the "mission-driven" focus of its multi-agency staff have created a community within a community—a courthouse, located in the center of a bustling metropolis, that, on occasion, feels like a small-town court.

Notes

1. One long-term objective of the Court is to promote dialogue between offenders and community groups, modeled after victim-offender reconciliation panels. Late in the research period, coordinating staff pilot-tested a community impact panel, bringing together selected prostitutes with multiple cases at the Midtown Community Court, community leaders and trained mediators. The panel was designed to help defendants understand the impact of quality-of-life offenses on the Midtown neighborhood, provide community members "with a forum for voicing their concerns and educating them about the underlying causes" of low-level offenses.

2. Because there was no information available about the correlates of community service compliance before the Court opened, planning staff initially developed procedures for assigning defendants to on-site and off-site community service projects based on common sense. Defendants with DATs and no open warrants were eligible for "low supervision" off-site placements if they were not homeless and had not been arraigned on drug or prostitution charges. Subsequent analysis demonstrated that many of the factors used in determining supervision level (case type, warrant status, homelessness and charge) were in fact correlated with the likelihood of compliance.
3. Additional analysis shows that the completion rate among prostitutes with sentences of five days or more (73%) was higher than their completion rate for shorter sentences (62%). This is partly because repeat offenders with a good track record of completion are likely to draw long community service sentences at the Court. Those who have failed previous alternative sanctions face a higher risk of jail sentences.
4. During the baseline period, there were no data available about the frequency of sentences mandating treatment participation in either the official state criminal justice information system, CRIMS or a CJA research database that compiles information on Criminal Court outcomes. Although these systems record information on the frequency of conditional discharges, they did not typically provide information on the conditions imposed. In recent years, both systems have added the capacity to count conditional discharges with an accompanying community service mandate. They do not, however, include information on social service mandates.
5. Voluntary participants come from a variety of sources: 20 percent sentenced to both community service and social service sanctions, 39 percent with social service sentences, 29 percent sentenced to community service and 12 percent who had not received an alternative sanction (defendants with other types of disposition/sentence, walk-ins, referrals made by local police, referrals made by treatment participants, etc.). In theory, the pool of potential voluntary treatment clients includes: defendants who completed at least one day of court-based social service or community service and who reported alcohol or substance abuse during the CJA assessment. By the end of January 1995, there were 1,055 defendants with these characteristics; over 10 percent of them (111) sought long-term treatment through court-based case managers.

CHAPTER FIVE

PROJECT IMPLEMENTATION

Before assessing the impacts of the Court on case outcomes, community conditions and community attitudes, it makes sense to examine whether difficulties in implementing components of the project impeded the Court's ability to reach its operational objectives. As highlighted in Chapter 1, much of the early debate about the project gave rise to predictions that the Court would have little impact. Critics argued that there would be too few cases to justify the establishment of the Court; that defendants' ability to "forum shop" for more lenient outcomes would make it difficult to change sentencing patterns; and that too few defendants would comply with community service sentences to affect community conditions. Before the Court opened, there was considerable speculation among outside observers about whether the project would be able to implement its extremely ambitious agenda.

By the end of the first year, it was clear that the Midtown Community Court closely embodied the planners' vision of what a community-based urban court might be. As expected, the Court introduced an array of intermediate sanctions that pay back the community harmed by crime and that use social services to address the underlying problems of defendants. Community members were enlisted as vital partners in the development and operation of community restitution projects and court-based social services. Technology emerged as a central tool in expanding the information available in the courtroom and in promoting strict accountability for intermediate sanction programs. And judges working at the Court made substantial use of these programs to provide a graduated, proportional response to low-level offenses.

Most of the predictions of the Court's early critics proved unfounded. As planners expected, the Court had little difficulty arraigning defendants within 24 hours of their arrest. Although some criminal justice personnel predicted widespread adjournments in response to the Court's new sentencing options, roughly 75 percent of cases were disposed at arraignment—a substantially higher aggregate disposition rate than in the Downtown court, where roughly 60 percent of misdemeanors and violations were disposed at arraignment.[1] Contrary to critics' predictions, the large majority of defendants completed community service sentences and efforts to engage community members in new ways did not serve to promote a desire for "vigilante justice."

Although there were relatively few barriers to implementation, several key issues needed to be addressed. Continuing effort was required to ensure that the new Court came close to its anticipated caseload of roughly sixty arraignments per day. There were concerns about the frequency of "forum shopping" among unlicensed vendors and prostitutes. Court technology staff confronted challenges in their efforts to introduce an ambitious new computer network. Procedures for scheduling and operating court-based alternative sanction programs evolved in response to developing problems, including backlogs in the issuing of declarations of delinquency and the need for rigorous tracking of participants in long-term substance abuse treatment.

This chapter reviews issues and themes that arose during the implementation process and the gradual evolution of central components of the Court. It also reviews local changes that may have supported the Court's effort to develop constructive responses to quality-of-life crimes and improve conditions in the Midtown area.

IMPLEMENTATION ISSUES

Reaching the Projected Caseload

Planning staff initially estimated that the new Court would arraign approximately 15,000 cases per year (60 cases per day).[2] In the early months, the Court's caseload was built slowly and deliberately. New sub-groups of cases were added one-by-one to permit revision and modification of procedures. In 1994, the Court's first full calendar year, it arraigned approximately 80 percent of the anticipated case-load. Some members of the criminal justice community were concerned that the phase-in process moved too slowly, reducing the project's ability to demonstrate how many cases could be handled per shift.

Even after the phase-in process was complete, caseload volume remained a concern. Although planners had accurately estimated the volume of cases arising in Midtown, roughly 20 percent of these continued to be arraigned Downtown. Around fifteen Midtown cases per day were tracked to the Downtown court because the prosecutor required a face-to-face interview with the arresting officer. In the summer of 1995, video-conference technology was introduced and was expected to eliminate the need for sending cases Downtown. But an analysis of data provided by

CJA showed that almost 3,000 cases per year, consisting primarily of low-level drug cases, petit larceny and traffic charges, continued to be arraigned at the Downtown court after its installation.

Project staff met repeatedly with local criminal justice officials to develop mechanisms for ensuring that appropriate cases were sent to Midtown. They also proposed adding other groups of cases (e.g., prostitution cases from other precincts, which were added in October 1994; cases from an adjoining eastside precinct) that could enter the Court's caseload without compromising the focus on a self-contained target community. This effort to add appropriate cases was driven by the fact that the Court had the capacity to handle a larger caseload and a concern about the continuing pressure on the Downtown court.[3]

Case Processing Issues

Members of the local criminal justice community raised questions about other key aspects of case processing. Before the Court opened, project staff needed to resolve issues related to the confidentiality of assessment information about defendants.

CJA interviews and attorney concerns There was considerable early discussion about the legal status and confidentiality of the expanded pre-arraignment interviews conducted by the Criminal Justice Agency. Some attorneys voiced concerns about the assessment information maintained on the Court's computer system:

> *... at the DA's Office we have... privacy concerns. We have huge amounts of confidential information that we use in prosecution.... We can't have it be some place where it can be accessed. We are obligated to keep it private....*

CJA interviewers at the Court handle more groups of defendants (defendants with DATs; defendants charged with prostitution) and gather more information from each defendant (prior substance abuse, health status, history of homelessness) than at the Downtown court. Although responding to the interview was voluntary, defense attorneys were not present during the CJA assessment interview. They were particularly concerned about the potential impact of information about prior substance abuse on case outcomes.[4] However, one early concern proved groundless: an assessment made at the Court does not follow a defendant if a case is continued to another arraignment part.

The intensity of these concerns faded after the Court opened. Some observers continued to question the appropriateness and costs of conducting CJA interviews with defendants who had received DATs. Yet, over time, respondents came to view assessment interviews as just another aspect of how the Court conducted business.

Adjournments The possibility of "forum shopping" at the Court also received considerable attention. There were two primary concerns that a broad increase in adjournments would raise system costs and that this would affect the project's ability to promote more constructive sentence outcomes.

Concerns about the frequency of forum shopping for vendors and prostitutes reflected an accurate assessment of which charges had high rates of adjournment at the Court, compared to baseline measures. These concerns were limited to two offenses only and were linked primarily to concerns about maximizing the Court's use of community restitution.

Some criminal justice professionals, recognizing that the new Court had produced a relatively high *aggregate* disposition rate, attributed it to caseload differences. Most criminal justice observers were aware that arraignment disposition and adjournment rates differed greatly by charge. They pointed out that the types of offenses concentrated in Midtown were more likely to be disposed at arraignment than offenses arising in other parts of Manhattan. For example, the Court arraigned a relatively small proportion of assault cases, which were typically adjourned at arraignment because of the need for corroborating interviews with complaining witnesses. There was little concern that overall adjournment rates had increased, putting extra pressure on the court system as a whole.

New Technology, New Players and New Information

Before the Court opened, there was considerable interest among clerks and attorneys about technology:

> *It's going to be incredibly computerized. And the computer system, if successful, will be extended to the other courts, Downtown. So I would just as soon learn them before they are introduced Downtown. Get a leg up.*
>
> *I'm looking forward to the computers ... the idea of a paperless court. Hard to imagine it. It's exciting.*

The technology has been an essential tool in reshaping how the Court does business. It was designed to serve a number of purposes, including facilitating the flow of cases, supplying the information necessary to support informed sentencing decisions and ensuring strict accountability for intermediate sanction programs. Project staff summarized it thus:

> *The Court application was designed to help criminal court judges make decisions rapidly and analytically and help the Court communicate with the public and outside agencies. Judges can quickly review electronically transmitted arrest, complaint and criminal history information; dispositional recommendations; and assessment information about defendants' homelessness, substance abuse and other problems. Flashing buttons alert judges and attorneys to information about defendants' prior court appearances, their sentence compliance and participation in social services. Case management screens help judges monitor defendants sentenced to long-term drug treatment. Large-screen TVs provide public information about all calendared cases. (Application to Windowsworld Open, March 1995).*

By the end of the first year, the Court's technology had been fully integrated into every stage of the court process from pre-arraignment case preparation through post-sentence monitoring.

But the effort to create New York City's first "paperless" court was not without significant "growing pains." Particularly in the early months, court proceedings were held up by delays in transmitting electronic "rap sheets" to the Court. Court clerks were frustrated by frozen screens, system crashes and the continuing need to assemble paper files for the Downtown court. The attempts to have CJA staff directly enter interview responses into hand-held computers, and to automate the calculation of a release-recommendation score, were unsuccessful as was the effort to transfer Midtown data to CJA's own computerized database.

Court clerks and attorneys were quick to express their frustrations with the new system:

> *I would spend more time on the computer systems up front, before starting operations. 'Cause they caused a lot of problems, and they still are....*

> *As far as computers go, there is still work to be done. In planning stages, people didn't realize what a daunting task it was.... This was a project in which they had nothing to refer to, no models. Everything was a first. Naturally, something like that requires a lot of fine-tuning to get it where you want. What needs most fine-tuning is the computer area....*

By the end of the first year, it was increasingly evident that the Court's technology was more valued by habitual users (the judge, clerks, the resource coordinator, coordinating staff) than by occasional users (defense attorneys, assistant district attorneys).

Attorneys proved particularly resistant to using court technology. Although defense attorneys had requested and received a new computer module that would simplify the process of making bail applications, they typically paid little attention to the computer system. Neither defense nor prosecuting attorneys relied extensively on color-coded assessment screens but deferred to the resource coordinator to review information about defendants' underlying problems. Attorneys typically saw little connection between their work at the Court and the information available on the Court's computer system.

> *... the defense attorneys don't use the computer (or) the DAs ... Maybe the clerks use it a little bit. And the resource coordinator uses it.*

They complained about excessive "down time," "sitting around and waiting" for rap sheets to be sent and for complaints to be scanned in:

> *All the rap sheets, all the information that we get from the computer is scanned in at some point ... all that paper.... So, there we are, all these lawyers, waiting for the stuff to get scanned in... So that we won't use it.*

For other Midtown staff, technology played a central role, effectively restructuring how they did their job. Both the resource coordinator and the judge routinely reviewed assessment screens, information about prior court appearances and prior compliance with previous sentences, case management notes and information about participation in mandatory long-term treatment. One judge working at the Court relied on technology to provide "a better quality and range of information. We don't have to rely on guesses as much." Court-based community service and social service staff relied upon immediate printouts showing case dispositions to help them schedule defendants in appropriate programs. Both court clerks and staff on the Court's alternative sanction floor depended upon technology to maintain and review information about program compliance. The ready access to this information streamlined the process of issuing declarations of delinquency and warrants for non-compliance. Technology as a whole ensured that Court staff would have detailed information about the defendants before the court.

Midtown staff continued to develop and expand the Court's technology application. During the first year, new modules were created to help court-based case managers assess candidates for the mandatory long-term treatment/case management program, identify appropriate community-based treatment providers, monitor defendants' participation in substance abuse treatment programs and provide information about the results of urine tests to the Court. In addition, technology staff, supported by a grant from the State Justice Institute, began the process of developing additional components, including:

- a mapping screen demonstrating the community context of the offense, such as whether it took place on a residential or business block, in a high crime area or near a school, etc.;
- a module showing compliance rates in various alternative sanction programs for selected types of defendants—defined by charge type, criminal history, substance abuse problems, etc.;
- up-to-date information about the defendant's involvement with different criminal justice and service agencies (Probation, Parole, Corrections, etc.); and
- electronic links to local police that would allow the Court to transmit information about dispositions, sentences and outstanding warrants for individual defendants.

The Court's software received considerable attention both locally and nationally for its role in re-shaping Court operations, including a prominent feature in *Wired* magazine. In March 1995, the Court's software application won the 1995 WindowsWorld Open competition, sponsored by Microsoft to recognize innovation and excellence in the application of technology to new settings. The development of customized software for the Court has made a substantial contribution to both statewide and national-level debates about the potential functions of court technology providing an impetus for longer-term systemic change.

Ensuring Accountability

Procedures for ensuring accountability for both community service and social service sentences evolved gradually. In the early months of the project, on-site research staff documented a growing need to respond more rapidly to non-compliance:

> *There's been a problem keeping up with warrants for community service. A substantial number of cases have*

> *been kept open before Declarations of Delinquency were issued. This was partly a staffing problem. The community service coordinator was initially overburdened— responsible for instructing community service participants about the terms of their sentence, and for scheduling, assigning and monitoring their community service compliance, as well as for issuing Declarations of Delinquency. A community service assistant started working with him a few weeks ago. Since then, staff have been catching up on overdue warrants for both community service and social service.*

During the first year, it also became apparent that the Court needed to develop new procedures to track defendants' participation in long-term treatment. Therefore, a new computer module was developed to ensure regular monitoring of treatment status and provide up-to-date information to the judge. When defendants sentenced to long-term drug treatment/ case management reappear in court for the judge to review their treatment status, information about that status is also immediately visible on the court computer. Court-based case managers monitor participation in treatment readiness, detox and treatment programs and provide electronic notes to the judge about defendants' participation. At subsequent court appearances, a "notes" button on the computer screen flashes, to alert the judge to electronic messages about client status.

In addition, a case management tracking module was developed to show the judge a defendant's treatment involvement day-by-day along with information about urine test outcomes. This screen displays a calendar of activities, including attendance at court-based treatment readiness sessions, participation in detox or treatment programs, excused absences and delinquency which is highlighted in red. The client tracking module is designed to help case managers maintain detailed records about defendants and the extent of their participation in local treatment programs. It also provides a directory of local treatment programs, information about various treatment modalities offered by each, their individual entrance requirements and an electronic "rolodex" of staff contacts.

According to attorneys and judges, the level of accountability at the Court ensures that non-compliance with sentences to intermediate sanctions issued in Midtown elicits a tougher response than non-compliance with such sentences issued Downtown. Local judges point out that because Midtown staff are known to monitor compliance closely, warrants issued by the Court for nonparticipation in community service and social service programs are taken seriously, when they are returned to either the Court or the Downtown court.

EMERGING THEMES

The Changing Nature of the Courtroom Work Group

The expanded information available in the courtroom, together with the long-term assignment of courtroom staff to Midtown, has influenced the nature of the courtroom "work group." Observers often comment that judge plays a far more active role in the misdemeanor arraignment process than judges in traditional arraignment courts. Armed with information about defendants' substance abuse, homelessness and other problems, as well as their previous participation in intermediate sanction programs, judges at the Court play a determining role in bringing cases to disposition and sentence and in monitoring compliance with sentence conditions.

For some defendants, the Midtown judge acts more like a drug court judge than an arraignment judge. Cases of defendants in mandatory long-term treatment are scheduled monthly for updates and judicial monitoring. Hearings can be held to review violations of conditional discharge. These activities represent "add-ons" to the arraignment court calendar. In addition, judges attend Community Advisory Board meetings and meet frequently with coordinating staff to review developing programmatic initiatives. Judges concur that their role at Midtown is a far cry from "business as usual."

The continuity of assignments for judges, attorneys and other court personnel at the Court also contributed to a shift in the nature of courtroom interactions. In contrast to the Downtown court, where assignments rotate frequently, many staff members have had long-term assignments in Midtown. During the first eighteen months, a single judge presided over most of the calendar, with back-up from four additional judges who covered vacations, sick days, holidays and night-court assignments. A small pool of defense and prosecution staff had either long-term or rotating assignments to Midtown.[5] A contingent of court clerks and court officers have permanent assignments at the Court. The result is a courtroom team that is unique in New York City arraignment courts, where courtroom personnel rotate frequently from part to part.

There were mixed opinions about the role of the resource coordinator, a new position in the courtroom. The resource coordinator was seen by Court planners as a critical new player, the linchpin in efforts to identify appropriate alternative sanctions. Other observers initially believed that the adversarial process would drive the resource coordinator to the margins. Indeed, early on several courtroom staff were only vaguely aware of the resource coordinator and her function.

Over time, some attorneys working at the Court became convinced that the presence of the resource coordinator had partly supplanted their role in the adversarial process:

> *[The] bottom line is that we found in better than 90 percent of the cases compliance by the Court with the recommendations made by the resource coordinator. We have an adversarial system ... [defense], prosecutor—those are the only entities that have official standing to discuss what's going on.*

Some assistant district attorneys raised objections to the role of the resource coordinator as an "outside party" influencing decision-making:

> *There is the resource coordinator [who] puts a recommendation for sentencing into the computer for the judge. It's a silent party which I think is inappropriate... I think it takes away part of the judicial functions....*
>
> *The problem is adding this additional party. [The defense] is supposed to give the judge reasons why she should sentence the defendant to... [a specific program]... It is my job to tell him to sentence the defendant to, or not to something. And here you have the two of us doing this. And the judge is looking at a screen and getting an outside party's position on what the sentence should be....*

Yet there was growing appreciation of the resource coordinator among the defense bar. Defense attorneys particularly appreciated the resource coordinator's efforts to link defendants to appropriate programs:

> *It's a good thing that there's someone who has training to look into these things, to actually talk to these people and find out what the problem is.... The idea behind the Community Court was to change the lives of these people, to turn them around.*

Court observations suggest that the presence of the resource coordinator ultimately served to enhance the role of the judge. It quickly became apparent that decision-making at the Court was more judge-driven than customary. The judge relied on the resource coordinator to provide information about the alternative sanctions available at the Court, arrange assessments for defendants being considered for long-term treatment as an alternative to jail, ensure immediate placement in detox or treatment facilities and verify information about compliance with alternative sanctions. Combined with the expanded information available on Court's computer system and the close monitoring of intermediate sanctions provided by coordinating staff, the resource coordinator position served to put the judge "in the driver's seat."

Although the support provided by the resource coordinator proved a valuable support, according to Midtown judges, it did not in itself *determine* case outcomes. Instead, the judge closely monitored information about case outcomes and alternative sanction compliance, became knowledgeable about the social service options available on-site and, ultimately, controlled the process of determining appropriate plea offers.

The difference in the judge's role was clear to defendants at the new Court as well as informed criminal justice professionals. They soon became aware that the Midtown judge was armed with more information than Downtown judges. Defendants reported that judges at the Court "know everything about you."

There were other changes. Over time, defense attorneys also grew familiar with the alternative sanction programs available at the Court and began initiating recommendations to draw upon on-site resources. Although generally the resource coordinator or the judge would recommend that a treatment alternative be considered, attorneys began calling upon the resource coordinator in their efforts to link clients to drug treatment as an alternative to jail.

Expanding Social Services

Early on, coordinating staff held weekly "wrap-up" meetings to review developing procedures in the courtroom and on the alternative sanction floor, identify problems and test potential solutions. These "debriefing" sessions were central to the evolution of and development of court-based programs.

In some sessions, staff conducted case conferences about individual defendants—a heroin addict with a lengthy history of shoplifting arrests, placed by Court staff in residential treatment;

a woman with multiple convictions for prostitution who reported being ready for change. These reviews helped court-based staff respond appropriately to individual clients and improve procedures for assessing client needs, matching them to appropriate services and monitoring outcomes. Coordinating staff recognized that inclusion of multiple social service providers at the courthouse provided a solid platform to build on but continuing efforts were required to respond to the complicated needs of a troubled population.

Particular attention was paid to addressing gaps in the range of services that might address defendants' problems. Although project staff had assembled an array of social service partners to provide direct services at the courthouse, the vocational services available to the defendant population were seen as insufficient. In pre-arraignment assessment interviews, over 40 percent of defendants reported wanting help with employment or vocational training. Both the resource coordinator and the community service coordinator repeatedly reported that defendants wanted help finding work.

The absence of readily available vocational services limited the new Court's ability to address one of the most pressing problems of the defendant population. Early on, coordinating staff established some capacity to conduct job readiness training, provide job referrals and link defendants to a program providing vocational services to a population between the ages of 16 and 24. However, there were few vocational services available for older defendants. In response to this gap, project staff developed an internship program that used the court-based mailhouse as an informal training site for a small number of defendants who demonstrated a strong commitment to building vocational skills. Beginning early in the Court's second year, coordinating staff focused on planning a more formal job training program, Times Square Ink, which began operating early in 1997.

Providing primary health care Although the Court established a capacity to provide medical testing, health education and referrals early on, it took longer to develop direct medical services at the courthouse. By the end of 1995, the New York University School of Nursing, in collaboration with the Court, had received funding from the Department of Health and Human Services to place a Nurse Practitioner at the Court to provide primary health care, including physical and gynecological exams, mental health screening and nutritional counseling.

The Role of the Coordinating Team

In describing the array of community partnerships established at the Court, project documents refer frequently to court-based social service providers and local supervisors of community service projects. Yet, relatively little text has been devoted to the primary partnership involved in the planning and development of the Court—the core relationship between administrative staff from the Unified Court System (UCS) and coordinating staff from the Fund for the City of New York (FCNY).

The joint UCS-FCNY coordinating team, in itself, represents a unique public-private collaboration. Members of the coordinating team have described the relationship as "seamless." During the planning and start-up periods, FCNY coordinating staff, working in close collaboration with the Administrative Judge of the New York City Criminal Court, played an unprecedented role at the courthouse, as the developers and coordinators of court-based community service and social service initiatives, technology and community outreach. The strong commitment of the Chief Judge of the State of New York helped ensure system-wide acceptance of this central alliance.

The coordinating team serves as an acknowledged intermediary between the Court and the community, establishing a channel for communications. Independent coordinating staff provide a "buffer zone" that helps shield judges from the perceived threat of undue community influence on decision making.

A central objective of the UCS-FCNY partnership was to produce a direct connection between the courtroom and court-based alternative sanction programs. The Court's integrated technology, which provides rapid feedback about defendants' participation in court-based alternative sanction programs, helps build this connection. At the Court, alternative sanction programs are not external add-ons, but an intrinsic part of court operations, broadly conceived.

At the end of 1994, internal changes within UCS posed a potential challenge to this central partnership. The Administrative Judge of the New York City Criminal Courts, Robert G.M. Keating, who had primary responsibility within UCS for overseeing the Court, was reassigned as the Administrative Judge for the Second Judicial District of the New York State Supreme Court. Judge Keating's reassignment ultimately had little effect on the coordinating team. In his new role, Judge Keating retained authority over the Court and other innovative projects involving court-community collaboration. The strong commitment of the UCS leadership to both the Court and the partnership with FCNY coordinating staff promoted a general acceptance of the team's effort to build broad court-community collaboration.

UNANTICIPATED FACTORS: OTHER INFLUENCES ON QUALITY OF LIFE IN MIDTOWN

The local political and economic context in which the project developed is an important part of the story. Any study of the Court's impacts must take into account both the barriers to and supports for project objectives that emerged during the implementation period. The multiplicity of local influences complicates the analysis of preliminary impacts on court outcomes, quality-of-life conditions and the enforcement of low-level offenses.

Broad influences on sentence outcomes During the research period, there was a growing commitment throughout Manhattan to using short-term alternative sanctions for low-level offenses at the Downtown court. This trend was partly stimulated by the local debate about the Court and its objectives. Because of this trend, it is important that analysis identify both impacts and trends in sentencing patterns for quality-of-life offenses. Therefore, the research database includes both baseline data and contemporaneous comparison data about case outcomes at the Downtown court.

Broad influences on local conditions In addition to the Court, several concurrent initiatives contributed to a general upgrading of Times Square and the surrounding area. Business Improvement Districts played a growing role in delivering enhanced sanitation and security in the Midtown area. The long-planned redevelopment of 42nd Street began attracting a growing number of new businesses to the Times Square area, following the announcement that the Disney Corporation would establish a hub for family entertainment. Increasing economic development began to transform sections of Midtown that had resisted the gentrification that swept Manhattan during the early 1980s. The Manhattan real estate market gradually emerged from a lengthy period of recession.

The Court began operating during a period of substantial transition in the local criminal justice community as well. The city's new mayor and police commissioner mounted a widely publicized campaign to take quality-of-life offenses seriously, leading to increased enforcement of "squeegee" window washers, panhandling in the subway, soliciting prostitution and other quality-of-life offenses. As discussed, the number of quality-of-life cases entering the courts increased citywide.[6]

Both of these trends—economic development and an increased focus on enforcing quality-of-life offenses—contributed to improvements in the quality of life in the Midtown area. As shown in Chapter 7, respondents to panel interviews and focus group participants were well aware that multiple influences, including the Court, contributed to making the streets of Midtown safer and cleaner.

Influences on quality-of-life enforcement One of the expressed objectives of the Court was to encourage police enforcement of low-level offenses. As discussed, local enforcement of quality-of-life crime increased substantially in response to the citywide policies of a new mayor and new police commissioner, who strongly endorsed aggressive enforcement of quality-of-life crime. These intensified policies provided an unanticipated support for the Court's effort to treat quality-of-life offenses seriously. The Court's growing collaboration with local police, discussed in Chapter 4, also served to encourage enforcement of low-level warrants.

Analysis of the Court's effects on quality-of-life enforcement needs to take into account the strong influence of policy initiatives at the New York City Police Department. It also needs to consider other influences on arrest levels in the Midtown area. As discussed in Chapter 7, prostitution arrests in Midtown dropped substantially in response to sentence outcomes at the Court and an increased number of "john" arrests. Although the Court sought to encourage quality-of-life enforcement, the drop in prostitution arrests in the Midtown area represents a successful project outcome.

Overall, there is no reason to believe that any of the implementation issues reviewed above substantially affected the Court's ability to achieve its objectives. The following chapters analyze the Court's preliminary effects on case outcomes, community conditions and community attitudes in a changing community context.

Notes

1. There are substantial differences between the two courts in adjournment rates for specific charges. Although the Court produces a substantially

larger percent of arraignment dispositions than the Downtown court, much of this difference is explained by underlying differences in the caseloads at the two courts.

2. There is no single arraignment part with a caseload that matches the caseload at the Court. Downtown arraignment parts which specialize in DATs rather than summary arrest cases have disproportionately high volume. The busiest Downtown arraignment part, which arraigned the bulk of DATs, averaged roughly 89 arraignments per day from January through October 1994. DATs are generally the quickest cases to arraign. Other arraignment parts, particularly those handling later shifts and arraigning mixed misdemeanor and felony caseloads, had substantially lower volume. Average caseload for all Manhattan arraignment parts was roughly 60 per day, the Court's target number. The "mix" of cases (DATs, misdemeanor summary arrests and felony arrests) handled Downtown varies from arraignment part to arraignment part.
3. After the first eighteen months, the Court's caseload continued to fluctuate in response to changes in police enforcement and charging policies that were largely beyond the control of the Court. The intensity of enforcement for specific offenses (panhandling, soliciting prostitution, turnstile jumping) shifted substantially during the demonstration period, affecting the total number of cases entering the Court and the overall caseload "mix." In October 1995, the number of arrests for turnstile jumping fell sharply, following a widely publicized incident in which an elderly woman from Pennsylvania, arrested for farebeating, was detained overnight; the drop in farebeating arrests substantially reduced the caseload volume. Subsequent changes in DAT policy have had a direct effect on the number of cases arraigned at the Court. For example, in the spring of 1996, tightened policies about the issuing of DATs increased the proportion of cases receiving summary arrests; as a result, failure to appear at arraignment dropped and arraignment volume increased.
4. In New York City, a defendant's responses to pre-arraignment interviews can be used for impeachment purposes only.
5. Four defense attorneys work at the Court each day, two from the Legal Aid Society (LAS) and two from the city's Assigned Counsel Plan. By the end of the research period, two LAS attorneys had been permanently assigned to the Court. Attorneys from the city's Assigned Counsel Plan were drawn from a pool of ten attorneys whose assignments at the Court rotate. Assistant District Attorneys are assigned to Midtown for a week at a time; they are guided by a senior paralegal from the District Attorney's office with over sixteen years of experience at the Downtown court.
6. A substantial reduction in crime rates in New York City has been widely documented and attributed to multiple factors, including increased enforcement of quality-of-life crime; the waning of the crack epidemic; demographic trends; steady growth in the New York State prison population; and other factors (Anderson, 1997; Horowitz, 1993).

CHAPTER SIX

COURT OUTCOMES IN A COMPARATIVE PERSPECTIVE

This chapter summarizes the findings of a comparative analysis of case outcomes at the Midtown Community Court and the Downtown court. It reviews differences between the two courts in case processing and case outcomes and examines the effect of the new Court on disposition rates at arraignment, conviction rates and sentence outcomes.[1]

It addresses key questions that arose during the planning period. Would defendants be more likely to adjourn their cases in search of a more lenient response Downtown? Would the Midtown Community Court be able to increase the frequency of community service and social service sentences in its effort to "pay back" the community and to help solve defendants' underlying problems? If so, how would the change in sentencing patterns affect the frequency of jail sentences and the frequency of "walks" (cases with no sanctions imposed)?

The analysis needed to control for key differences in the caseloads handled at the two courts—differences in caseload composition (the kinds of cases heard) and the type of arrest (DAT or summary arrest). Charge type and arrest type were associated with important differences in case outcomes. For example, assault cases have high adjournment rates because they require a post-arraignment interview with the complaining witness; defendants who receive DATs are less likely to be convicted, because they typically have little prior criminal justice involvement; and defendants charged with shoplifting are relatively likely to receive jail sentences because shoplifting has traditionally been seen as more serious than other misdemeanor offenses.

To control for caseload differences at the two courts, the research used multivariate statistical techniques in examining the Midtown Community Court's influence on case outcomes. These techniques allowed the research to consider multiple factors simultaneously. In essence, they permitted the research to ask how case outcomes would have differed if the Midtown and Downtown courts handled the same caseloads.

The analysis considered six key decision points:

- whether defendants given a DAT show up as scheduled;
- whether the case is disposed at arraignment or is continued;
- whether disposition is through a dismissal, an ACD[2] or conviction;
- whether the sentence involves an alternative sanction (e.g., community service), a more traditional sentence (e.g., jail or fine) or no sanction;
- whether jail sentences are imposed, and, if so, the average length of jail sentence in the two courts; and
- whether sentenced offenders comply with alternative sanctions.

DATA SOURCES

The research drew upon three large databases to analyze arraignment outcomes and used smaller data sets to examine compliance with alternative sanctions. The large databases each contain comprehensive information about cases scheduled for Criminal Court arraignment in Manhattan through the first disposition and sentence. Because the Midtown Community Court functions primarily as an arraignment part, the analysis focused on arraignment outcomes. Databases are described below:

Baseline: a 10 percent random sample, provided by New York City's Criminal Justice Agency (CJA), of all non-felony arraignments in Manhattan during the twelve months prior to the opening of the new Court (October, 1992 through September, 1993: N= 5,841).
Comparison: a sample of all non-felony arraignments held at 100 Centre Street (Downtown), also provided by CJA, during the Court's first twelve months (N = 15,125). The comparison data set included all cases from the three Midtown target precincts and a 10 percent random sample of Downtown arraignments from other precincts. This ensures sufficient numbers of cases to conduct analyses of the differences between the two courts that control for precinct of arrest, as well as charge, arrest type and prior criminal history. In descriptive tables below, the cases which originated in the three Midtown precincts received weights of one. All other cases were given a weight of ten (N = 15,125, re-weighted N = 51,188).

Midtown: data for all cases arraigned at Midtown during its first twelve months (N = 14,533).

Compliance: to help measure compliance rates for alternative sanctions at the Downtown court, the Management Information System (MIS) Division of the New York District Attorney's Office provided several case-level databases drawn from the mainframe system tracking sentences and the microcomputer system maintained by the Downtown Alternative Sanction Office; the New York County Borough Chief Clerk's Office provided us with information as well. Though the original intention was to merge this information with the defendant databases provided by CJA, there were substantial problems in merging these data sets with each other or with CJA databases because of inconsistencies in the specification of common case identifiers. Information about compliance at Midtown was drawn directly from the project's information system.

CASELOADS, CASE PROCESSING AND CASE OUTCOMES

Differences between the Midtown and Downtown Courts

There were key differences between the two courts in terms of the caseloads handled. During its first year, the Midtown Community Court operated five arraignment shifts per week, handling over 14,500 cases (about 22% of the misdemeanor caseload in Manhattan). The Downtown court, operating between 28 and 30 arraignment shifts per week, handled the balance, along with felony arraignments.

The caseloads of the two courts varied substantially by charge. The Midtown caseload included a higher proportion of petit larceny, prostitution, theft of service and unlicensed vending charges than the Downtown caseload, and a lower proportion of assault, drug and "other" charges (such as soliciting a prostitute and disorderly conduct) (see Figure 6.1).

Caseloads at the two courts also differed substantially in terms of the precinct of arrest (Midtown or not). Virtually all (96%) of the Midtown caseload stems from an arrest in one of the three Midtown precincts. As shown in Figure 6.2, arrests from non-Midtown precincts at Midtown were most common for prostitution and theft of service cases.[3] A substantially smaller proportion of Downtown cases arose in Midtown (21% overall). Midtown cases were heard Downtown for a variety of reasons: during the Midtown

Figure 6.1 Composition of Charges
(Percentages in Parentheses)

	Midtown		Downtown		Total
Assault	204	(1.5)	3,877	(7.9)	4,081
Drugs	468	(3.3)	10,931	(22.2)	11,399
Other	1,434	(10.2)	13,944	(28.4)	15,378
Petit Larceny	2,433	(17.3)	4,450	(9.1)	6,883
Prostitution	1,100	(7.8)	2,508	(5.1)	3,608
Theft of Service	5,405	(38.5)	10,860	(22.1)	16,265
Unlicensed Vending	2,992	(21.3)	2,579	(5.2)	5,571
Total	**14,036**		**49,149**		**63,185**

Community Court's early months, some types of cases (e.g., drug cases involving summary arrests) had not yet been transferred to the new Court; summary arrests made in specified weekend hours were not eligible for the Court; and some cases were initially heard Downtown because the District Attorney required an interview with the arresting officer. Figure 6.2 shows that the percent of cases from Midtown precincts at the Downtown court varied substantially by charge, ranging from 13 percent for assault cases to 52 percent for prostitution cases (an offense which has traditionally been concentrated in Midtown).

Caseloads at the two courts also differed significantly in terms of arrest type: 70 percent of Midtown cases were generated through a DAT, compared to 33 percent of Downtown cases (Figure 6.3). There are several reasons for this difference. First, since October 1993, Midtown police precincts scheduled *all* DATs (weekday *and* weekend arrests) at Midtown; in contrast, weekend summary arrests made in Midtown were sent Downtown. In addition, because some summary arrests were gradually phased in at the new Court, the Downtown court received a substantial number of summary arrests from Midtown precincts for some charges (e.g., assault, drugs).

Figure 6.4 shows the distribution of sentences at arraignment at the two courts. At Midtown, sentences are heavily weighted toward intermediate sanctions. In contrast, at the Downtown court, both traditional punishments (jail, fines) and "walks" (sentences of "time served," conditional discharge with no specified sanction) are more common. For all charges, "walks" are far less common at Midtown than Downtown, where they account for roughly half of all sentence outcomes. Intermediate sanctions account for the large majority of Midtown sentences for all charge

Figure 6.2 Comparing Area of Arrest by Charge

		Midtown Community Court Percentage			Downtown court Percentage	
Charge	**Cases**	**Arrest Inside Midtown Precincts**	**Arrest Outside Midtown Precincts**	**Cases**	**Arrest Inside Midtown Precincts**	**Arrest Outside Midtown Precincts**
Assault	190	97	3	3,877	13	87
Drugs	415	96	4	10,931	22	78
Other	1,268	94	6	13,944	20	81
Petit Larceny	2,232	99	1	4,450	32	68
Prostitution	1,029	91	9	2,508	52	48
Theft of Service	4,872	96	4	10,860	16	84
Unlicensed Vending	2,032	99	1	2,579	19	81
Total	**12,038**	**96**	**4**	**49,149**	**21**	**79**

Figure 6.3 Comparing Case Type of Arrest by Charge

		Midtown Community Court Percentage			Downtown court Percentage	
Charge	**Cases**	**DAT**	**Summary**	**Cases**	**DAT**	**Summary**
Assault	204	99	1	3,877	18	82
Drugs	468	55	45	10,931	19	81
Other	1,434	56	44	13,944	25	75
Petit Larceny	2,433	60	40	4,450	26	74
Prostitution	1,100	1	99	2,508	2	98
Theft of Service	5,405	86	14	10,860	65	35
Unlicensed Vending	2,992	82	18	2,579	58	43
Total	**14,036**	**70**	**30**	**49,149**	**33**	**67**

Figure 6.4 Prevalence of Imprisonment, Intermediate Sanctions and Unconditional Sentences, by Charge and Court*

Charge	Imprisonment		Fine		Intermediate Sentence		Unconditional Sentence	
	Midtown	Downtown	Midtown	Downtown	Midtown	Downtown	Midtown	Downtown
Theft of Service	5%	11%	0%	2%	82%	41%	13%	46%
Unlicensed Vending	1%	2%	1%	24%	70%	17%	29%	57%
Drugs	17%	22%	0%	1%	76%	30%	7%	47%
Petit Larceny	17%	43%	0%	1%	76%	25%	7%	31%
Prostitution	11%	16%	0%	3%	87%	18%	2%	63%

* The percentages in each row sum to 100% (or as close to that total as rounding error permits). Arraignments involving charges of assault are omitted because only one defendant was sentenced for that charge during the Midtown Community Court's initial year.

types, but less than a third of sentences for most charges Downtown (the single exception is theft of service). Jail sentences and fines are infrequent at Midtown, representing at most 17 percent of the sentences imposed for any charge at arraignment. Downtown, jail sentences and fines are more prevalent, together ranging from 13 percent (for theft of service) to 44 percent (for petit larceny) of arraignment sentences. Overall, there are clear differences in sentence outcomes at the two courts. For most misdemeanors and violations, the Midtown Community Court makes far less use of jail, fines and "walks" and far more use of intermediate sanctions than the Downtown court. Determining the strength of these differences however, requires the use of multivariate statistical techniques.

USING MULTIVARIATE STATISTICAL ANALYSES TO COMPARE OUTCOMES AT THE TWO COURTS

For each of the six decision points, the research examined whether or not a particular event occurred. Did the defendant show up at arraignment when a DAT was issued? Was the case continued at arraignment or disposed? If disposed, was the defendant convicted? Was an alternative sanction imposed? Was a jail sentence imposed? Was the case disposed without any conditions being imposed on the defendant? To answer these questions, the research employed logit analysis—the appropriate technique for predicting whether or not an event occurs based on a set of categorical explanatory factors.

Decision 1: The Frequency of Failure to Appear at Arraignment

The first inquiry considers a decision over which the courts have little control: whether a defendant with a DAT appears at arraignment. In the first year, the Midtown and Downtown courts were mirror images of each other in terms of the frequency of DATs: roughly two-thirds of Midtown cases were DATs compared to roughly one-third of Downtown cases. This difference affected the overall distribution of sentences at the two courts: for example, having a DAT precludes a sentence of "time served." In addition, summary arrests are more likely than DATs to result in convictions.

The Midtown Community Court opened at a time of a slight increase in failure-to-appear (FTA) rates (from 48% in 1992 to 50% in 1993). For most offense categories, the FTA rate in Manhattan courts was somewhat lower in the year before the new Court opened than during the first year of operations; growth in FTA rates was substantial only in the category of "other" charges.

Although the FTA rate at Midtown for DATs during the first year was higher than Downtown (54% compared to 47%), this reflects long-standing differences between Midtown and other Manhattan precincts. In the year before the Court opened, the FTA rate for defendants from Midtown precincts was also higher (52%) than for other Manhattan defendants (45%). The growth in FTA rates was roughly equal in Midtown and non-Midtown precincts.

Charge type Figure 6.5 shows the frequency of DAT arrests for each charge at the two courts. The table shows that the bulk of DATs scheduled at Midtown (86%) are for theft of service (52%), unlicensed vending (18%) and petit larceny (16%). In contrast, these charges account for only 60 percent of the cases Downtown. DATs for drug (13%) and "other" charges (22%) are substantially more common Downtown than at Midtown (3% and 8% respectively). Prostitution cases almost never result in DATs at either court.

After controlling for charge type, analysis showed no statistically significant differences in "no show" rates between Downtown and Midtown except for unlicensed vending cases. To illustrate findings about DAT FTA rates, research staff calculated the "derivative from mean," a measure that illustrates differences in outcomes for comparable cases.[4] Based on this calculation, Figure 6.6 compares the probability of a DAT warrant being ordered at the two courts for specified charges. The probability that a defendant will not appear at arraignment for unlicensed vending cases is substantially higher Downtown than at Midtown (69% compared to 52%).

Figure 6.5 Charge Distribution for DAT Cases at the Two Courts

Charge Type	Downtown	Midtown	Overall
Assault	4%	2%	4%
Drugs	13%	3%	10%
Petit Larceny	7%	16%	10%
Prostitution	0%	0%	0%
Theft of Services	44%	52%	46%
Unlicensed Vending	9%	18%	12%
Other	22%	8%	17%

Figure 6.6 The Warrant Ordered v. No Warrant Ordered Decision

	Derivative from Mean	
Charge Type	**Downtown**	**Midtown**
Assault	.21	.16
Drugs	.54	.60
Petit Larceny	.53	.54
Theft of Service	.51	.51
Unlicensed Vending	.69	.52

The analysis demonstrates that, overall, the new Court had no effect on DAT appearance rates. It also serves to demonstrate that the difference in aggregate appearance rates at the two courts is largely a function of underlying differences in charge composition and arrest location. Although there were initial hopes that the Midtown Community Court might improve appearance rates for DAT cases, there is no evidence that it did so.[5]

Decision 2: Case Adjournments

Continuances (or adjournments) are a cost to the system. They prolong cases and demand more court, corrections and prosecutorial resources to reach a disposition. Very few misdemeanor arraignments in Manhattan (less than 2%) ultimately result in a trial. Most continuances are sought in pursuit of some advantage—a dismissal or a better offer—rather than a trial.

Adjournments "buy time" in both courts. "Buying time" can be important for misdemeanor offenders who have open cases and outstanding warrants and are facing substantial jail sentences. For some defendants, adjournments can represent "forum shopping," a decision to seek a more lenient judge. "Forum shopping" happens at both courts.

Yet the dynamics of adjournment may differ somewhat at the two courts. There is relatively little room for defense attorneys to maneuver at Midtown. The kinds of cases processed there generally do not involve witnesses or civilian complainants. (The clear exception, assault cases which require an interview with the complaining witness, are continued in large numbers at both courts.) Because of the smaller volume of cases and the use of electronic records, files are unlikely to be mislaid. The strength of District Attorney's case is more often clear at the time of arraignment. These factors remove some incentives to continue.

Figure 6.7a Percent of Cases Continued by Court

Court	Cases Not Continued	Cases Continued	Total
Downtown	24,373 (59.1%)	16,896 (40.9%)	41,269
Midtown	5,590 (73.0%)	2,072 (27.0%)	7,662
Total	**29,963 (61.2%)**	**18,968 (38.8%)**	**48,931**

Figure 6.7b Percent of Cases Continued by Charge

Charge	Cases Not Continued	Cases Continued	Total
Assault	191 (4.9%)	3,687 (95.1%)	3,878
Drugs	6,566 (65.3%)	3,483 (34.7%)	10,049
Petit Larceny	3,405 (64.4%)	1,882 (35.3%)	5,287
Prostitution	2,673 (77.9%)	758 (22.1%)	3,431
Theft of Service	8,918 (89.6%)	1,040 (10.4%)	9,958
Unlicensed Vending	1,747 (64.1%)	978 (35.9%)	2,725
Other	6,463 (47.5%)	7,140 (52.5%)	13,603
Total	**29,963 (61.2%)**	**18,968 (38.8%)**	**48,931**

Yet some observers suggested that the Court, in its effort to increase the use of intermediate sanctions, might promote continuances for offenses that typically received no sanction at the Downtown court. Defendants wishing to avoid community service in Midtown might simply adjourn their case Downtown. This issue was of central interest in the analysis.

It was clear that aggregate continuance rates at the two courts differ substantially: 27 percent of Midtown cases are continued compared to 41 percent of Downtown cases (see Figure 6.7a). Overall continuance rates vary substantially by charge, however, ranging from a high of 95 percent for assault to a low of 10 percent for theft of service (Figure 6.7b).

For this decision point, two different models were used to examine court effects. The local policy audience was particularly interested in the Midtown Community Court's *net* effect on adjournment rates, given the concern that "forum shopping" might increase system costs. Therefore, we first examine *overall* court effects on adjournment rates. In contrast, the second model isolates specific charges at the two courts and examines the effect of the new Court on adjournments for each charge.

Continuance Decision: Model 1 The first model examines whether the Court had an overall effect on adjournments without looking at how that effect may have varied for specific charges. Variables used to predict whether there was an effect include the location of arrest, case type (DAT or summary arrest), charge type and whether the case was handled at Midtown.

In model one, analysis showed that charge type, arrest location and arrest type are all influential in determining the continuance rate, but that the arraignment court (Midtown or Downtown) does not have an *overall* impact on the continuance rate. Therefore, despite the large difference in the continuance rates between the two courts (shown in Figure 6.7a), when other differences (e.g., charge, arrest type) are taken into account, the impact of the arraignment court *by itself* is insignificant.

Continuance Decision: Model 2 Although the new Court had no *net* effect on adjournment rates, the first model conceals some charge specific differences in adjournment rates at the two courts. To develop a detailed picture of the differences in continuance rates between the two courts, it is necessary to examine court effects for different charges. The second model looks at the effect of the arrest location, case type, charge type and the *interaction* of charge type and arraignment court. Analysis shows that assault cases are far more likely to continue than other cases, a finding that was true at both courts. It also showed that defendants with unlicensed vending, theft of service and prostitution cases are *more* likely to adjourn cases at Midtown than Downtown and that defendants with drug and petit larceny charges are *less* likely to continue their cases at Midtown than Downtown. Together, these charge-specific differences in the Midtown Community Court's influence on adjournment rates produced the finding that there is no *net* difference, as shown in the Model 1 discussion.

Figure 6.8 The Continue v. Dispose Decision

Charge Type	Derivative from Mean Downtown	Midtown
Assault	.95	.97
Drugs	.34	.25
Petit Larceny	.40	.29
Prostitution	.20	.34
Theft of Services	.10	.12
Unlicensed Vending	.23	.56

Charge-specific differences are illustrated by analysis of the derivative from means (Figure 6.8) which shows that the probability of a petit larceny case being continued is 29 percent at Midtown and 40 percent Downtown. Overall, individuals appearing at Midtown are more likely to continue their cases (compared to Downtown) when the charge is prostitution or unlicensed vending, less likely to continue the case when the charge is drug possession or petit larceny, and about the same when the charge is assault and theft of service, holding constant the impact of case type and arrest location.

For two offenses, prostitution and unlicensed vending, there was evidence that the Midtown Community Court may have increased the likelihood of adjournments. This finding supports the perceptions of Court personnel, who reported that defendants charged with these two offenses were most likely to engage in "forum shopping." For other offenses, however, there was no evidence of an increase in adjournment. In fact, the likelihood of adjournments for drug and petit larceny cases was significantly reduced.

Decision 3: Disposition—ACD or Conviction

In New York City, there are three possible case dispositions for non-felony cases at arraignment: dismissal, conviction or ACD.[6] Dismissal is rare, recorded in 2 percent of the arraignment dispositions Downtown and 3 percent at Midtown. The ACD is expungeable. If the defendant is not convicted of another offense during the next six months and if specified conditions are met (community service/social service), the record of the ACD is automatically dismissed.

Variables used in the analysis The analysis, which is limited to individuals whose cases were disposed at arraignment, estimates the probability of conviction as opposed to an ACD. Given the rarity of both dismissed cases and of assault cases disposed at arraignment, these cases have been dropped from the analysis.

As judges explain it, the ACD-conviction decision is largely driven by criminal history. ACDs in New York City are seen as appropriate for defendants who are relatively new to the criminal justice system. Therefore, the analysis of this decision included variables that distinguish between the extent of prior misdemeanor and prior felony convictions. To control further for differences between defendants, three types of extra-legal factors are also included: gender, race-ethnicity and age.

What determines how a case is disposed? The conviction decision can be best understood in the context of the formal and informal policies and practices within the New York City Criminal Court that structure the use of ACDs and convictions at arraignment, as explained by local judges. ACDs are likely for first offenders charged with misdemeanor offenses; a second arrest is likely to result in escalation in the court's response—the defendant might plead guilty to a violation (e.g., disorderly conduct) rather than a misdemeanor offense; and a third case is likely to produce a plea to the misdemeanor charge.

Analysis showed that several variables were significantly related to the likelihood of conviction, including charge, case type (i.e., DAT arrest), "prior record" variables, age and gender. Drug and prostitution charges were associated with a high likelihood of conviction at both courts. Variables describing the defendant's previous interaction with the justice system support the "conventional wisdom" about the ACD-conviction decision: the likelihood of conviction increased with the extensiveness of prior convictions. The effect of race appears to be negligible.

The impact of charge and the court part of disposition are illustrated by derivatives from the mean in Figure 6.9. The probability of conviction is significantly lower at Midtown for two charges: petit larceny (Midtown, 76%; Downtown, 84%) and theft of service (Midtown, 65%; Downtown, 80%). Yet, unlicensed vending defendants are somewhat *more* likely to be convicted at Midtown (99%) than Downtown (92%).

Decision 4: Sentencing and Sanctioning Options

Sentences and sanctions Sanctions can be imposed both for defendants who are convicted and for those who receive an ACD (adjournment in contemplation of dismissal). Conviction leads to

Figure 6.9 The Convict v. ACD Decision

Charge Type	Derivative from Mean Downtown	Midtown
Drugs	.95	.93
Petit Larceny	.84	.76
Prostitution	.99	.98
Theft of Service	.80	.65
Unlicensed Vending	.92	.99

the imposition of a sentence at arraignment. In addition, ACDs can require that specified conditions be met before dismissal (for example, one day of community service or social service).[7] For convicted cases, the most frequent outcomes at both courts include a conditional discharge with no conditions imposed; a conditional discharge with community service and/or social service; sentences of "time served"; and jail sentences. Fines are infrequent for all charges, except unlicensed vending cases Downtown.

These outcomes can be divided into four categories: (1) imprisonment, (2) fines, (3) intermediate sanctions and (4) unconditional outcomes ("walks," including conditional discharge with no conditions imposed, sentences of "time served," and ACDs with no conditions imposed). In the years before the new Court opened, jail, fines, sentences of "time served" and other types of "walks" were the traditional court responses to misdemeanors.

For purposes of analysis, the research distinguished between "traditional" and "alternative" sanctions. Traditional sentencing options include jail, a fine, "time served" or a conditional discharge. Alternative sanctions include community service, social services and a combined package of social service (typically an educational program) and community service. Probation is rarely used for defendants arrested for misdemeanors. In recent years, even before the new Court opened, intermediate sanctions (community service and social service sentences), which are less severe than jail but more severe than a "walk," have been increasingly common, particularly for DATs.[8]

Variables used in the analysis This section considers two sentencing models. The first model looks at the factors that determine who receives outcomes with no conditions imposed (an ACD only, conditional discharge or "time served") compared to those receiving alternative sanctions, jail time or a fine. The second model examines factors that affect the decision to impose an alternative sanction rather than a more traditional sentence.

Sanction Decision: Model 1 The first model examines factors related to the likelihood of receiving a sentence in which no conditions are imposed (commonly referred to as a "walk"). Analysis showed that defendants whose cases are disposed at Midtown have a substantially greater chance of receiving active punishment, and less chance of receiving a "walk," than those sentenced at arraignment Downtown. Other factors that are significantly associated with a reduced likelihood of a "walk" include having a DAT; having a drug charge or petit larceny charge; the number of prior misdemeanor convictions (a defendant with more prior misdemeanor convictions is less likely to receive a "walk"); and age (an older defendant is less likely to receive a "walk"). In contrast, defendants charged with prostitution, theft of service and unlicensed vending are significantly *more* likely to receive "walks" than others.

The estimated probabilities in Figure 6.10 demonstrate differences between the two courts in the likelihood of receiving a "walk" for specific charges. At Midtown, the likelihood of a "walk" was substantially less than at the Downtown court for all charges. The table shows that unlicensed vending is the only charge type at Midtown where the probability of a defendant getting a "walk" exceeds 20 percent. In contrast, at the Downtown court, the likelihood of a "walk" ranges from 23 percent for petit larceny to 70 percent for unlicensed vending.[9] The differences between the two courts are large and significant for all charges.

Sanction Decision: Model 2 The second model of the sanctioning decision examined whether or not defendants received an alternative sanction (a community and/or social service sentence). Overall, 42 percent of the cases at the two courts were given an alternative sanction. There is a considerable difference, however, in the use of alternative sanctions at Midtown (81%) and Downtown (31%).[10]

Arrest type, charge type, extensiveness of prior record and extra-legal factors comprise the set of variables used in the analysis of this decision point. Several factors—case type, criminal history, charge and arraignment court—were associated with the likelihood of an alternative sanction being imposed. As

Figure 6.10 "Walk" v. Sanction Decision

	Derivative from Mean	
Charge Type	**Downtown**	**Midtown**
Drugs	.39	.05
Petit Larceny	.23	.06
Prostitution	.55	.01
Theft of Services	.50	.15
Unlicensed Vending	.70	.23

predicted by Court personnel, analysis showed that individuals arraigned on a DAT are significantly more likely to receive an alternative sanction than others. In addition, the extensiveness of prior record is negatively and significantly related to the probability of a community/social service sentence. Individuals with more than five prior misdemeanors are more likely to receive a traditional sentence than those with fewer prior misdemeanors, controlling for all other factors. Gender and age are not statistically significant. For all charges, the effect of the new Court on the likelihood of an alternative sanction being imposed is large, positive and significant. This finding reflects the strong commitment to using alternative sanctions at Midtown.

Analysis also showed that unlicensed vendors are less likely to receive a sentence of community or social service. By contrast, drug and petit larceny cases are *more* likely than other charges to receive alternative sanctions.

Figure 6.11 shows large and significant differences between the two courts in the predicted frequency of alternative sanctions for defendants with similar characteristics, defined as the mean values for arrest type, prior record and extra-legal variables, for specific charges. For example, the table estimates that 69 percent of defendants charged with unlicensed vending and 95 percent of those charged with prostitution would receive an alternative sanction at Midtown, compared to 18 percent and 25 percent respectively Downtown.

Decision 5: The Jail Sanction

Jail time is the most severe sanction for misdemeanor offenses in New York City. It is also the most costly. This section examines the use of jail at the Midtown and Downtown courts using two approaches. First, it provides a descriptive profile of the prevalence of jail sentences, jail sentence length by charge and the

Figure 6.11 "Alternative Sanction" v. Traditional Sanction

	Derivative from Mean	
Charge Type	**Downtown**	**Midtown**
Drugs	.37	.83
Petit Larceny	.30	.78
Prostitution	.25	.95
Theft of Service	.27	.75
Unlicensed Vending	.18	.69

Figure 6.12 Top Arraignment Charge by Court (Column Percentages in Parentheses)

Charge	Midtown	Downtown	Total
Drugs	224 (3.8)	6,241 (26.4)	6,465
Other	688 (11.6)	5,571 (23.6)	6,259
Petit Larceny	1,082 (18.3)	2,278 (9.6)	3,360
Prostitution	732 (12.4)	1,953 (8.3)	2,685
Theft of Service	2,472 (41.8)	6,513 (27.5)	8,985
Unlicensed Vending	716 (12.1)	1,091 (4.6)	1,807
Total	**5,914**	**23,647**	**29,561**

total number of jail days ordered in the two courts. Next, it reviews the findings of multivariate analysis of the impact of case characteristics, arraignment court and defendant characteristics on (1) the probability of receiving a jail sentence and (2) the length of jail sentences imposed at the two courts.

Descriptive profile Figure 6.12 shows the distribution of charges at the two courts for all defendants whose cases were disposed at arraignment during the Court's first year.[11]

Figure 6.13 shows the arraignment outcomes at the Midtown and Downtown courts for these cases. Of more than 29,500 cases, just over 4,600 (16%) received a jail sentence (Midtown, 8%; Downtown, 17%). Jail sentences constituted a substantially higher proportion of arraignment outcomes Downtown, while community and/or social service sentences constituted a substantially higher proportion of outcomes at Midtown.

Figure 6.14 presents information about jail sentences at the two courts. The upper two tables show the number and percent of jail cases by charge. For example, 18 percent of the drug cases disposed at Midtown received jail sentences compared to 14 percent of drug cases Downtown. Overall, the Downtown court imposed a higher proportion of jail sentences for all charge types. The table in the lower left shows the mean numbers of jail days imposed for specified charges at the two courts; jail sentences in the aggregate tend to be longer at Midtown. Finally, the lower right hand table displays the total number of jail days imposed for each charge at the two courts.

Determinants of the frequency and length of jail sentences The analysis of the jail sentence decision was conducted in two

Figure 6.13 Case Outcomes at Arraignment by Court (Column Percentages in Parentheses)

Sentence	Midtown	Downtown	Total
ACD Only	302 (5.1)	2,790 (11.8)	3,092
Conditional Discharge	313 (5.3)	3,029 (12.8)	3,342
Community and/or Social Service	4,744 (80.0)	6,894 (29.2)	11,638
Fine	17 (0.3)	1,012 (4.3)	1,029
Jail	469 (7.9)	4,140 (17.5)	4,609
Probation	—	38 (0.2)	38
"Time Served"	69 (1.2)	5,744 (24.3)	5,813
Total	**5,914**	**23,647**	**29,561**

steps. The first step examines the impact of characteristics thought to influence whether or not a defendant is sentenced to jail. The second step focuses only on those who were sentenced to jail and examines factors that influence the length of jail sentences. Because it is likely that common factors influence the probability of receiving a jail sentence and the length of jail sentences, the models contain common variables.

Stage 1: The jail versus no jail decision The research used logit analysis to estimate the probability that a particular defendant would be sentenced to jail. It showed that jail is less likely for all charge types at Midtown, except for unlicensed vending (where the probability of jail is low and essentially identical at the two courts) and drug charges, where the effect is negative but not statistically significant. In addition, the prior record variables show that the probability of a jail sentence increases with more prior misdemeanors. Racial differences are clearly not a factor in the jail decision.

The derivative from mean results (Figure 6.15) show that the probability of a jail sentence is uniformly lower at Midtown than Downtown, except for unlicensed vending. On the whole the Midtown Community Court makes less use of jail, holding other factors constant. The differences are largest for petit larceny and prostitution cases.

Stage 2: The length of jail sentence This step used linear regression analysis to estimate the impact of various defendant characteristics on the length of jail sentence received. Analysis found that case type, charge, prior record and age were

Figure 6.14 Aggregate Data about Cases with a Jail Sentence

Number of Cases Receiving a Jail Sentence

Charge	Midtown	Downtown
Drugs	40	1,297
Other	46	787
Prostitution	79	313
Petit Larceny	162	987
Theft of Service	118	730
Unlicensed Vending	7	18

Percent of All Cases Receiving a Jail Sentence

Charge	Midtown	Downtown
Drugs	18%	21%
Other	7	14
Prostitution	7	14
Petit Larceny	22	51
Theft of Service	5	11
Unlicensed Vending	1	2

Mean Days of Jail Incarceration

Charge	Midtown	Downtown
Drugs	19	19
Other	9	27
Prostitution	15	5
Petit Larceny	79	49
Theft of Service	10	9
Unlicensed Vending	11	6

Total Days of Jail Incarceration

Charge	Midtown	Downtown
Drugs	775	24,379
Other	428	21,279
Prostitution	1,190	1,709
Petit Larceny	12,819	48,212
Theft of Service	1,207	6,434
Unlicensed Vending	77	102

Figure 6.15 Jail v. Other Sanction Decision

Charge Type	Derivative from Mean Downtown	Midtown
Drugs	.18	.15
Petit Larceny	.44	.22
Prostitution	.15	.04
Theft of Services	.17	.12
Unlicensed Vending	.01	.02

significantly associated with jail sentence length. It also demonstrated that, all else being equal, petit larceny cases at Midtown receive jail sentences that are 31 days longer than similar cases Downtown, and that jail sentences for prostitution cases tended to be longer at Midtown than Downtown.

Decision 6: Compliance with Intermediate Sanctions

Ideally, an analysis of the Court's influence on compliance with intermediate sanctions would merge information about case characteristics and defendant characteristics with information about compliance and control for underlying differences in the populations receiving intermediate sanctions at the two courts. This could not be done, however, because the data sets available for the comparison of intermediate sanction compliance rates at the two courts are not equivalent.[12] Although the Midtown database merged compliance information with data about defendant and case characteristics, a merged data set is not available for cases arraigned Downtown.[13] This made it impossible to control for underlying differences in charge, arrest type, number of days assigned or other case and defendant characteristics when analyzing differences in compliance at the two courts.

With the cooperation of the Office of the District Attorney for New York, research staff obtained case level information on the number of community service and treatment days assigned and the number of days completed. Yet inconsistencies between record keeping systems used to record sentence outcomes and to monitor alternative sanction compliance made it impossible to match data about case and defendant characteristics (charge, arrest type, disposition, defendant demographics) with Downtown compliance data for sampled cases.[14] Therefore, to examine aggregate differences in compliance rates at the two courts, research staff gathered supplementary information on alternative sanction outcomes from the New York County District Attorney's Alternative Sentence Office and the New York County Borough Chief Clerk's Office.

Community service compliance: aggregate differences For all community service sentences, the 1993–1994 completion rate Downtown was 50 percent. Community service failures at the Downtown court include two groups: those who did not present themselves at the Alternative Sentence Office (17%) and those who received their assignment but did not complete all of the days assigned (an additional 33%). At Midtown, the completion rate was 75 percent.

Some of the differences in aggregate community service compliance rates are related to procedural differences at the two courts. Defendants at Midtown are escorted by court officers to the equivalent of the Alternative Sentence Office. This reduces the likelihood that they will not report for scheduling although they are free to leave the scheduling office.[15] In addition, alternative sanction staff at Midtown schedule many defendants to start their sanction within 24 hours of sentencing, substantially faster than Downtown where defendants often begin serving their sentences three weeks after sentencing.

Differences in the populations receiving community service sentences at the two courts There are substantial differences in arrest type, charge and prior criminal history among the populations sentenced to community service at the two courts. As shown in Figure 6.16, defendants receiving community service sentences at the two courts differ substantially in terms of charge.

Those at the Downtown court are more likely to have been charged with drug and "other" offenses and less likely to have been charged with unlicensed vending, prostitution and theft of service than Midtown defendants.

Defendants receiving community service sentences at arraignment at the two courts also differ in terms of criminal history and arrest type. In some respects, defendants sentenced to community service at the Downtown court appear to pose a higher risk of non-compliance than those at Midtown: 67 percent have three or more prior misdemeanor convictions, compared to 22 percent at Midtown; half have summary arrests, compared to 39 percent at Midtown. Yet a larger proportion of Midtown defendants sentenced to community

Figure 6.16 Charges for Defendants Receiving Community Service — Downtown and Midtown

Charge	Downtown	Midtown
Drugs	12%	1%
Petit Larceny	5	8
Prostitution	4	11
Theft of Service	31	46
Unlicensed Vending	1	11
Other	46	12
Total	**99%**	**99%**

service have prior felony convictions (14%) than Downtown defendants (9%).

The two courts do not differ substantially, however, in terms of community service sentence length. At the Downtown court, 56 percent of community service sentences are for one day, 25 percent for two days and 19 percent are for three or more days.[16] The distribution of sentence lengths for Midtown defendants is similar to that Downtown: 60 percent, 20 percent and 20 percent.

The implications of these differences are not easily interpreted. In several respects, the Downtown court has a higher-risk population of community service defendants—one with more extensive criminal histories, a higher proportion of drug charges and a lower proportion of DATs. In other important respects—sentence length, the proportion of prostitutes receiving community service sentences—the population at Midtown is as "tough" or "tougher." Overall the data available are insufficient to support a more detailed analysis, delineating the factors that affect community service compliance and the difference in compliance rates for comparable populations at the two courts.

Social service compliance The types of short-term social service sentences available at the Midtown and Downtown courts differ substantially. At the Downtown court, judges can sentence defendants charged with drug offenses or prostitution to a six-hour treatment readiness program (one day for prostitutes; one or two days for drug offenders). At Midtown, a greater variety of social service sanctions were available during the first year—health education groups for prostitutes and "johns," single session treatment engagement groups, a four-hour treatment readiness program (ranging in length from two to eight days). Social service sentences at Midtown can be handed out to all defendants, regardless of charge; no single charge type accounts for more than a third of the sentences. In contrast, 90 percent of treatment readiness sentences Downtown are for drug cases.

Because the nature of programs offered at the two courts differ in terms of content, duration and clientele, comparisons of compliance rates are difficult to interpret. In addition there is less reason to anticipate a substantial Midtown effect on social service compliance than on community service compliance for two reasons: first, the treatment readiness program Downtown maintains a high level of accountability and produces high rates of compliance for a difficult population; second, social service sentences at Midtown rarely begin the same day as sentencing, reducing the potential impact of a "same-day" start on compliance.

The aggregate data for the Downtown treatment readiness program show compliance separately by charge and number of days assigned, permitting some controlled comparisons of social service compliance. Completion rates for one-day social service sentences were 68 percent for defendants charged with prostitution at both the Midtown and Downtown courts. Compliance rates for defendants charged with drug offenses at Midtown were substantially higher than Downtown for one-day sentences (94% compared to 59%) and somewhat lower for two-day sentences (48% compared to 57%). These aggregate comparisons do not control for underlying differences in criminal history, arrest type or demographic characteristics.

Overall the conclusions that can be drawn about differences in sentence outcomes at the two courts are far stronger than the conclusions that can be drawn about differences in compliance rates, given the absence of data sets that merge information about case characteristics, defendant characteristics and alternative sanction participation for the Downtown court.

SUMMARY

The development of the Midtown Community Court gave rise to a debate among criminal justice system officials about whether the new Court would make a difference in the handling of misdemeanor cases in Manhattan. The analyses reviewed above help answer key questions raised in that debate: Would the Court's effort to expand the use of intermediate sanctions serve instead to increase the frequency of adjournments at arraignment? Would widespread adjournments reduce the Court's ability to make a difference in sentence outcomes? Employing multivariate statistical techniques to control for underlying differences in the caseloads at the two courts, the research demonstrated that the new Court had no net impact on adjournment rates and substantially increased the use of community service and social service sentences.

The analysis uses multivariate statistical techniques to distinguish between differences in case outcomes that are due to the arraignment court (Midtown or Downtown), and differences that are related to case and defendant characteristics, including charge, arrest type (summary or DAT), arrest location (Midtown or other Manhattan precincts), prior record and extra-legal considerations (age, race, gender). In addition, the chapter reviews differences in compliance with alternative sanctions.

When interpreting the results in this chapter, it is necessary to keep in mind some of the basic differences between the two courts in volume, charges and arrest type. In its first year, the new Court primarily handled petit larceny, prostitution, theft of service, and unlicensed vending cases; the bulk of assault and drug cases are handled Downtown. In addition, 70 percent of Midtown cases originate as DATs in contrast to Downtown, where one-third of the cases begin as DATs.

Is there a Difference between the Two Courts in Whether Defendants given a DAT Appear as Scheduled?

In the aggregate, warrants were ordered in 54 percent of Midtown DAT cases and 47 percent of Downtown DAT cases. There are significant differences in the "no show" rate for specific charges. Assault cases are the least likely to result in a warrant ordered (roughly 20% fail to appear). Other charges cluster around 50 percent.

Multivariate statistical analysis does not point to consistent differences in the "no show" rate at the two courts. After controlling for differences in charge, defendants with DATs who are arrested in a Midtown *precinct* have a greater likelihood of failing to appear at arraignment, regardless of whether the case is scheduled in Midtown. After controlling for charge and arrest location, the Midtown Community Court has a significantly *lower* "no show" rate for unlicensed vending. There are no significant differences in DAT "no show" rates for other charges at the two courts.

Is there a Difference between the Two Courts in Continuance Rates?

A central question raised in the debate about the new Court was whether it would substantially increase aggregate adjournments at arraignment and, thereby, raise system costs. In the aggregate, fewer cases are adjourned at Midtown (27%) than Downtown (41%). More detailed analysis shows that there are significant differences in adjournment rates at the two courts for specific charges. Holding the impact of arrest type and arrest location constant, defendants at Midtown are more likely to continue their cases (compared to Downtown) when the charge is prostitution or unlicensed vending; less likely to continue when the charge is drugs or petit larceny; and equally likely to continue when the charge is assault and theft of service. Overall, these charge-specific differences have no net impact on the frequency of adjournment.

Is there a Difference between the Two Courts in Conviction Rates?

During the planning period, there was some debate about the Court's potential impact on conviction rates. Several criminal justice professionals suggested that the expanded availability of social services sentences at the new Court might "coerce guilty pleas" among defendants who were eager to be placed in drug treatment. In response, court planners pointed out that court-based services were not restricted to defendants who pled guilty but were available to *all* defendants.

There was no evidence that the Court increased the frequency of guilty pleas at arraignment. In fact, overall conviction rates are somewhat lower at Midtown (67%) than Downtown (79%). Multivariate analysis shows that conviction rates vary significantly by charge, arrest type, criminal history, defendant age and gender. Convictions were more likely for summary arrests; defendants with drug, prostitution and unlicensed vending charges; defendants with more extensive criminal histories, older defendants and male defendants. After controlling for these factors, there is little difference in the probability of conviction at the two courts for drug and prostitution cases. In contrast, defendants have a *lower* likelihood of conviction for petit larceny and theft of service at Midtown and a *higher* probability of conviction for unlicensed vending compared to Downtown.

Is there a Difference between the Two Courts in the Frequency of Intermediate Sanctions and the Frequency of "Walks" (Sentences with no Conditions Imposed)?

The Midtown Community Court makes much greater use of intermediate sanctions (81% of disposed cases) than the Downtown court (31% of disposed cases). After controlling for underlying differences in arrest type, charge, criminal history and defendant characteristics, the Court handed out significantly more intermediate sanctions for all charge types. Other factors also affect the frequency of intermediate sentences at the two courts: individuals arraigned on a DAT are more likely to receive an alternative sanction than those with a summary arrest; and the extensiveness of prior record is negatively (and significantly) related to the probability of an intermediate sentence.

One consequence of the new Court's commitment to using intermediate sanctions is a reduction in the frequency of sentences in which no conditions are imposed (ACD only, conditional discharge with no specified condition, and "time served"). In the aggregate, substantially more cases receive such sentences Downtown (47%) than at Midtown (10%). Multivariate analysis shows that the likelihood of receiving a "walk" varied significantly according to arrest type, charge, criminal history and defendant age. All else being equal, "walks" were significantly less common for summary arrests (DATs cannot receive "time served" sentences); defendants charged with drug and petit larceny offenses; defendants with extensive records of prior misdemeanor convictions; and older defendants. The probability of a "walk" was significantly higher at the Downtown court for all charges.

Is there a Difference between the Two Courts in the Likelihood of Receiving a Jail Sentence and if so, in the Length of that Jail Sentence?

Jail sentences represented a substantially higher proportion of arraignment sentences Downtown (18%) than at Midtown (8%). Multivariate analysis shows that jail sentences for all charge types are less likely at Midtown, except for unlicensed vending (where the probability of jail is essentially identical at both courts) and drug offenses, where the effect is not significant. In addition, the probability of a jail sentence increases with more prior misdemeanors.

On average jail sentences tend to be somewhat longer when imposed at Midtown, although sentence lengths vary substantially by charge. After controlling for differences in arrest type, charge, criminal history and defendant demographics, there is little difference between the two courts in jail sentence length for defendants convicted of drug, unlicensed vending and theft of service offenses. Yet defendants convicted of prostitution and petit larceny at Midtown face significantly longer jail sentences than those convicted Downtown.

Is there a Difference between the Two Courts in the Extent of Compliance with Intermediate Sanctions?

Court planners anticipated that a variety of procedural differences at the new Court—escorts to the scheduling office, brief "lag time" between sentencing and the onset of an intermediate sanction, strict accountability—would improve compliance with short-term intermediate sanctions. There is clear evidence that aggregate community service compliance rates are higher at Midtown than Downtown (75% compared to 50%) and that social service compliance rates were higher for some populations. Yet the data available for Downtown were insufficient to control for underlying differences in charge, criminal history and arrest type (summary or DAT), making it difficult to generate precise estimates of the extent of the Court's impact on compliance rates for a matched group of cases.

Notes

1. The methods used and the findings of that analysis are described in detail in a separate report on the evaluation of the Midtown Community Court (Sviridoff et al., 1997). This chapter reviews the major issues explored and summarizes the key findings.
2. According to New York State Criminal Procedure Law 170.55, an adjournment in contemplation of a dismissal is an order which releases the defendant on their own recognizance with the promise of a dismissal if specified conditions are met. Unless the prosecutor applies to have the case restored to the court's calendar within six months, the case is automatically dismissed.
3. As discussed, the Midtown Community Court began receiving prostitution cases from all Manhattan precincts in August 1994. In addition, theft of service cases were brought to the Court from designated transit police districts which were not precisely coterminous with NYPD precincts.
4. The derivative from the mean is calculated by first setting variables that are not related to charge at their mean level and setting all charge type variables at zero, and then calculating the probability that a warrant will be ordered. These methods are described in detail in the evaluation report (Sviridoff et al., 1997).

5. As discussed in Chapter 3, the Court's experiment with shortening the time between arrest to scheduled appearance (from three weeks to one) had no effect on appearance rates.
6. Acquittal is not one of the possible case dispositions because an acquittal is a trial verdict and trials never occur at arraignment.
7. For purposes of analysis, conditions imposed with an ACD are combined with conditions imposed as a sentence.
8. Between the baseline year and the Court's first year, the increased use of intermediate sanctions (and a concomitant decrease in "walks") was substantially greater for cases arising in Midtown precincts than for other cases. The impact of the Court is particularly apparent for DATs because all DATs from Midtown precincts were transferred there. (By contrast, summary arrests occurring in Midtown precincts on weekends continued to be arraigned Downtown.)
9. Given the substantial difference between the two courts in the likelihood of a sanction being imposed, the fact that adjournment rates do not vary more is surprising.
10. The data analyzed here overstate the Midtown Community Court's impact on intermediate sanctions for drug cases. This is because existing databases do not maintain information about sentences to the treatment readiness program (TRP) at Downtown arraignment. Aggregate data on TRP show that over 2,300 defendants convicted of misdemeanor drug charges were sentenced to TRP in 1993. (Ninety percent of TRP sentences Downtown involve drug cases.) These sentences were imposed either at arraignment or at a subsequent appearance. In addition, some defendants arrested on felony charges who were convicted of misdemeanor drug charges received TRP. If data on arraignment sentences to TRP were available, it is likely that the difference in the use of intermediate sanctions at the two courts for drug cases would be sharply reduced.
11. The analysis was restricted to defendants who were at risk of receiving a sentence or a sanction. As a consequence, the analysis excluded DAT "no shows," continued cases, and cases with missing data on the arraignment sentence. It did *not* exclude ACDs because they are "at risk" of an intermediate sanction. Assault cases were also excluded from this analysis because very few resulted in an arraignment disposition and sentence.
12. In contrast to Midtown, compliance data for the Downtown court includes information about a substantial number of cases sentenced to community service after arraignment. Unlike Midtown data, Downtown community service compliance data sets also include felony arrest cases that were disposed as misdemeanors and sentenced to community service. Because the Downtown community service data sets are not linked to other court information, cases comparable to those at Midtown can not be selected for purposes of comparison.
13. The fact that sentence compliance cannot be easily tracked Downtown is not just a research problem, but is an "Achilles' heel" of the New York City criminal justice system. Lack of accountability has led some observers to conclude that alternative sanctions are essentially meaningless. As discussed in Chapter 2, one of the impacts of the technology used at Midtown is dramatically improved case monitoring. Computerization at Midtown has supplanted the traditional "paper

trail." As a result, because Midtown defendants don't easily "fall through the cracks," accountability is enhanced. Defendants will complete their sanctions or else face the consequences.

14. Despite repeated efforts, it proved impossible to merge compliance information and case characteristics with sufficient assurance that all relevant defendants were included and correct information was available for each defendant.
15. Even for those who reported to the scheduling office at the Downtown court, compliance rates were substantially lower than aggregate rates at Midtown (61%).
16. Percentages are based on a random sample of 508 arraigned misdemeanor cases from 100 Centre Street during the summer of 1993.

CHAPTER SEVEN

COMMUNITY IMPACTS

This chapter reviews the effects of the Court on quality-of-life conditions in the Midtown area. It documents changes in offenses such as street-level prostitution and unlicensed vending—offenses that are linked to neighborhood markets with a steady customer base. It looks closely at selected hot spots of illegal activity—geographic areas with high concentrations of quality-of-life offenses. It also examines the effect of community service work on concentrations of graffiti in the Court's target area.

The chapter also examines information drawn from street observations and interviews about what happened on Midtown streets over the first eighteen months, supplemented by analysis of arrest trends, documenting substantial reductions in arrest frequency for prostitution and unlicensed vending in the target area. Combined with information from individual and group interviews with community members, structured observations and offender interviews, the analysis of arrest frequency documents a substantial reduction in the frequency of market-based quality-of-life offenses in the Midtown area.

Methodology Changes in quality-of-life conditions are difficult to measure. The two most widely used methods for assessing changes in offense frequency—victimization studies and analyses of variation in criminal complaints—are not applicable to low-level offenses. Victimization surveys, designed to measure the volume of underreported offenses, such as rape, provide little information about quality-of-life offenses (e.g., prostitution) which victimize *communities* rather than individuals. Analyses of complaint data are also inadequate for monitoring changes in low-level offending, because quality-of-life offenses rarely generate individual incident reports. Arrest records are typically the only official police record of such activity.

Research staff recognized that shifts in arrest volume (in contrast to complaint volume) do not *necessarily* reflect changes in the volume of offending. For example, an increase in arrest frequency may reflect changes in police priorities or in staffing levels rather than an increase in criminal activity. Therefore, the research sought to bolster analysis of arrest data with structured observations and interviews about perceived changes in community conditions and in levels of local enforcement.

Three primary methods were used to monitor the Court's effects on local conditions: (1) a series of individual and focus group interviews with community leaders, residents, local police and other criminal justice officials, designed to review expectations about the Court's potential impact on community conditions and to track perceived changes; (2) urban ethnography, designed to document changes in levels of offending and review perceived reasons for market changes in the Court's first eighteen months; and (3) analysis of quantitative data from the New York City Police Department and the Court database, documenting trends in the volume of arrests for specific offenses.

PRELIMINARY EXPECTATIONS AND PERCEIVED CHANGES IN LOCAL CONDITIONS

Awareness of Quality-of-life Problems

Before the Court opened, there was a general consensus among community members that quality-of-life conditions in Midtown were bad and possibly getting worse:

> *In the Times Square area, it's everything from low-level drug dealing to just regular scam artists, from scalping to Three Card Monte. When you go to the more residential areas where there is less tourist traffic, scams decrease and every day crimes like drugs and prostitution become more apparent.... It's also homeless people who leave large amounts of rubbish on your sidewalk and kids who... spray graffiti on buildings and... spit on restaurant windows.*

> *Prostitutes move from block to block, avenue to avenue, and honestly, in the last year, at least in Hell's Kitchen, it's gotten worse ....*

> *Midtown is in worse condition than it's ever been. Tourists say they never saw gates [before] on Fifth Avenue....*

> *All these people lying around on the streets ... It's the volume of drugs and prostitution, particularly in our neighborhood.... For the limited number of police there are, they are fighting as hard as they can. It's just that they are outnumbered.*

There was a general recognition among respondents that courts typically provided few constructive responses to these problems. As one respondent put it: "Quality-of-life crimes are important. And the judges do not consider them important."

Expectations about Potential Effects on Street Conditions

Community leaders clearly hoped that the new Court would contribute to their effort to improve area living conditions. Yet initial expectations about the Court's ability to affect local conditions were modest. There was initially little expectation that the Court might have a deterrent effect on local quality-of-life offenders or that community service projects might substantially improve local conditions.

These restrained expectations sprang in part from community awareness that previous law enforcement and community improvement strategies, designed to address local quality-of-life problems, had produced disappointing results. Respondents also had a realistic vision of how difficult it would be for any sentence in a misdemeanor court to make a difference in the life of a defendant. Sentences to incarceration for a misdemeanor are typically set in days, not months. Intermediate sanctions at the Court featured brief educational programs or short stints of community service. There was also some speculation among a few members of the local business community that, if the Court were more punitive toward misdemeanor offenders, quality-of-life offenders would either congregate in other parts of the city or adjourn their cases in large numbers. It was recognized that displacement might have a positive effect on local conditions, although it might not represent an effective solution to citywide quality-of-life problems. Predictions of displacement were not widespread. Most observers believed that the lure of the Midtown area for street-level offenders would outweigh the costs imposed on offenders through arrest, detention and punishment.

Two quality-of-life offenses—drug addiction and prostitution—were of most concern to community members. There was little expectation that the Court could have much impact on local drug markets, because drug trafficking cases (with the exception of those involving marijuana sales) are felony offenses in New York State and, therefore, ineligible for the Court. There was also considerable skepticism before the Court opened about the Court's ability to affect prostitution markets or to change entrenched habits of offending:

> *Most of us agree that prostitutes are not going to be rehabilitated. There is nothing you can do with them.... They'll just keep doing it ....*

> *Nobody expected that this court is going to stop prostitutes from working. Nobody expected to stop prostitution. If you can get somebody to be punished soon after they committed*

> *the crime, they will at least see cause and effect. It doesn't mean they'll never do it again, but you make a point.*
>
> *The people committing these petty crimes are just going to change their M.O. They'll get cagier, figure out ways to skirt around this .... From my heart, gut, I don't think anything's going to change ....*

Although there was considerable skepticism about the likelihood that changes in court procedures alone could make a difference in entrenched patterns of behavior and community conditions of disorder, there was some hope that other aspects of the Court—the availability of court-based services, community restitution—might have an influence. These expectations are reviewed below.

Expectations about the effects of social service interventions Community leaders expected that the Court might affect community conditions by providing services to high-rate offenders with significant problems, particularly substance abuse.

> *One of the most important things is the drug treatment, because so much crime comes from drug addiction. So if you stop just one person from using drugs, you can stop 100 cars from being broken into....*
>
> *If you can solve a few people's problems early on, the community will benefit in the long run....*

Some respondents were frankly skeptical:

> *That's a pretty heavy burden to put on the system, [to] change people and turn them into law abiding citizens. I think that's too much of a burden....*

Expectations about community service impacts Some respondents also pointed out that community service work might have a direct effect on local conditions:

> *They are supposed to sweep the streets and clean graffiti....*
>
> *They'll definitely think twice about spraying the same wall again after cleaning it off....*

There was considerable skepticism about whether offenders would actually carry out community service orders:

> *You're going to have to walk them there and watch them do it, or they are not going to do it....*

If now they can get people to actually do their community service, maybe get it to have some impact on their lives, even if it were only ten percent, that would be good....

The hardest will be... monitoring all these defendants. If the Court really begins to process 50 defendants a day, they may have at any given time 250 defendants working in the Midtown area. For whom they will be responsible .... And they do not have 200 people to watch these 250....

Because of early skepticism both about compliance rates and about the Court's ability to supervise large numbers of defendants, there were, at best, modest expectations about whether community service work could make a difference in local conditions.

Perceived changes in local conditions: community perceptions After eighteen months, community members had recognized substantial improvements in local quality-of-life conditions. Local police and community leaders reported substantial reductions in the volume of prostitution and unlicensed vending activity. A few community leaders reported that they had kept early doubts about the potential for positive effects on local conditions to themselves (as one said, "in my heart of hearts"). They persevered in hoping for the best because they liked the basic concept of a community court. After a year, one community leader who "didn't think the New York courts could do it" found the new Court to be "a rational, intelligent and appropriate response to quality-of-life crimes."

The head of one local business organization noted that merchants doing business on Eighth Avenue, Midtown's "troubled spine," felt that the area was becoming safer. In a survey conducted a few years before the Court opened, only 10 percent of merchants reported that security was "okay"; after nine months, half reported that security was "okay," a substantial improvement in perceived safety.

Perceived effect on prostitution Some individuals and organizations that monitored local prostitution reported a dramatic improvement in area conditions. In a five-block area close to the Court, regularly monitored by a neighborhood watch group, an activist estimated that street prostitution had dropped to one-tenth of its 1992 level after a year. After two years, this activist estimated that the decline in prostitution activity was even steeper—from 250 sightings to twelve. This respondent, who had actively campaigned for a more effective police, prosecutor and court response to local street prostitution, reported that the Court had produced "a phenomenal effect" by providing immediate sanctions and court-based social services. The respondent saw a mandatory health education group for prostitutes as one particularly effective strategy for leading some individuals to "opt out" of prostitution and the associated lifestyle.

Local police also reported a substantial change in the concentration of street-level prostitution:

> *During the day time, there is not that much prostitution out there anymore—used to be a lot midday and before twelve. Now it's more late into midnight. And on the weekends it's heavy, because the Midtown Community Court is closed on the weekend, and they know that. So the girls are terrified of coming up here, 'cause they don't want—and their pimps don't want them—to do community service. 'Cause it cuts into their time and earnings. So the Court ... has really made a big dent in prostitution in the 10th precinct. The girls are ... working shorter periods of time ... so they don't have to face this court.*
>
> *In Chelsea, it has definitely made a difference. Say you have guys coming out of Madison Square Garden after hockey games—some drunk, rowdy, looking for girls. Usually we get some fights, maybe the pimps bust their heads with baseball bats, some get robbed.... Well, now you don't have that as much, because the girls aren't there. Not there, because they don't want to appear in the Community Court.*
>
> *Pimps with ten, fifteen girls making thousands upon thousands a day. They don't want them to come up here because if she does community service work it cuts their profits.*

Some local police officers reported that prostitution activity had shifted to weekend hours, when the Court was closed and arrested offenders were sent to the Downtown court:

> *You can see the difference ... I go out on the street, I don't see any prostitutes out. But if I go out after six [on Friday] it's like a free-for-all. Because they know if they get collared then, they'll get taken Downtown—not the Court. Weekends—forget it. You can't walk down Eleventh Avenue. It's out of control.*

Effects of community service work Community members were also convinced that the Court's community service crews had had a marked impact on conditions of disorder. Community leaders, residents and local police attributed a marked reduction in graffiti to the Court:

> *On Ninth Avenue, there's a lot less graffiti because some is being painted over.*
>
> *I saw them painting over the graffiti sprayed on the store window gates, the shutters. Painting them silver again. And I asked who they were.*
>
> *There's a lot less muck out there now. I see them working around there [the Court] all the time.*
>
> *I was sitting in a merchant's office and a group of these people passed, wearing the vests. And he interrupted, 'Wait a minute. I want those people, I want those people.' He wanted them to fix the graffiti. So people know now.*
>
> *I found out about it just a few days ago, reading the 48th Street Block Association Newsletter .... There was a notice with a number saying if you have a problem with graffiti to call them and they'll send someone to paint it over. Which I think is wonderful.*

STREET-LEVEL CONDITIONS

Local police and community residents began to report specific changes in the concentration of prostitution and unlicensed vending at known "hot spots" in the Midtown area shortly after the Court opened. Local police reported that one of the most active prostitution locations, near upscale Midtown hotels, had closed down completely. Community members reported a belief that street-level prostitution had been "displaced" to other precincts which were not served by the Court. These early reports and rumors were ultimately corroborated by both ethnographic interviews and observations and by arrest data.

This section includes information from the ethnographic component of the research, which documents a substantial reduction in prostitution and unlicensed vending during the research period and examines contributing factors. It also examines evidence from the analysis of arrest data about changes in the frequency of these offenses.

Although field researchers concentrated primarily on these two offenses, they also monitored other quality-of-life conditions—squeegee window-washers, gamblers (primarily three-card monte games)—that were prominent in the target area when the Court opened. Defendants charged with these offenses, however, rarely appeared at the Court, either because activity had substantially diminished by the time the Court opened (squeegee window-washers) or because arrests were infrequent (gamblers).

Ethnographic Research: Research Design and Methods

The ethnographic component of the research was designed to document changes in street-level conditions in Midtown Manhattan, particularly those related to the establishment of the Court. Interviews were designed to provide insight into the daily lives of street offenders, to elicit their opinions about the Court and to examine how the street scene had changed in Midtown Manhattan. In addition, a standardized observation protocol was used to count the numbers of people involved in activities at specific Midtown locations.

Learning the Midtown ropes The first several months of fieldwork were spent learning about the "geography of offending" in the Midtown area and the different sub-categories of offenders. For example, unlicensed vendors fell into several sub-groups, differentiated on the basis of what they sell (T-shirts versus handbags versus perfume), whether they are sedentary or mobile and whether they sell: (1) a product they made; (2) a legal product they bought; (3) an illegal product they bought; or (4) a product they stole.

Commercial sex workers also differ greatly. For example, "upscale" commercial sex workers have pimps, wear fur coats, drive expensive cars, own property and command hefty prices for the services they render. There are others who work alone at a "mid-level" stroll in the theater district and charge moderate prices ($20 for oral sex, for example). Those at the bottom are addicted to crack and/or heroin and can be convinced or coerced to perform sex acts for less than $5. Further, there are commercial sex workers who target specific clients and work only on specific days, i.e., days when Social Security checks arrive. In short, through preliminary fieldwork, several different types of unlicensed vendors, commercial sex workers and gamblers were identified. It was first necessary to distinguish the various types of actors before specific observation sites could be chosen and intelligent and appropriate questions asked. Once this was done, systematic observations and interviewing began.

Over the course of the research period, interviews with commercial sex workers focused on several themes or topics including: (1) a description of the "market" in which they participated, including working conditions, clients and their perceptions of market changes over the past year; (2) why they choose to work in the Midtown rather than other local sites; (3) how much income they generated, how they spent it (especially drug consumption), recent changes in earnings and any additional income generating activities; (4) their arrest and incarceration history; and (5) their experiences with and feelings about the Midtown Community Court, especially compared to other criminal court experiences.

Interviews with vendors focused on their perceptions of the structure of economic opportunity in New York City, specifically why they risked arrest by selling on the street rather than seeking legitimate employment. In addition to questions about their experiences with the Court, they were asked to describe their target clientele and to describe how changing conditions made it harder or easier to reach them. They were also asked to identify lucrative spots to work, to define why these locales were profitable and to discuss their ability—as individuals and groups—to avoid detection and arrest.

Though it was the intention of the research to interview people who "squeegee" car windows, an intensive crackdown on these activities by the police department in the months preceding the opening of the Midtown Community Court made them virtually non-existent since the beginning of the research period. Very few squeegee men (and no women) were encountered over the research period, and most of these were reluctant to be interviewed for fear that they might be arrested. Several panhandlers were interviewed about their former squeegeeing activities, but none were observed actively pursuing this form of generating income. The following excerpt from fieldnotes is typical of the limited and somewhat retrospective information gathered regarding squeegeeing activities in Midtown:

> *I walked down Eleventh Avenue to 49th Street where I bumped into three panhandlers, only one of whom was active at the time. The other two guys were sitting on the sidewalk sharing a 40 ounce bottle of malt liquor. This particular corner was formerly the site of a lot of squeegeeing, but I haven't observed that happening for some time now. I started talking with the white guy, George, who appeared to be in his late 40s. He was approaching cars stopping at the light on 49th Street to ask for change. George said, 'I used to squeegee, but that's illegal now. So, I carry a cup. I don't like to do this, but what the hell.' He indicated that he would prefer to*

> *squeegee windows to make money since it gives him the feeling that he has somehow earned it. He admitted that there were some squeegee workers who were very aggressive toward motorists, and he felt that they were the ones who ruined it for everyone else. He said that he was not that type of squeegee worker. Instead, he said that he had regular customers whose car windows he washed on a daily basis. George said that the police were familiar with the activities that occur on that corner and that they have been patrolling the area to make sure that they don't get out of hand.*

Though squeegeeing appears to have been nearly eliminated from Manhattan streets, it remained common in the outer boroughs. Several squeegee men were interviewed in Brooklyn (near the Atlantic Avenue Men's Shelter) and in the Bronx (near the Jerome Avenue exit of the Cross Bronx Expressway) to explore whether there had been any visible displacement of squeegeeing from Manhattan to the outer boroughs. While none of those interviewed reported newcomers to their locations, there was widespread knowledge that squeegeeing was no longer tolerated in Manhattan.

The observation sites The sites which were ultimately chosen for systematic observations were as follows:

1) *Unlicensed vending*: Broadway between 49th and 50th Streets was chosen as the primary site to observe unlicensed vendors. The primary reason for choosing this site was that many vendors lived in a nearby single-room occupancy hotel which provided an opportunity to observe vendors as they began or ended their selling day.
2) *Commercial sex work*: Based on police reports, community sources and preliminary ethnographic observations, three sites, each corresponding to a different "style" of prostitution, were chosen for systematic observation of commercial sex work. The first site, near 56th Street and Sixth Avenue, was located near expensive hotels in Midtown. The commercial sex workers who frequented this site were reported to spend time in the bars of these expensive hotels, wear fancy clothes and command high prices for their services. By the time that systematic observations began, however, most of the commercial sex workers had moved to other locales. After several weeks of fruitless visits, regular systematic observations at this site were discontinued.

The second site for systematic observation of commercial sex work was on 27th Street and Eleventh Avenue, in a warehouse district. The workers at this site, all of whom had "pimps" who managed them, represented the pinnacle of street-level workers in terms of earning potential. They generally dressed in expensive clothing (full length fur coats, high heels, etc) and asked upwards of $50 for their services. They also regularly worked out of "houses," to which they were more than happy to refer clients.

The third site for systematic observation of commercial sex work—characterized in this report as a "mid-level stroll"—was on Ninth Avenue between 44th and 45th Streets. This site was worked by a combination of veterans and newcomers (mostly young women from out of New York State). Unlike the higher priced strolls, most of the women at this location used drugs, usually crack.

There were several other places where lower echelon commercial sex workers were observed to work, including strolls located around Hell's Kitchen Park and the Port Authority bus terminal, but these locations did not receive the same level of systematic observation as the sites which were initially chosen.

Findings of Ethnographic Fieldwork

Several changes in street conditions in the Midtown area suggest that the Court and increased street-level enforcement activities were beginning to have an effect. The following section examines the changes that took place in Midtown Manhattan for each of the various activities targeted by this research.

Commercial sex work Each segment of the commercial sex market showed changes in the ways in which business was conducted, and some of these changes represented dramatic shifts over a short amount of time. The ways that the different strolls changed over the research period are described below.

Mid-level stroll The mid-level stroll, located on Ninth Avenue between 44th and 45th Streets was the most dramatically affected by stepped up enforcement and the existence of the Midtown Community Court. This stroll was located near a busy commercial strip where many trendy restaurants had recently opened and there was a residential district where residents were actively involved in community affairs, including a neighborhood watch group formed to combat blatant street-level sex markets. Observations and interviews suggest that the number of women working along this stroll decreased markedly over the research period, from about twenty to fewer than ten "regulars." There was also substantial turnover: several commercial sex workers dropped out (going home, to jail or to rehab); some newcomers arrived. In addition, street activity became less blatantly visible, as methods were developed to avoid arrest and punishment.

While several factors were responsible for the downsizing and decreased blatancy of the mid-level stroll, the two primary factors were the increase of street-level enforcement by the police and pressures imposed by the Court. Several commercial sex workers complained that community service sentences made major demands on their time—especially sentences of a week or more—and made it extremely difficult to maintain their "regular" pace of evening work.

Ethnographic data suggest that the presence of the Court was a factor which encouraged commercial sex workers to explore other options (legal and illegal) for earning income and helped discourage them from staying in the business. Some respondents complained strongly about the toll that multiple days of community service had taken. Laurie, for example, was a young white commercial sex worker who often solicited "dates" on Eleventh Avenue. She had already been to the Court several times and had become accustomed to serving community service sentences. She complained about getting worn down working two "jobs":

> *This really sucks. I've had to work all day in the basement of the courthouse stuffing envelopes and when I get out of work, I'm tired. And my man is waiting outside for me in his car, expecting me to go out to the Avenue and work all night for him. Hey, I can't do this for too many days in a row before I'll drop from exhaustion.*

Ethnographic fieldnotes illustrate a similar point:

> *I had gone to 46th Street to look for Angie. The last time I had done an interview with her, business had been pretty slow. She had recently finished a stint of community service at the Court and looked quite stressed. I wanted to interview her to see if things had changed in the last couple of weeks. I was not surprised when I didn't immediately see her standing on the corner since it had become more difficult to simply hang out in*

the area. I spotted a couple of other women who I recognized but didn't really know... (clearly working, but trying to be inconspicuous). When I approached and asked if they had seen Angie, they were cautious at first about giving me information. I eventually convinced them that I wasn't the police. (Apparently, Angie had told them about the guy who comes around to do interviews.) They told me that after the last couple of months that had gone so badly for her—arrests, court appearances, community service and fewer 'dates'—Angie had gone home to try and make a go of it there. They wished her well and said that they didn't expect her to come back. One of them said that she too was thinking about getting out of the Midtown scene because things were not the same as they once were.

In contrast to 100 Centre Street (referred to as "Downtown"), women who were taken to the Court quickly learned that they could not easily get away with using aliases nor shirk the responsibilities that came with the sentences they received there. Surprisingly, however, despite their perceptions of being more closely scrutinized and monitored at the Court than Downtown, nearly all the women said that they preferred to be taken to the Court because it was "fairer," "cleaner" and "quicker" than elsewhere.

The opinion of Peppa, who worked the mid-level stroll, was perhaps characteristic of what was regularly voiced by the others:

Peppa had been to the Court several times in 1994 and generally preferred it to "going Downtown." She said that the Court was: "a quick system. It only takes about two or three hours to see the judge. And it's always a female judge. She's a bitch. I think she's harder on us because we're females like her." Peppa complained that, "community service is all day (her emphasis)—cleaning toilets and stuffing envelopes. I think it sucks, but its easier than going to Central Booking. Even though I hate doing it, I guess the community service is fair."

While business at the mid-level stroll had been characterized by "milling around" behavior in past years, stepped up enforcement, increased punishment and harassment by neighborhood residents had made prostitutes who worked this stroll much more mobile over the research period. Women no longer lingered on corners or sat on stoops waiting to proposition "dates" as they passed by. Instead, they walked briskly up and down the block, as though they were on their way to an appointment. Though they would try and catch the eye of a potential date as they passed on the sidewalk, they almost invariably waited for the date to make the first move, a significant change from the previous year. They had become so wary that the first question that they always asked the ethnographer was whether he was a police officer.

Over the research period, almost all of the women who worked this stroll were arrested numerous times and had been to the Midtown Community Court at least once. They complained that their business had suffered dramatically. .

Increased enforcement of "johns" for soliciting prostitution also took a toll. According to several workers, many potential dates were also much more cautious about how they sought sexual services. Rather than walking directly up and having women proposition them or propositioning women themselves, potential dates were driving (or walking) around the area for some time before they became convinced that a woman who they had their eye on was not a police officer. This "jumpiness" on the part of customers dramatically slowed transactions and affected the amount of income that many of these women expected to earn.

> *Lucy said that in the short amount of time that she has been here, and from what she has 'heard from the other girls, the cops are harassing people a lot more out here. There are fewer dates. They're scared to stop.'*

> *Peppa complained that it has become difficult to work this stroll because 'you can't tell the police from the dates. Also, there's lots of female decoys who get all dressed up to bust the dates. We can spot them right away, but the dates don't seem to be able to tell the difference. Since things have gotten tough out here, I only work about two hours a day, make my money and then chill.'*

Unlike many of the women working at this stroll, Peppa was still able to pay her bills even when she began working fewer hours. Others were forced to look for different economic opportunities to try and make ends meet. For example, one woman said that she had begun shoplifting to earn extra income, while another said that she had begun to help a drug dealer—acting as a lookout—to make a few more dollars.

A central outcome of the increased pressure on this commercial sex market was that workers' behavior became more discreet. The women were less visible because they were no longer stationary and less likely to proposition potential customers. As the following interview with Stacey suggests, because it was becoming increasingly "costly" for buyers and sellers to meet, commercial sex workers began cultivating more repeat "clients" who made appointments and they tried to rely on fewer anonymous, spontaneous dates.

> *I have a lot of friends in jail right now. There's not that many customers any more. The walking patrol keeps girls off the stroll and discourages customers from stopping. I'm lucky that way. I'm young and look good; most of my dates are steadies. I don't really have to walk the stroll looking for work. In fact, I have one date that comes every day who pays me $100, so if I don't want to come outside, I don't have to.*

Over the research period, the decreased visibility and downsizing of the commercial sex market were precisely the types of outcomes which suggested that recent court and police initiatives were beginning to have a significant impact on the street.

One vignette helps illustrate this change on the street:

> *The ethnographer had arranged to interview a commercial sex worker one Thursday at 8 p.m. When he arrived at the agreed upon place there was a commotion on the sidewalk. The woman who was to be interviewed was being arrested for a street altercation with her boyfriend. As officers were placing the handcuffs on her, the ethnographer wedged his way through the gathered crowd and asked her what had happened. After she responded tersely, protesting her arrest, the ethnographer instructed her to call him as soon as she had an opportunity. The ethnographer did not see the arrested commercial sex worker for several weeks. When he finally reestablished contact with her, she had been to the Midtown Community Court, completed her sentence of community service, returned to her hometown in search of 'legitimate employment' and reluctantly returned to New York City when she could not 'make a go of it at home.'*

To summarize, the mid-level stroll experienced significant changes over the research period which led to a smaller, more discreet market. These changes appear to represent a response to several sources of pressure, including: (1) increased street-level enforcement; (2) the economic revitalization of the neighborhood; and (3) the presence of the Court.

Low-level stroll The low end of the commercial sex work continuum, represented by the stroll around Hell's Kitchen Park, was also substantially altered over the research period. Many of the women who participated in this market had previously managed to earn the majority of their income from performing sex acts. With increased enforcement in the vicinity of their hang out spots (which were near drug distribution centers) their business had declined to the point where many of them had given up commercial sex work as a "regular" occupation. Most of the women interviewed at these sites continued to engage in such work when the opportunity presented itself, but found it too difficult to continue to work the streets consistently. The increase in street-level enforcement and monitoring of sentences by the Midtown Community Court had made a wide range of street behaviors risky. People who had once solicited "dates" and consumed drugs and alcohol in public with impunity, had now begun to moderate their routines or face increasingly stiff sentences when caught. The segment below, from an interview with a 37-year-old Latina who was once an active commercial sex worker on the stroll near Hell's Kitchen Park, illustrates how difficult this area had become for sex workers. On this night, the ethnographer encountered her sitting on a stoop, depressed by the lack of money-making opportunities, and suffering from heroin withdrawal pains.

> *Lucy reported that the police were starting to ticket people for seemingly "minor" offenses and that earlier in the day, her "friends got ticketed $45 for a bottle of beer." She went on to say that she had been arrested four times in the last year; once for "soliciting" and "three times for possession [of drugs] within the last three months." Each time, she was taken to the Court.*

Upper-level stroll Shortly after the Court opened, the upper echelon strolls—those where commercial sex workers wore fur coats and charged $50 and up for services rendered—switched out of the hotel district and consolidated in a commercial area, where neither business persons nor residents were likely to complain about their presence. At the beginning of the research period, the area around 56th Street and Sixth Avenue had been identified by members of the police department as one of the most prominent "hot spots" for commercial sex workers. By the time the researchers entered the field, however, this location had dried up completely. Many of these workers relocated to a warehouse district.

Activity in this location did not appear to change significantly during the research period. Although there was evidence that some of the women were working fewer hours, business in this area remained fairly constant over the research period, despite fairly intense enforcement efforts. Though the numbers of commercial sex workers and times they worked varied considerably more from day to day at this stroll than others, it remained a viable market place, evidenced by the nearly constant lines of cars mysteriously circling the block in this rather deserted warehouse district. Ethnographic observations made in the dead of winter documented that even sub-zero weather seemed have little effect on the number of stiletto-heeled, flesh-flashing streetwalkers on parade at this location.

In general, all the commercial sex markets located in Midtown Manhattan were affected by changes in local conditions during the research period and consequently, they became more discreet and smaller. Some of these changes were simply the result of seasonal variation—e.g., when it is colder, people are less likely to spend a lot of time on the street. Other changes seemed not to be the result of seasonal variation or temporary fluctuations in market conditions, but rather, the outcome of recent initiatives, particularly increased street-level enforcement and the presence of the Midtown Community Court.

Volume of prostitution arrests Findings from street ethnography, individual interviews and group interviews, pointing to a drop in the volume of prostitution in Midtown were reinforced by analysis of arrest volume for specific offenses in Manhattan. Figure 7.1 shows that the volume of arrests for street prostitution in Midtown began dropping dramatically when the Midtown Community Court opened, and continued to drop throughout the research period—a 56 percent decline compared to a comparable baseline period.[1] As shown in Figure 7.1, six months after the Court opened, prostitution arrests had dropped 25 percent in Midtown and 19 percent overall; a year later, prostitution arrests had dropped 56 percent in Midtown and 35 percent overall. Although the volume of arrests in the rest of Manhattan increased, this increase was small compared to the decreased number of arrests in Midtown.

There appeared to be a limited amount of displacement to other areas. Respondents arrested for street prostitution in Midtown reported that other parts of Manhattan simply could not support the type of prostitution stroll to which they were accustomed. Prostitutes in Midtown Manhattan command substantially higher prices than prostitutes in other parts of town. There weren't that many places that they found appropriate for

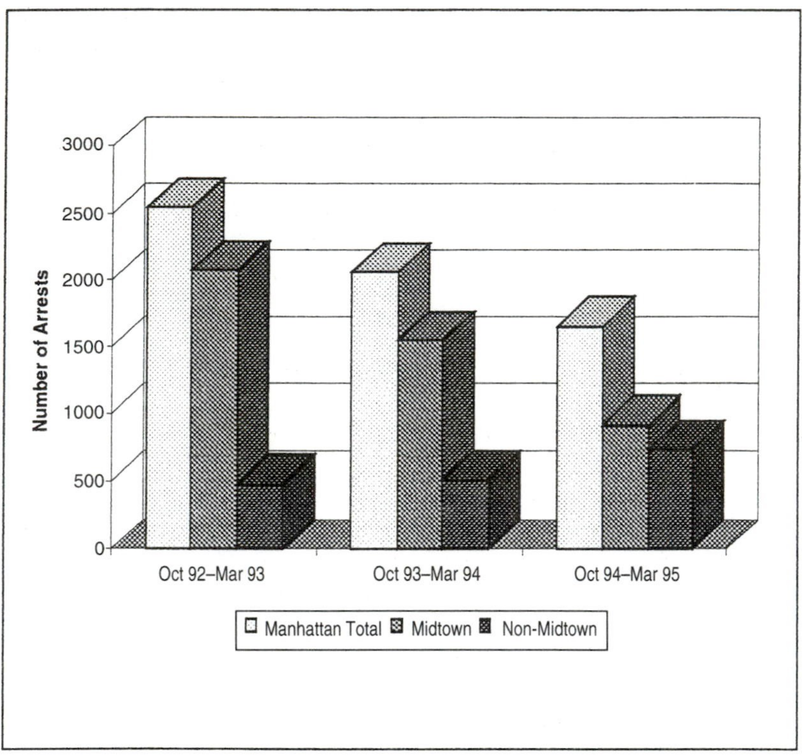

Figure 7.1 Manhattan Prostitution Arrests: Three Comparable Six-Month Periods

business. The increase in arrests in the rest of Manhattan reflects a moderate amount of displacement to adjacent precincts and a substantial citywide increase in quality-of-life enforcement.

Unlicensed vendors Like commercial sex workers, unlicensed vendors participate in distinct markets. Some of these markets saw little change over the research period, while others witnessed major upheavals. In general, people for whom vending was only an occasional activity did not seem to have been affected by increased enforcement in Midtown nor the presence of the Midtown Community Court. For example, those vendors who occasionally roamed the streets selling a case or two of items that "fell off a truck" were unlikely to be arrested because they spent little time on Midtown streets. The occasional vendors who were interviewed were all aware that there are penalties involved in getting caught engaging in such activities, but they were unaware of the presence of the Court. The following excerpt from fieldnotes presents one example of the few "occasional vendors" interviewed:

> *I spotted two African American guys selling men's cologne out of a paper bag standing outside of the Blimpie's on the corner of 34th Street and Eighth Avenue. It was getting dark outside and one of them was acting as a lookout while the other tried to attract customers. They were hawking the product to men en route to a Rangers hockey game at Madison Square Garden. They asked if I wanted to buy a bottle for my wife and I told them no. I then told them that I would be interested in interviewing them and briefly described the nature of my research, and Herb, the seller, followed me into Blimpie's for a brief interview. Herb said that he's from Nelson Avenue in the Bronx and he works unloading trucks in the Hunt's Point section. Once in a while, a few boxes of merchandise happen to "fall off the truck" and he sometimes takes them into Midtown Manhattan to sell them. According to Herb, this happens infrequently; about once every few months or so. He noted that "hustling on the move is easier than standing in one spot because there's less pressure." Though he knows that it is illegal, he said that he had never been arrested for selling without a license. But he added that even having a license doesn't guarantee that a vendor will not have problems with the police. He went on to describe how he recently witnessed a licensed vendor get his merchandise seized by the police because he was unwittingly selling on Port Authority property. Even with this example, however, Herb noted that if he ever intended to sell in one spot on a regular basis, he would get a license.*

Vendors who sat on the sidewalk and made their own product were also largely unaffected by increased enforcement and the Court. For example, Rail, a Panamanian bracelet maker worked daily at the 50th Street and Broadway site throughout the research period and was arrested only once for vending during that time. He consistently reported that police officers did not bother him and he spent no effort looking for them, while on the same block, knots of anxious Senegalese T-shirt and watch vendors were constantly looking for plainclothes and uniformed officers. The following description of Rail's business gives a sense of how different his business was from the vendors who were the constant targets of police and repeat clients of the Midtown Community Court.

> *Rail is a Panamanian immigrant who has carved out a little niche for himself making beaded bracelets which he sells for $6 apiece on Broadway near 50th Street. He works seven days a week sitting on a milk crate near the bus stop. Though he speaks little English, he has established something of a clientele and carries with him a series of small notebooks where clients write a name and/or draw a picture of what they want the bracelet to look like. At any one time, he carries between fifteen and twenty commissioned bracelets in his waistband and displays another eight to ten bracelets for pedestrians to look at and buy. Rail spends his time sitting on the sidewalk listening to a walkman playing salsa music and happily making his commissioned works. If a new client approaches him with a request, he can make a bracelet from scratch in about 20 minutes. On a good day he can earn about $140; on a bad day about $50.*
>
> *Rail has worked this location for approximately six months and has been arrested only once for vending during that period. He was arrested on a Saturday and sent to 100 Centre Street where he received "time served" and a small fine. He was clearly unhappy about losing his materials and a day of work, but he chalked it up as the price one must pay to work Midtown. Rail says that he is wary about working on Saturdays because the same arresting officer "hassles" him sometimes, but normally police officers say little to him. He has never heard of the Midtown Community Court, though his lack of English language skills may be partially responsible for this. He said that he had been arrested only once for vending, but claimed to have about fifteen citations for smoking on the subway platform and jumping the turnstile. Rail said that all of these infractions took place in the outer boroughs and he has never bothered to answer the desk appearance tickets that were issued. When asked if he was worried that the tickets might come back to haunt him, he shrugged his shoulders and laughed.*

While these notes, taken from early in the research period, reflect little knowledge on Rail's part of the Court, it is significant that he never learned much more about it, even though he continued to work every day, cheek by jowl, with other vendors who had considerable experience at the courthouse. This suggests that police officers may have been selective in their enforcement of vending statutes, but also attests to the lack of a sense of "community" between different types of unlicensed vendors. Of course, language barriers may, to a large degree, account for the lack of communication between different types of vendors, but the ethnographer never saw Rail speak or try to speak with any of the other vendors who frequented the block, though he clearly recognized them by face was somewhat familiar with their daily routines.

The most targeted of the unlicensed vendors were those who sold cheap imitations of expensive name-brand products like fake Rolex watches and imitation Pierre Cardin sweatshirts. All such vendors who were interviewed were aware of the Court and most of them had been there several times. The excerpt from fieldnotes below illustrates vendors' familiarity with going rates at the Court:

> *I spoke with Ali, a Senegalese watch vendor, while we were observing a team of gamblers hustling tourists. Ali commented that the gamblers 'make good money' and that the team was very good at their trade. He noted that the 'cops never catch them; always my people.' When asked whether he had been to the Midtown Community Court, Ali replied, 'many times.' He said that the usual sentence he and other vendors receive is a fine [surcharge] plus one day of community service.*

Ultimately, the increase in enforcement and the presence of the Court clearly had a significant impact on this segment of the vending population. Where these vendors were nearly ubiquitous on the streets of Manhattan at the beginning of the research period, by the end the ethnographer was hard pressed to find many of them. A few Senegalese vendors who were interviewed in early 1995, opted to go through the trouble of getting a license (a difficult process in Midtown Manhattan) rather than suffer repeated arrests and increased community service sentences. They complained that renewing their licenses quarterly was troublesome and cost them a few hundred dollars, although it was ultimately cheaper than getting arrested and having to perform so many days of community service. Because the number of licenses available to general vendors is very limited (capped at 853 in 1979: Sontag, 1993), this option was not widely available.

Another way that many vendors appeared to be coping with the increase in enforcement was by forging alliances with small shop owners and kiosk operators. By the end of the research period, many such businesses had positioned a former vendor as a "salesperson" standing in front or to the side who watched any items that the owner might put out on the sidewalk. In return, the store owners allowed the "salesperson" to add his own line of merchandise to whatever the store had to offer. Such accommodations reduced the risk of arrest, the confiscation of merchandise and a day lost to community service at the Court.

Arrest volume: unlicensed vending It was somewhat more difficult to analyze changes in the volume of arrests for unlicensed vending than for prostitution because the NYPD does not maintain separate precinct-level information about arrest volume for this offense. Analysis of the changes in the number of illegal vending cases entering the Court provides a reasonable proxy for official NYPD data. This is because the vast majority of individuals arrested for unlicensed vending in Midtown during the research period were sent to the Court.[2]

Figure 7.2 shows that arrests for unlicensed vending in the Midtown area, as measured by the number of vending cases at the Court, dropped by 24 percent from the Court's early months (11/93–3/94) to a comparable period in the Court's second year (11/94–3/95). For vending cases, there are no comparable data for non-Midtown precincts.

Overall, the ethnographic research, analysis of arrest data and focus group and individual interviews with local police, community leaders and residents pointed to a substantial improvement in local quality-of-life conditions during the Court's first eighteen months. According to community members:

> *There is a much better feeling generally. People are feeling better and safer. Rents have gone up a little, the streets seem cleaner.*
>
> *On Ninth Avenue, there's less graffiti because some is being painted over. The girls I always saw coming home? Definitely fewer of them.*

There were several other factors that appeared to have contributed to this improvement, including increased police enforcement, clean-up crews provided by Business Improvement Districts and general economic development in the Times Square Area. Community members and local police acknowledged that the Court was a substantial contributor to the recognized improvement in quality-of-life conditions in the Midtown area.

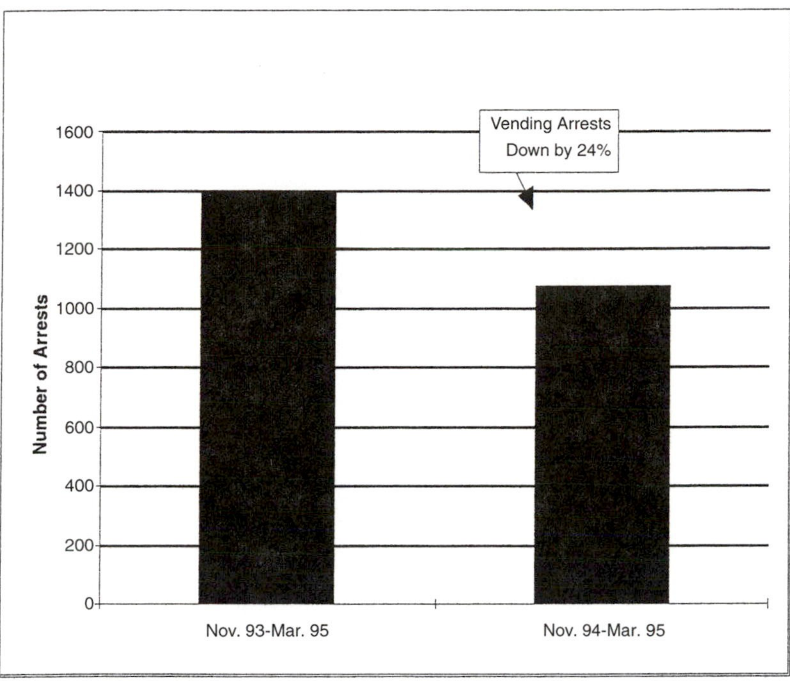

Figure 7.2 Unlicensed Vending Arrests, Midtown: Two Comparable Periods

Notes

1. Between 1993 and 1994, prostitution arrests in the Court's target area dropped by over 35 percent—all during a period in which enforcement of low-level offenses in New York City had intensified. Although the number of arrests in other precincts increased in response to heightened enforcement, the total number of prostitution arrests in Manhattan as a whole dropped by 1,000, or 21 percent. Subsequent analysis shows that the volume of arrests for prostitution continued to decline sharply in subsequent months.
2. Baseline data supplied by the NYPD during the Court's planning period showed that over 80 percent of arrests for administrative code offenses (almost entirely for unlicensed vending) were DATs. *All* Midtown DATs are sent to the Court. The only Midtown vending cases sent to the Downtown court involved summary arrests made during the weekend hours that were ineligible for the Court. At least 60 percent of Midtown summary arrests for unlicensed vending are made during eligible hours. Therefore, it is reasonable to assume that roughly 90 percent of vending arrests made in Midtown are sent to the Court.

CHAPTER EIGHT

COURT OUTCOMES: EXPECTATIONS AND PERCEPTIONS

The community served by the Midtown Community Court was broadly defined by the Court's planners as including community members (leaders, residents, merchants); local criminal justice professionals (senior criminal justice officials, judges, attorneys, court clerks, court officers, CJA personnel and local police); and defendants. This chapter examines expectations for and perceptions of court operations and case outcomes at the Midtown Community Court among these various groups. It examines three areas: hopes and expectations for the Court, including the criteria proposed for assessing its success; perceptions of court procedures and case outcomes; and key differences among respondent groups in attitudes toward the Court and its response to low-level offenses.

Because the chapter focuses primarily on courtroom activity, it draws more heavily on the attitudes of criminal justice personnel than on those of community leaders and residents.[1] Perceptions of the Court's role in target neighborhoods will be examined in the next chapter.

Methodology Chapters 8 and 9 draw upon two primary data sources, designed to track opinions as they changed from before the Court's opening through its first two years. These include (1) a series of interviews conducted at regular intervals with a panel of involved community members and criminal justice officials over a two-year period and (2) two sets of focus groups with community leaders, residents, attorneys, local police officers and other criminal justice personnel. The first set of focus groups was held just before the Court opened; the second was held about one year later. In addition, research staff conducted a set of individual interviews with defendants at both the Downtown court and the Midtown Community Court to gather information about defendants' perceptions of the differences between the two courts. Research staff also convened a group meeting of judges who had worked at the Court to discuss perceived differences between the Midtown and Downtown courts.

Individual and group interviews focused on identifying perceptions of how the Court differed from "business as usual" at the Downtown court. Baseline interviews sought to identify hopes, expectations and concerns about the new Court. Subsequent interviews tracked changing perceptions of the effect of the Court on case outcomes, compliance rates and community conditions and the perceived value of alternative sanction programs.

Overview of Changing Themes As reviewed in Chapter 1, much of the debate about the Midtown Community Court took place during the two-year planning period. At that time, there were clear divisions between project supporters (community groups, senior court personnel, the mayor's office and senior police management) and project opponents (the prosecution and the defense bars). Attorney groups initially opposed the development of the Court, arguing that it was unfair to devote resources to a single neighborhood and that project funds might be better spent on improvements at the centralized court. Other stakeholders raised different issues, including whether the Court could operate efficiently, whether it could actually affect case outcomes and whether defendants would comply with intermediate sanctions. The focus of respondents' concerns shifted substantially over time from questions about whether the new Court would "work" to an examination of the implications of the project for other New York City courts.

Early Concerns Before the Court opened, both criminal justice and community respondents posed a series of "can it be done?" questions: Could cases be routed successfully to the new Court? Could the Court handle its caseload in a single shift without unduly stretching arrest-to-arraignment time? Was it possible to change "going rates" for low-level offenses? Would any defendants actually perform community service? There was considerable skepticism about whether such objectives could be achieved.

Some opponents of the project suggested that the new Court might indeed affect sentence outcomes. They argued that the relatively rich resources available—on-site services, state-of-the-art technology—would produce an "unfair advantage" over the Downtown court.[2] They also argued that the high quality of the personnel selected to work at the Court—from the judge to the court officers to the defense attorneys—would have a strong influence on outcomes. A representative of the District Attorney's office commented that the "elite" staff assigned to the Court could produce more constructive case outcomes for misdemeanor cases in any setting: "With these judges, I could hold court in my living room."

The Court quickly demonstrated a capacity to promote a broad use of community-service and social-service sentences and to ensure that the vast majority of sentenced offenders complied. Early on, informed respondents switched their focus to specific operational issues, including caseload volume, adjournment rates, the role of the resource coordinator, the value of technology, levels of community service supervision, the visibility of community service projects and the amount of feedback that the Court provided to the community (see Chapters 5 and 9).

Follow-up Interviews By the time the Court was eighteen months old, respondents' focus had shifted toward the Court's perceived impacts, including an increased use of alternative sanctions. Respondents attributed changes in case outcomes to a variety of factors, including the Court's infrastructure for assessing, matching and monitoring defendants in alternative sanctions and the role of the Resource Coordinator in promoting a wider use of community service and social service sentences. Several respondents suggested that the small scale and community base of the Court helped promote an expansion of intermediate sanctions and increased compliance with those sanctions.

In follow-up interviews, both criminal justice professionals and community members raised questions about whether specific components of the Midtown model might be successfully adapted to other local courts. They asked whether individual components of the Midtown model were essential to its ability to transform case outcomes: Could centralized courts expand the use of community and social service sentences without the Court's information system? Could they improve compliance without escorting defendants from arraignment to the scheduling office or establishing the capacity for "same-day" community service?

Overall, there was a general recognition that the project had promoted more constructive case outcomes than "business as usual" at the Downtown court. There was also substantial support for the Court's effort to use community service and social service sentences to "pay back" the harmed community and help solve the underlying problems of defendants. For most respondent groups, early skepticism about what the Court might accomplish gave way to increasing expectations about the Court's ability to "turn lives around," promote constructive sentences and improve community conditions.

HOPES, EXPECTATIONS AND CRITERIA FOR SUCCESS

Hopes and Expectations

Many respondents in panel interviews drew a distinction between their hopes and expectations for the new Court. Most *hoped* that the project would succeed in reducing recidivism, changing lives, reducing the frequency of quality-of-life offenses and providing appropriate, proportionate punishment. Expectations were substantially more restrained than expressed hopes. As one criminal justice professional put it: "Nearly any kind of change is going to be incremental. You are not going to change the world."

Many representatives of both the community and the criminal justice system had high hopes for the Court. Some anticipated a fundamental change in the arraignment process, resulting from the effort to think holistically about the work of the Court. They hoped that the Court would promote the use of constructive sentences, including community service and social service sanctions; that social service agencies at the Court would intervene in unhealthy lifestyles and criminal behaviors; that defendants would think about the impact of their actions on the community; that the community would see something positive being done about central community problems; and that the attitudes of police officers toward the courts would improve.

Expectations about the project's ability to influence court outcomes, promote compliance with community service sentences or help defendants "transform their lives" were far more modest. Several respondents expected little change in "business as usual." According to the focus group facilitator, predictions about what the Court could accomplish through its social service component were "guardedly optimistic." Respondents were particularly restrained in their predictions about the project's ability to influence defendants with high rates of recidivism and a strong economic stake in their criminal behavior. It was recognized that little was known about levels of recidivism for low-level offenses at the Downtown court.

Baseline Criteria for Judging Success

Respondents in focus groups and individual interviews suggested similar criteria for judging the success of the project, including reducing recidivism, changing court outcomes to provide "appropriate punishment," "changing lives" and improving community conditions. There was little difference among respondent groups in the criteria proposed and no clear consensus about the relative priority of these criteria.

Respondents in individual interviews proposed a variety of criteria for evaluating the Court. Some looked for quantitative impacts, such as reductions in the rate of recidivism and changes in the Court's use of intermediate sanctions and jail. Others proposed more qualitative criteria, including reducing the extent of community alienation from the courts and improving the efficiency of court operations. Cost-benefit issues were centrally important to organizations that had provided financial support to the Court and to criminal justice officials, particularly those critical of the decision to invest resources in a satellite facility.

In baseline interviews, respondents said that they would judge the project a success if the following criteria were met:[3]

If recidivism were reduced Before the Court opened, a number of respondents, particularly court clerks, attorneys and police officers, reported that they would judge the success of the new Court by the extent to which it managed to slow down the "revolving door" of repeat offending.

If the Court changed case outcomes to provide appropriate punishment Respondents wanted to see more constructive responses to low-level crime at the Court. Community members were particularly supportive of the concept of community restitution, but desired a tough response—specifically jail sentences—to non-compliance and recidivism. In interviews conducted before the Court opened, there was widespread dissatisfaction with "business as usual": "I don't think judges care. I don't think they consider any of this important ... "; "All judges are interested in is clearing their calendar...."

If the Court "changed lives" Some respondents reported that they would regard the Court as a success if it made offenders aware of constructive options and succeeded in "saving" a few.

> *This is a very realistic group. So, if five people come in off the streets and get in the drug program and stop dealing on the corner.... If there was a decrease of activity in the streets, if these offenders were reluctant to come into the Times Square area ... [instead of] tourists.*

Many respondents believed that intervention efforts would be most effective for defendants whose criminal careers were just beginning:

> *They will be given a chance to help themselves early on in the process.... If you can stop them before they commit 30 shoplifts, maybe you can stem it right there....*

If community conditions improved Some residents reported that they would judge the Court by conditions in the area. If there were less street crime or if the deterioration of quality of life were halted, they would find the Court a success:

> *I will judge success if the types of complaints change. Let's say prostitutes and drug dealing complaints are down and there now are more about car alarms. Then I would say 'Great.'*

PERCEPTIONS OF COURT OUTCOMES

At the time the Court opened, even leading critics of the project were well aware of fundamental problems with the traditional handling of low-level offenses. According to a senior member of the District Attorney's office, "The history in this building over the last ten years has been that misdemeanor offenders have learned that crime pays. We have given the courthouse away" (Horowitz, 1993). During the planning and start-up period, there was general agreement that misdemeanor courts should develop mechanisms for promoting more constructive responses for misdemeanors. The debate centered around (1) the appropriateness of the Court as a locus for developing and testing such mechanisms, and (2) the ability of a community-based arraignment court to make a difference in case outcomes.

Shortly after the Court opened, informed criminal justice staff and community leaders recognized that the new Court was having a substantial effect on the use of alternative sanctions. Critics and supporters alike indicated that the new Court focused more intensively on quality-of-life offenses and promoted the use of intermediate sanctions for cases that would have had no conditions imposed Downtown. By the end of the first year, respondents familiar with the Midtown and Downtown courts acknowledged that their hopes for an increased use of alternative sanctions had been met: "[Downtown] what they get is 'time served' and they are out. Here, you never get 'time served.' You always get community service...." Early predictions that there might be little impact on case outcomes proved unfounded.

Respondents raised a variety of other issues about sentencing as well. Were sentence outcomes internally consistent? Would defendants comply with alternative sanctions programs? Would enough defendants benefit from social service sentences to justify the creation of court-based services? Was the new Court "tougher" or "softer" on misdemeanants? The following sections review community opinions about these issues.

Consistency in Sentencing

There were two concerns expressed about the Court's potential for disparity in sentence outcomes: first, that the new Court might produce substantial inequity in sentencing (e.g., different case outcomes from Downtown for defendants arrested in Midtown) and, second that it might produce inconsistency in sentencing (e.g., disparate sentences *within* the Court for defendants with comparable charges and criminal histories). Attorneys' concerns about equity were not shared by community members who hoped that the Court experiment *would* produce different, individualized, constructive outcomes for misdemeanor cases heard in Midtown. In fact, Court planners and community members saw differences between the Midtown and Downtown courts in case outcomes (e.g., increased use of alternative sanctions) as a key indicator of project success.

By the end of the first year, some attorneys reported that the judge's access to expanded information and the greater availability of sentence alternatives in Midtown had indeed had a substantial effect on sentencing. There was general agreement that the Midtown Community Court produced substantially different sentence outcomes than the Downtown court. Although this finding represented a success to community groups and criminal justice professionals who hoped for a more constructive response to quality-of-life offenses, it also represented sentencing disparity for defendants processed in Midtown—a key concern of some local attorneys.

The fact that sentences at Midtown differed from those at the Downtown court, however, did not mean that they were *internally* inconsistent. Criminal justice professionals who predicted inconsistent outcomes at the Midtown Community Court argued that misdemeanor sentencing was relatively unconstrained, compared to felony sentencing, giving rise to substantial judicial discretion.[4] To avoid inconsistency in sentencing at the Downtown court, the

District Attorney's office used guidelines to ensure that misdemeanor pleas consistently reflected "going rates" based on prior record and charge. Although the DA's office used identical guidelines at the Midtown and Downtown courts, there was speculation that guidelines would play a lesser role at Midtown, where expanded information and resource coordination served to promote judicial control (see Chapter 5).

By the end of the first year, there was general agreement that sentencing at the Court was being carried out consistently. Respondents acknowledged that a new set of "going rates," specific to the Court, had been established. In fact, some attorneys reported that the Court's information system, isolation and small scale made it easier to reach consensus about "going rates" for specific offenses, producing even greater consistency in sentencing in Midtown than Downtown.

Social Service Sentencing

Most respondents initially believed that a relatively small proportion of defendants would make substantial changes in their lifestyles after being sentenced to participate in court-based social services. Community members and criminal-justice professionals believed that the Court could help only *motivated* defendants leave the life of prostitution, drug addiction or petty theft. There was little expectation that a misdemeanor court could force a person to make that decision. Several respondents were skeptical about the likelihood of social service success:

> *My concern is that what the Court does won't be enough. If someone is driven to commit a crime, will the Court providing a service and possibly providing some self-esteem—Is that going to be enough to turn somebody around ... [with] no other way to make a living except dealing drugs....*

In spite of this skepticism, there was considerable support for the Court's effort to help solve defendants' underlying problems:

> *If the root is a drug problem, then go at it, give it a shot upstairs. And monitor it, see if this person comes back again.... And if he fails again and again, now you have a record of it through the computers....*

Court planners, some courtroom personnel and social service providers saw the Court as offering help at a moment of crisis when a small number of defendants might be particularly receptive to assistance. As a member of the courtroom staff put it:

> *A lot of the defendants in this court do respond well if treated like an individual and given some sort of structure and some sort of job. Unfortunately, we are not in a position to provide jobs for people. The social services are excellent. They are doing very well. We have an English as a Second Language class.... And they have kids walking in off the street to learn English.... We have a lot of people on drugs coming into the programs.*

Some respondents initially hoped that the availability of on-site services might affect recidivism rates, although no one expected large numbers of defendants to make dramatic changes in their lives. Because community leaders set a modest standard for court-based services, the response to the Court's first success stories were highly positive: "wonderful things are happening to individuals there"; "close to a miracle." Over time, community leaders began to expect a somewhat larger number of success stories than initially predicted.

Awareness of success stories did not promote a broader expectation that aggregate recidivism rates would be substantially reduced. In fact, expressed hopes about the Court's ability to have a broad impact on recidivism diminished between the first and second focus group, particularly among courtroom staff who saw a number of high-rate repeat offenders return to court.[5] Ultimately, criminal justice personnel and community leaders focused more on the impact of services in changing a relatively small number of lives than on broad reductions in recidivism rates.

Compliance with Alternative Sanctions

Expectations about the Court's potential impact on compliance with alternative sanctions were mixed. Some respondents predicted increased compliance because of procedural improvements —court officers escorting defendants to the scheduling office, the possibility of "same-day" sentencing and the availability of on-site work crews for participants at high risk of non-compliance. Some suggested that efforts to match a defendant with the appropriate type of sanction might encourage completion. Yet, others argued that the widespread use of alternative sanctions at the Court for some groups believed to be at risk of noncompliance (e.g., prostitutes) would result in *lower* completion rates than Downtown.

By the end of the first year, community members were often uncertain about whether the new Court had affected compliance with alternative sanctions. Some remembered hearing that compliance rates were "very good." Others either professed too little knowledge or believed that compliance rates were roughly equal to rates Downtown. Inside the Court, on the other hand, the judge, clerks and coordinating staff monitored community service compliance rates closely and were well aware that aggregate compliance rates were substantially higher than aggregate rates Downtown. Attorneys were also aware that tightened procedures had helped promote compliance:

> *When someone is given community service, he's not sent away with, 'Go and sin no more.' He has to sit in the front row, is brought up with a group and starts community service that day. And they do it.*

Although there was some concern that the Court's initial positive effect on compliance might dissipate over time, regular review demonstrated that compliance remained at a consistently high level.

Perceived "Toughness"

Given the Court's effort to move sentencing to the middle ranges between "nothing" and jail, it is not surprising that respondents held mixed opinions about whether the new Court would be "tougher" or "softer." Before the Court opened, many respondents, aware that the Court would use intermediate sanctions for cases that would have received no punishment, saw such sanctions as more severe than "business as usual."

At the same time, some criminal justice professionals also recognized that the Court might substitute intermediate sanctions for jail, a "softer" response. There were mixed opinions about potential reductions in the use of jail. To some criminal justice professionals, particularly the District Attorney's office, reductions in the frequency of jail sentences represented excessive lenience. To others, jail alternatives represented a valuable, systemic cost-saving. For many years, the New York City criminal justice community has worked to develop mechanisms for diverting non-violent, jail-bound offenders into constructive alternatives in an effort to reduce overcrowding at local correctional facilities. Supporters of the Court pointed out that intermediate sanctions would provide a valuable alternative to very short-term jail sentences (one to five days) which produced little actual jail time, after subtracting pre-arraignment detention time and "good time."[6]

Before the Court opened, community members and criminal justice professionals also expected an aggressive response to non-compliance. As one community member put it:

> *The Court is set up to do not only community service but health and drug rehab and the wide array of social services. But—it also says that if the three-card monte guy fails to be responsive—he goes to jail.*

There were two distinct points of view about the use of jail as a response to non-compliance. Some community members and local police saw such jail sentences as sending a valuable message about accountability at the new Court. Other criminal justice professionals were concerned about the potential costs of jail sentences, imposed on defendants who failed alternative sanctions. They saw "secondary" jail sentences as a threat to the Court's potential ability to reduce system costs by providing alternatives to incarceration.

"Tougher" sentences After the first year, many respondents acknowledged that the Court frequently imposed community service and social service sentences as an alternative to "nothing" —sentences of "time served" and other non-punitive responses. In contrast, they typically saw Downtown misdemeanor courts as lax in response to low-level crime, ineffective with repeat offenders and unable to produce constructive solutions.

> *My experience with prostitution and drug dealing [Downtown] is that it is 'time served' for prostitutes. For drug dealing, a lot of times law enforcement itself won't press the case unless it's something major.*

Both community members and criminal justice professionals noted that Downtown quality-of-life cases were dwarfed by the sheer number and variety of more serious charges. They believed that cases which received low priority Downtown were taken seriously at Midtown.

Although community members and many criminal justice personnel supported the Court's efforts to promote intermediate sanctions as an alternative to "nothing," some defense attorneys objected that "tougher" sentencing had hurt their clients. One defense attorney complained that it was nearly impossible to get a case dismissed at the Court. Yet this attorney saw other advantages for his clients:

> *While overall it's bad for my clients, there are a few who have really benefited. They definitely did. They got into a drug program.*

"Softer" sentences Early on, the District Attorney's office voiced objections to perceived reductions in the frequency of jail sentences at the Midtown Community Court, particularly for repeat offenders. Over time, the District Attorney's office increasingly pointed to reductions in the use of jail and criticized the new Court as "too soft" on repeat offenders.

Some attorneys recognized that the Midtown Community Court was both "tougher" and "softer." As one put it, "I don't like to use the word 'lenient.' I'd call it different." In focus groups, one ADA, who acknowledged the widespread use of community service instead of jail at the Court, also recognized that those who failed alternative sentences at the Court were treated more harshly than they would have been Downtown:

> *Sentencing that comes out of 100 Centre Street [the Downtown court] is quite different from what comes out of Midtown. There [at Midtown] you get community service under circumstances in which no one would ever get community service at Centre Street. People can come through the system—jail cases...—and come out to do community service. But then the flip side is, people who are afforded community service at Centre Street, if they fail to do their service, they get much more lenient penalties than [Midtown] defendants.*

Responding to non-compliance By the end of the second year, attorneys working at both the Midtown and Downtown courts were convinced that the new Court responded more toughly than the Downtown court to non-compliance with alternative sanctions:

> *As others have indicated, they get more strict [at Midtown] in what you get [if] you fail your community service. Then you're going to jail ... whereas you might not Downtown.*

According to informed respondents, non-compliance with alternative sanctions did not *automatically* result in "secondary" jail. Judges and attorneys reported that defendants who failed to complete their initial sentence and returned to the Court on warrants were either given a second chance or offered increased days of alternative sanctions rather than jail time. For others, particularly those who failed the long-term treatment case management program, "secondary" jail sentences were consistently imposed. (The second stage of the research will include an analysis of the extent of secondary jail at the two courts.)

General Assessment of the Court's Effects on Case Outcomes

Overall, community members and criminal justice personnel acknowledged that planners' early vision of the role of alternative sanctions at the new Court had been realized. This success led some community members to recommend that a broader array of misdemeanor offenses—cases from other precincts, weekend cases, summary arrests still kept at the Downtown court—should be arraigned at Midtown. It also led to a continuing discussion about whether aspects of the Midtown model could be adapted to a centralized setting.

GROUP DIFFERENCES IN EXPECTATIONS AND ASSESSMENTS

The expectations for and assessments of case processing and court outcomes at the Midtown Community Court among criminal justice professionals, defendants and community members varied substantially by group. In discussing their general assessments of the project as a whole, most criminal justice professionals and defendants tended to focus primarily on courtroom issues, whereas community members and local police officers were more likely to focus on community impacts and on the overall role of the courthouse in the community.

Judges The small group of judges who worked at the Court reported that working in the courthouse substantially improved their ability to do their job. They pointed to several aspects of the Court that represented an expansion of resources—more information about defendants, more alternative sanction programs and a greater ability to monitor alternative sanction compliance. Judges referred to the "barrenness" of available sentencing alternatives at the Downtown court. As one judge put it, "Better things can happen here."

Accountability was seen as an important component. Midtown judges reported that judges Downtown were aware that the Court provided strict accountability for alternative sanction programs. They reported that failure to comply with a Midtown sentence "means more" to Downtown judges than failure to comply with a comparable sentence, imposed Downtown. They pointed out that comparable information about compliance at the Downtown court was hard to come by. Judges reported feeling more comfortable taking risks at the Court, because they were confident that they would receive accurate feedback about what happened.

Judges also reported that working in Midtown gave them a better sense of the community context of offenses—for example, whether an offense took place at a recognized community hot spot. They drew a clear distinction between having a broader understanding of the community context of an offense and community pressure to be "tougher." Midtown judges were committed to the principle of independent judicial decision-making. They reported that there was little community pressure for greater "toughness." According to Midtown judges, involved community members were generally aware of jail overcrowding and supported the Court's use of alternative sanctions.

Judges held mixed opinions about whether the Court required a particular type of judge. One judge suggested that the availability of resources at the Court helped promote a broader range of sentences, "independent of ideology." Conceding that some judges were "better at sentencing" than others, he suggested that many judges could work—and work well—at the Court, because the resources available would help promote consistent sentencing. Others pointed out that some Downtown judges would not be "comfortable" with the expanded judicial role required at the Court. According to one judge, many Downtown judges would resist the role of a Drug Court-style judge and prove unwilling to talk directly to defendants mandated to participate in long-term treatment. Claiming that judges must "want to" use the resources available in Midtown, she pointed out that Downtown judges were often leery of alternative sanction programs and characterized the Midtown approach as judicial "social work." This contrast between the

Midtown and Downtown judicial styles bespoke a clear recognition of an emerging cultural shift—a redefinition of judicial priorities and procedures.

Attorneys Officials from both the District Attorney's Office and the Legal Aid Society had initially taken a critical public stance toward the Midtown Community Court. In individual interviews and focus groups, attorneys were less likely than other groups to change their initial views, particularly about issues that they viewed as fundamental: equity for defendants across *all* arraignment parts and across neighborhoods.

Before the Court opened, ADAs and defense attorneys differed in their views about how the Court might affect their roles. Defense attorneys generally welcomed a changed role:

> *Now in criminal court you don't think in my job like a social worker.... This [court] will make us think more like that. You have to look beyond the complaint itself.*

> *The only reward a defense attorney gets is to win a case, but winning the case doesn't necessarily do the person good. Whereas with all the intervention, maybe they'll actually change their lives....*

ADAs were more resistant to a change in roles, stressing the need for continuity between practice Downtown and in Midtown:

> *I think it [the Court] might make everybody involved be more innovative, more willing to try something new. But the balancing concern for DAs will be a concern with fairness, with uniformity. Treating like crime alike. There are crimes on this list that are committed all over the city and geography alone is not enough of a distinction for us to agree to vast differences in treatment.*

After the first year, defense attorneys and prosecutors differed in the extent to which their personal views departed from the official positions of their respective offices. ADAs generally echoed the issues raised by their office—the fairness of handling Midtown misdemeanors differently, concerns about reductions in the frequency of jail sentences. Although ADAs recognized advantages in the facilities and services available at the Court (one spoke of "a certain degree of dignity"), these advantages were generally perceived as inequities: "People in the rest of the system are forced to suffer another type of justice."

Defense attorneys (a mix of Legal Aid attorneys and attorneys from New York City's panel of indigent defense attorneys) were more likely to distinguish their personal views from those initially expressed by Legal Aid. Some defense attorneys believed that improvements in holding cells, in the speed of disposition and in court facilities made the Court a better place for defendants. Defense attorneys also valued the expanded range of alternative sanctions at the Court.

As a group, attorneys remained acutely aware of the issues that surrounded the Court in the planning stages. To some, the Court represented a valuable experiment which might ultimately help improve the system as a whole. As one attorney put it:

> *I think it's helped because the debate is important. It is important for us not to accept the status quo. We are unhappy with the way things are and ... that we haven't played enough of a role. And we are, all of us, the experts in this area. But to the extent that people are engaged in a debate, I think that is extremely positive, and I think that from this we are going to learn things that we can give to the whole community.*

Other Courtroom Personnel Court staff were initially troubled by operational issues in the Court's early months, although they became increasingly satisfied with the Court as time went on. Some initial concerns (e.g., questions about the Court's ability to handle its caseload in a single shift; concerns about the ability to build connections between data systems; early worries about the confidentiality of assessment information) quickly proved not to be a problem. Other initial operational concerns related to the Court's information system (e.g., delays in receiving "rap" sheets) remained. Some court professionals also expressed an initial concern with the ability of intermediate sanction programs to provide sufficient services to defendants and sufficient feedback to the Court:

> *The hardest thing will be not so much for the Court, but for the programs. Can they deliver? They are making promises.... A person needs educational help. Will they be able to deliver?*

> *The programs will have to keep very accurate stats and providers have to be watched. To see exactly what they are doing—whom they are servicing, where those people are going.*

Over time, courtroom staff increasingly recognized the accomplishments of community service and social service programs based at the Court. By the end of the first year, courtroom staff were visibly pleased with the community service component at the Court and the positive effect of community service on the neighborhood:

> *I look at it from the point of view of the people that can be helped. And those are better helped in the Community Court than they would be Downtown. Because of the fact that the community service they have to do is right there; it's not put off a month, as it normally is. And, if a prostitute comes in and actually says to somebody 'I don't want him to bail me out'—we can help her.*

> *I work at night often, overtime, while defendants are doing their community service and I hear a lot of their comments and most of them like it very much. They compare it to Downtown and are very positive. A lot of them volunteer. They finish their sentence and they volunteer to come back.... I think a lot of them are looking for help and the resources are there for them.*

They were particularly satisfied with the immediacy of assignment and the ability to have higher-risk defendants work on-site, facilitating links to court-based services: "The fact that people start their community service the same day. That's a tremendous asset."

During the second round of focus groups, several respondents from criminal justice agencies working at the Court commented on the unique team atmosphere:

> *Being with something from the beginning.... It's unusual.... from having six cases a day to what we have today. And it is small. Everybody really helps each other. It's kind of intimate. Nice that way.*

> *They like working there. They like the environment. And we organize tours for others in our agency. They are impressed. They think that it is humane, as opposed to the big bureaucracy.*

Police Although police management and precinct commanders were strong supporters of the Court, local police officers were one of the most critical groups before the Court opened. The attitudes of local police changed dramatically once the Court began operating.

At first, local police officers voiced little support for the Court's philosophy and objected to its location, adjacent to one of their precinct houses. They were particularly concerned that their cars might be vandalized, that parking would be difficult to find and that the neighborhood would suffer from the large numbers of defendants who would be drawn to their area. There was considerable skepticism, rooted in experience, about whether the Court could have any impact on case outcomes or the behavior of the defendant population:

> *There is no trust among the average working police officer toward the whole building.... The services, the criminal justice part, the sentences.... Everyone is under the general idea that this whole thing is going to crash and burn.*

There was also skepticism about the possibility of line officers becoming engaged in any community-focused initiative that did not have strong support within the Department itself:

> *Success of this with the police will depend on where the idea was conceived. If it was conceived with input from the police in some form, they'll be more in favor of it. But if [it was] some goon from City Hall or some goon at the Community Board ..., it will be announced at the Precinct meeting, and the person in charge will leave the room and everyone will say, 'What a bunch of crap. More of the same old crap.'*

Such attitudes were not universal among local police officers. A few local police officers initially anticipated that the Court might improve the efficiency of community-based court processing, and create an incentive to treat quality-of-life offenses more seriously:

> *I think it's a good idea. Say you see a guy urinating. You know he has no ID, just wearing shorts, filthy, a bum. Normally, you might not want to get involved.... The desk officer is likely to say, 'I don't want you to put this guy into the system and make overtime. This is really a nonsense charge.' But, now this will be better. We won't have to go through the conversation in the car, 'Should we bring him in? Does it pay to get involved?'.... You'll be able to actually put handcuffs on the guy and stick him in front of somebody ... in two hours.*

By the second year, the extent of support for the Court among local police officers had increased substantially. Many local police officers attributed a marked reduction in prostitution to the Court and its effort to treat low-level offenses seriously.

> *Downtown prostitution is regarded as a very low-level thing. They don't realize the consequences of street prostitution. Up here, the judge is very harsh. Downtown the prostitutes get treated with kid gloves.*

Although police officers expressed concerns about "forum shopping" as a means of avoiding sentences at the Court and about perceived inconsistent policies about which misdemeanor cases (e.g., summary drug arrests) should be sent to Midtown, the Court was highly valued for its recognized ability to respond constructively to quality-of-life conditions.[7]

Defendants Individual interviews with defendants, arraigned at both the Midtown and Downtown courts, were designed to gather information about defendants' perceptions of the differences between the two courts. Defendants familiar with both courts generally reported that facilities were cleaner, cases moved faster and sentences were tougher. There was broad awareness that community service sentences were more common at Midtown than Downtown. There was also a recognition among Midtown defendants that "the people there care about you." A few defendants also mentioned differences in the level of available information and accountability at the two courts. As one defendant put it, at Midtown "they know everything about you."

Community leaders Many community leaders had been active partners in the development of the Court and were clearly committed to the project by the time interviewing began. Although they were excited by the prospect of changing "business as usual," they were restrained in their expectations about case outcomes, compliance with intermediate sanctions and recidivism. There was a general recognition that there was little to lose by attempting to change the status quo. As one community leader put it, "We felt we had to do something, because clearly what was happening wasn't working."

These restrained expectations were largely satisfied by the mere fact that the Court had been created. One respondent noted that, given the political and logistical problems faced during the Court's planning process, it was a substantial achievement that "this court didn't fall flat on its face."

Once the Court began operating, community leaders' expectations about what the Court might achieve expanded considerably:

> *I can say that I was really ambivalent when it started, feeling kind of iffy about its prognosis. Sitting here now, I feel much better informed and I think it is doing a good job. And, because I was so iffy, it has exceeded my expectations.... That's based on seeing the Court work and hearing the stories about people's lives turned around....*

> *I spoke to Judge X and he said that, other than the DA's office, everybody who's come into that Court and spent time looking at it—no matter how severely critical they were before they walked in—has gone away really impressed with the operation and feeling supportive of it. And I believe him.*

After the first six months, community leaders began citing individual success stories as evidence of the Court's efficacy:

> *In one instance, a person who lived in the Times Square Hotel was arrested and taken to Community Court and they contacted the hotel and the hotel staff worked with the resident to help him.... It was an example of the Court doing what it said it would do....*

By the end of the first year, several community leaders demonstrated a keen awareness of some unique features of the Court. A neighborhood leader, active in monitoring quality-of-life conditions, pointed to the importance of rapid scheduling of alternative sanctions and immediate access to court-based services. This respondent suggested that the immediacy of alternative sanctions might reduce the chance that defendants would be back on the streets committing offenses the same day.[8]

Community members were also aware that court-based service programs aimed to reach defendants at "a teachable moment," shortly after arrest. Within a year, expectations about the number of defendants whose lives might be "turned around" through Court-based service had grown.

Community Residents Community residents who had no institutional affiliation with the Court tended to know less about it than other groups both before and after the Court opened. In early focus groups, community residents, selected from a list of those who had ever attended key community meetings, had generally heard about the Court and remembered that it would be community-based ("like a satellite station"); would deal with low-level crime; would promote efficiency; and would use community service as "payback" to the community. Community residents were particularly supportive of the concept of community restitution, although they were concerned about the potential difficulties of supervision.

There was little apparent change in the expressed attitudes of community residents between the first and second focus groups. In follow-up focus groups, community residents continued to express support for community restitution projects—the feature of the Court that they knew most about:

> *I found out about it just a few days ago, reading the 48th Street Block Association Newsletter.... There was a notice with a number saying if you have a problem with graffiti to call them and they'll send someone to paint it over, which I think is wonderful.*
>
> *One of the things they have that's helping us is the mailing services. We've just given them a mailing to do....*

Overall, both criminal justice and community observers presented sophisticated analyses of how and why the two courts differed. They cited several distinguishing features of the Midtown Community Court—court-based services, pre-arraignment assessment interviews for defendants, the role of the resource coordinator and strict accountability for intermediate sanctions—that contributed to differences in sentencing. Respondents also reported a variety of differences in court procedures at the two courts—escorts to the intermediate sanction scheduling office, immediate assignment to community service—that helped promote a broader use of intermediate sanctions.

At the time of the Court's opening, a number of criminal justice system officials expressed a belief that there would be substantial differences between the new Court and the Downtown court. They anticipated that individual components of the Court would prove successful, including health services in the court building, the immediacy of intermediate sanctions, closer monitoring of community service sentence compliance and court-based substance abuse treatment services. Some argued that these components might work just as well in a centralized setting. Questions about which components of the project might work best locally and which might be successfully adapted to high-volume centralized courts were raised early and often in the ongoing debate about the Court.

Community members tended to voice different concerns than criminal justice professionals. Questions about the value of decentralization, equity and cost-effectiveness were of less concern to community leaders and residents who tended to view the Court as "something good for the neighborhood." They were particularly interested in the visibility of community service projects, the role of the Community Advisory Board and the amount of community feedback provided by the Court.

Notes

1. Issues related to case processing and case outcomes were particularly salient to senior criminal justice officials. All of the criminal justice officials interviewed knew one another and exchanged views and information regarding the Court's progress. Many criminal justice respondents saw themselves as stakeholders in the Court either because they were directly involved in the project or because their agencies had stationed staff at the Court. Criminal justice officials tended to focus on standard quantitative measures of arraignment outcomes—caseload volume, the failure-to-appear rate for DATs and adjournment rates for particular offenses—reviewed in previous chapters.
2. Several criminal justice professionals indicated that their primary focus was necessarily on the overall Manhattan caseload, including felonies, handled at the centralized court Downtown rather than what happened in Midtown. As one put it, "What happens at the Community Court doesn't keep me awake at three o'clock in the morning." Given the need of criminal justice agencies to focus on serious felonies, they noted that the Court had received an extraordinary level of support, even from agencies and groups that were critical of its establishment: "Everyone wants the Court to succeed. Everyone is working toward the same goal."
3. This section draws extensively upon the two reports prepared by the focus group facilitator (Eckstein, 1993 and Eckstein, 1995).
4. Senior criminal justice officials pointed out that misdemeanor sentencing afforded more flexibility than felony sentencing. For many serious felony cases, they reported, sentencing decisions were constrained by state sentencing laws, mandating prison terms under specific conditions. In contrast, sentencing recidivist prostitutes or addicted shoplifters permitted a more creative, holistic response.
5. It should be noted that there was no information available during the research period about the new Court's impact on recidivism rates, compared to the Downtown court. This analysis will be conducted in the second stage of the research. As discussed in Chapter 4, the vast majority of defendants (88%) appeared at the Court only once. Yet Court staff quickly became familiar with individual repeat offenders, particularly those charged with prostitution, who returned to the Court on new charges, to complete community service and to participate in court-based services. The familiarity with individual repeat offenders contributed to a growing cautiousness about the Court's ability to affect aggregate recidivism rates.

6. In New York City, jail inmates are credited with one day of "good time" for every two days served. This effectively reduces all jail sentences by a third.
7. The focus group facilitator commented on this change in attitude. One police officer who participated in both baseline and follow-up focus groups refused to believe that he and his colleagues had been so negative one year before.
8. This addresses a major frustration with the courts felt by those active in seeking to improve quality-of-life conditions. One respondent reported that before the Court opened, local residents traveled in chartered buses to 100 Centre Street in order to observe arraignments of those arrested in a police sweep of street prostitution. The prostitutes, it is claimed, arrived back in Clinton before the court observers.

CHAPTER NINE

COMMUNITY AWARENESS, INVOLVEMENT AND ASSESSMENTS

The key initial audience for the new Court included members of a network of public and private neighborhood improvement organizations active in Clinton, Chelsea and Times Square. One community leader in Midtown portrayed the Midtown Community Court as being oriented to "concentric circles of attentive publics." Community leaders formed the innermost circle, the primary target for involvement. Concerned residents and merchants, affected by quality-of-life crime, formed the next ring. The extensive publicity that the Court generated in both citywide and local news media provided an avenue for reaching the outer rings of the "attentive publics."

COMMUNITY AWARENESS

Although the Midtown Community Court was designed to break new ground in promoting improved court-community relations, experienced observers of New York City criminal justice programs were cautious in assessing the potential level of community awareness. Many respondents predicted that awareness of the Court would be slight among the general public, while community leaders would be very aware. Based on research on community policing in New York City, one criminal justice professional estimated that no more than a quarter of the community would be aware of the existence of the Court or of any community-focused, criminal-justice initiative.

Midtown Manhattan may be a particularly challenging location in which to promote broad awareness of the Court, given the high-density mix of residential, retail and institutional land use, and the large population (over 100,000) living in Midtown neighborhoods. Informal communication networks do not thrive in such an environment. Some felt that the various other efforts underway to improve conditions in the Times Square Area might affect community awareness of the Court. For example, the local Business Improvement District fielded highly visible sanitation and security crews in the area near the Court. Only a sophisticated local observer was likely to distinguish such efforts from those of the new Court.

Focus group sessions held weeks before the Court opened found a relatively high level of awareness among those community members who had ever participated in an organized community activity (e.g., a precinct-community council meeting or block watch group). The focus group facilitator reported that in the initial round of focus groups:

> *... awareness of the Court is quite high among the residents. All but one or two had heard something about a new court due to open in the area. Awareness may not be this high in the general community because the group members have attended at least one community board meeting and a few are active in neighborhood organizations and so may be more alert to community matters then other residents .... (Eckstein, 1993).*

Most residents were aware that the new Court would deal with "low-level" crime, and employ "community service" sentences as payback for offenses. Only a few residents, however, recalled hearing anything about court-based social services for offenders.

The level of awareness among community residents ranged from rumor to detailed knowledge about the proposed use of community service sentences:

> *There's going to be a brand new level of court in the 50s, in one of the schools I believe ... for crimes like lower drugs. Some prostitutes, some misdemeanors.... In order to expedite dealing with them, they will bring them into this courthouse and then send them back into the community... to wash windows, do things. They give buildings and community groups chances to recommend projects to be done.*
>
> *Adjacent to the Police Precinct, right? Instead of running them Downtown, they are going to bring them to this court. To have them do things, rather than lock them up.*
>
> *It's like a satellite station, a satellite police station ... Midtown Community Court they call it.*
>
> *I heard that these people will be available to do community service and mass mailings. You can bring it to their site, and they'll have these people stuff the envelopes.*
>
> *They are supposed to sweep the streets and clean graffiti under the supervision of the Times Square BID. This is for minor offenders—whom I'm sure they know where to track down. For misdemeanors and minor violations.*

Respondents in individual interviews believed that awareness of the Court was initially quite low among merchants. Three months after the Court opened, one community leader estimated that roughly 2 percent of local merchants were aware of the Court. Subsequent estimates suggested that outreach efforts and the visibility of community service work crews had significantly increased awareness on the part of local merchants.

Individual interviews held around the time the Court opened also suggested that awareness of the new Court among the broad residential community might be limited. For example, a local activist predicted that involved community members (e.g., those who attended police-community council meetings) would know about the Court, but that "ordinary" residents would not.

Over time, respondents continued to believe that awareness of the Court remained highest among residents who were active in community organizations and concerned about community issues. One community leader, who lived within a few blocks of the Court, said that she "would be surprised if people on her block [knew] about the Court."[1]

Community service work crews appear to have been the most effective vehicle for building awareness of the Court among residents. In the second round of focus groups, several community members reported having observed work crews in action. Indeed, several residents learned about the Court from such sightings; other residents saw workers in action, but were unaware of the source:

> *Yes, I see the same lot and I've seen these guys with the vests cleaning it out—but I had no idea who they were, that they have anything to do with any court. I've never heard of this court.*
>
> *I saw them painting over the graffiti sprayed on the store window gates, the shutters. Painting them silver again. And I asked who they were.*
>
> *I've heard other people comment there is less graffiti, and someone said that throughout the neighborhood the graffiti was being painted over more regularly.*
>
> *I knew nothing about it, except that the Court was there.*

COMMUNITY INVOLVEMENT

Community involvement with the Court generally was highest among individuals involved with Community Boards, neighborhood watch organizations and Precinct Advisory Committees. Members of such organizations were aware of the Court and discussed and monitored its progress. As one respondent put it in the second focus group:

> *As much as there is an organized community in Clinton, the Court has got to it. They did a wonderful job of getting back to them before [the Court opened]. They haven't been as good at getting back to people [since opening]. But, ... with the block associations, those people know that the Court is there. They're starting to feel a sense of ownership.*

Some community leaders expected that the Court would encourage frequent public observation of court sessions. Although that expectation was partly shared by Court planners, it was not central to their vision of the Court. There was a general awareness that the hours of Court operations (nine to five on weekdays) and the nature of misdemeanor arraignment proceedings (high volume cases lasting a few minutes) would not draw a broad community audience. Although project coordinators frequently hosted group tours of the Court, judges at the Court reported that few unescorted community observers visited the courtroom, other than an occasional community activist interested in a specific type of offense.

Community Advisory Board The main vehicle for structuring community involvement and assisting in the development of community service projects was the Court's Community Advisory Board (CAB), a central component of the project. The Board was structured to provide a formal connection between the Court and community leaders and, through them, to the organizations that they represent. During panel interviews, members defined two broad roles for the Board: to provide information about the Court to the community and to advise the Court's planners and managers about community concerns.

Members generally found the Board "extremely useful." Board members reported particular satisfaction with the commitment to dialogue shown by the Administrative Judge for the New York City Criminal Court and the judge assigned to the Court. Both judges attended all of the Advisory Board meetings, which "stunned" (according to one member) and greatly pleased the Board. This arrangement facilitated a broad-based dialogue about the Court's operations among community residents, business people, the Court's coordinators and judges. Board meetings precluded discussion of specific sentencing decisions with judges assigned to the Court.[2]

Some board members expressed concerns about the structure and content of CAB meetings. Several initially complained about irregular and "haphazard" scheduling. They also expressed concern about the adequacy of a ten-person Board to express community concerns (some felt that the Board should have doubled or tripled in size). There was also some concern about the balance between what one respondent saw as "a sales pitch" and substantive discussions about important emerging issues.

Concerns about the frequency and content of CAB meetings did not last very long. By the end of 1994, the Board's meeting schedule had been fine-tuned. Members expressed satisfaction that there was adequate follow-through on ideas and suggestions arising from meetings. Some members continued to feel that some topics—for example, the mechanics of scheduling community service and the sheer number of outdoor work crews—required more attention in board meetings. However, serving on the CAB was acknowledged to be educational for both the members and for the broader community reached through the member's extensive networks of local contacts.

Several members cited the same issue—the high adjournment rates for vendors at the Court—as an example of the Board's educational role. Vending cases were of prime concern to members of the CAB who represented the local business community. The session served to educate community leaders about the legal constraints in vending cases. CAB members learned that no "rap sheet" information is available for vendors charged with administrative code violations, which do not require fingerprints or photographs. This made it impossible for the Court to distinguish between first-time and repeat offenders in vending cases. Some Board members suggested that such knowledge could lead to advocacy by local organizations, to work toward change in law and practice.

Much discussion at CAB meetings centered on the Court's efforts to link repeat offenders to needed services. At an early meeting, a defendant who had been sentenced to drug treatment at the Court made a presentation. The success of that presentation, characterized as "educational," led members to request that a defendant speak at each subsequent meeting. Over time, however, some members sensed that the meetings were becoming "too much of a love-fest," as one expressed it. They believed that the presence of a defendant from the Midtown Community Court would be more appropriate as an occasional feature of the meetings.

Other Forms of Community Interaction The Court provided a number of other forms of community interaction. As discussed in Chapter 4, community members drew upon the Court as participants in mediation sessions and as recipients of community service. The second round of focus groups and panel interviews showed that these aspects of the Court were highly valued by the community.

> *The Court also has a mediation program which tries to settle disputes between residents and businesses and between businesses. They stepped in between that [porno] place they were going to open and the community groups....*
>
> *At the Community Board, we've taken advantage of that service a lot. In our role trying to mediate between various interests in the community, we've used the mediation service of the Court regularly. And they've been very responsive.*

As discussed in Chapter 4, some community members also took advantage of court-based services, including GED classes or weekly AA meetings. The Court's community liaison actively recruited business owners, interested in graffiti removal and other clean-up projects, and conducted outreach campaigns to expand the audience for the Court's newsletter.

COMMUNITY REACTIONS

The overall assessments of the Midtown Community Court made by community leaders were highly positive and became increasingly favorable over time. Eighteen months after it opened, the head of one community organization gave the Court "unbelievably high marks."

Reactions to Community Service

To community members, community restitution was the most important function of the Court. It was seen as a constructive form of punishment, in contrast to sentencing at the Downtown court, which was viewed as providing little punishment other than "time served."

> *I think it's the Court that has had this [positive] effect. Cops are doing a better job. On urination, on a lot of stuff. All these small quality- of-life offenses should be enforced by the cops and taken to the Community Court and the offenders put back in the area to clean up the streets—clean, paint—instead of being taken Downtown where they get nothing.*

According to a police officer with extensive community contacts, many residents who were quick to complain about local conditions had noticed that things were getting better. The officer associated this change with the graffiti removal and other visible community service work done by defendants from the Court.

Although there was general satisfaction with the new Court's use of community service sentencing, community members raised several concerns about community service. To the community, it was important that community service be visible, that the Court monitor compliance closely to ensure that it was sufficiently "punitive" and that participants be adequately supervised.

Visibility Community service sentencing was the single component of the Midtown Community Court that residents knew the most about. They valued aspects of the Court that served the community directly. Visible signs of "payback"—defendants at work painting over graffiti or maintaining street tree beds—were a primary source of community satisfaction with the Court.

> *I would put a banner in every tree pit that is cleaned up—with the name of the Community Court on it.*

Visibility was a central issue to the community. Leaders in the community and local criminal justice officials realized that much community service work took place inside the court building. They wanted more outdoor community service. From their perspective, visible payback to the community by defendants was an impact in itself, a sign that something was happening.

There was considerable discussion about "sightings" of crews in action. Some respondents had never seen or heard of the work crews. Other respondents had either noticed crews in action or noticed the effect of their work:

> *Don't worry. You'll soon be seeing them—shoveling snow, chopping out the ice, sweeping the streets.*

> *I was sitting in a merchant's office and a group of these people passed, wearing the vests. And he interrupted. 'Wait a minute. I want those people.' He wanted them to fix the graffiti.*

> *There is definitely less graffiti. And that's a result of the painting by the defendants from the Community Court, as part of their community service.*

> *One of the things they have that's helping us is the mailing service. We've just given them a mailing to do. We'll see how fast they do it....*

Concerns about punishment and compliance Before the Court opened, community members and criminal justice professionals were skeptical about the likelihood that defendants would actually perform community service:

> *All I've seen for the past twelve, fourteen years is a revolving door, particularly where it comes to community service. A lot of warrants, a lot of community service being imposed, but not getting done.... Not 100 percent of the people are going to get there, but ... if you can get a small amount now ... it may become a good thing. Do something that they are not doing Downtown.*

> *In all my years in the system, all I've seen is people coming back like a revolving door. How many people actually do their community service? I don't think it's a big number.*

> *You have to remember that the people committing these misdemeanors are the least able to be supervised.... You can round them up, if you can find them....*

Community members also wanted to be sure that community service was exacting sufficient punishment:

> *What do they have in place that really both serves the community and serves the purpose of making people be responsible for their actions?*

In the second round of focus groups, representatives of local agencies that supervised community service crews expressed satisfaction with the "toughness" of community service sentences, compliance rates and mechanisms for ensuring accountability:

> *We've had folks up to three times and each time their sentence is longer. They must show up and we have a very good rate of completion. In cases of problems, the Court has been very good about telling us, 'This guy is not coming back to you, don't worry.'*

> *The last we heard, they have a very good rate of completion of community service sentences.... I think an 80 percent completion rate.*

Yet community leaders wanted even more information about specific work projects, the types of defendants assigned to each, the structure of the work and the customers served.

Concerns about supervision Some community members, particularly local police, were concerned about the quality of community service supervision. Although generally pleased with the positive effect that community service work crews had on the appearance of the neighborhood, some respondents believed that work crews were unsupervised and lackadaisical in their approach to work. Although these beliefs were based on scattered observations, a few respondents were adamant about their accuracy:

> *No, there were no supervisors. Not when I've seen them. Have you seen them or are you just taking somebody's word for that?*
>
> *I wonder if the Community Court people are being really supervised, or if it's just a matter of putting in a day.... It is hard to tell who's in charge and how accountable they are. They just seem to be shuffling their feet and going through the motions....*

The perceived value of community service to supervising agencies Community leaders regarded community service provision as a cooperative venture between the Court and community organizations. Some local organizations that provided community service supervision for the Court initially regarded their participation as an exercise of community responsibility, rather than as a source of cheap labor. Some agency representatives reported that the costs of scheduling and supervising defendants at least equaled the value of what they contributed to clean-up efforts. Over time, however, cutbacks in city services challenged that assessment. As city sanitation services were reduced, the efforts by not-for-profit organizations to promote quality-of-life conditions became more important. Although work performed through community service sentences helped, paid employees of local Business Improvement Districts were the mainstay of community-based sanitation efforts. Yet community service work was increasingly recognized as contributing to ongoing efforts to improve the quality-of-life in Midtown Manhattan.

Reactions to Court-Based Services

Community residents were less aware of Midtown's social service capacity than they were of other components of the Court. In both rounds of focus group interviews, community members needed prompting before discussing court-based social services.

In general, community members who knew about the services available at the Court responded favorably. They spoke approvingly of English as a Second Language (ESL) classes, former defendants serving voluntarily as interns in the Court's mailroom, referrals to treatment programs and other court-based services. In the second round of focus groups, supportive comments were often balanced with expressions of concern about the intractability of the underlying social problems being addressed:

> *There are some questions about the effectiveness [of social services].... It's trying to go to the base of the problem. Drug treatment, education—things of this sort might help. The things they should have gotten from home or school.*

> *Most useful, keeping a certain kind of defendant in mind, is that they will be given a chance to help themselves early on in the process. If you can solve a few people's problems early on, the community will benefit in the long run.*

In assessing the Court, community leaders stressed the importance of the "atmosphere," particularly on the Sixth Floor, in making the Court an effective place for delivery of treatment, educational and health services: "Such a welcoming place to come for services and support," where "defendants are treated like human beings and with feeling for their individuality." One provider of community service supervision described the Court as having "a milieu that is conducive to compliance."

Some community members suggested that the Court's effort to provide "help" conflicted with the punitive nature of the Court. They feared that a "settlement house" atmosphere might limit the Court's ability to promote general deterrence or support punitive objectives. For example, one respondent questioned whether holding ESL classes was appropriate for a criminal court. This respondent suggested that the non-threatening atmosphere necessary to promote voluntary engagement in services might be "too soft" to promote deterrence.

Community Hunger for Information

By the end of the first year, community leaders expressed a desire for more information and feedback about the Court.

> *The Community Court has a responsibility to make itself known and to the extent that it speaks to being a* community *court, its responsibility is to define who that community is and how to reach them. And in my mind they haven't done that as well as they might.*

Over the next few months, coordinating staff substantially increased the extent of community outreach: a first-year progress report was widely distributed; Board meetings were held more frequently; quarterly newsletters were disseminated; and a community newspaper began to run a monthly column about the Court. In addition, the Court began to attract a substantial amount of local, national and international media attention. Although these initiatives increased the amount of information available, community members remained hungry for even broader community feedback.

CONCLUSIONS

Focus group and panel interviews covered central issues of concern to community leaders and residents: the certainty and consistency of punishment, intervention through social services, "payback" to the community by defendants and changes in community conditions. By the end of the second year, there was considerable consistency in the community's perceptions of these issues and assessments of the Court's performance. Community reactions differed considerably from the reactions of criminal justice professionals, reviewed in the previous chapter. The reactions of both groups are summarized below:

Punishment For the most part, respondents who were familiar with the Court believed it provided a proportional, escalated response to low-level offenses. Most reported that sentencing was generally tougher than the Downtown court, driving an increase in adjournment rates for prostitution and unlicensed vending offenses at the Court. There was general agreement among informed community members and criminal justice personnel that the Court had produced more constructive sentence outcomes than the Downtown court.

Social Services The role of the Court as a gateway to services found strong support in every group. Most viewed the stationing of social services in the court building as an opportunity to help a small number of people. Although the number of dramatic successes might be small, many people seem to know at least one story. The defendants whose stories were known tended to have lengthy histories of convictions and an array of personal and health problems. Each success was, therefore, seen as fostering a potentially significant reduction in quality-of-life crime and community public health problems, such as the spread of sexually transmitted diseases through prostitution and IV drug use. Community members raised questions about the potential conflict between punishment and help. Assistant DAs argued that the full potential of court-based social services would be unrealized until services were located at the centralized court as well.

Community Service Although there was initial skepticism about whether defendants would actually complete community service sentences, there was some recognition that compliance rates at the Court were better than anticipated and a recognition that immediate scheduling made a difference. Primary concerns were that community service work be more visible and supervision be sufficiently stringent. By the end of the second year, the community wanted to see more work crews, closely supervised and working harder.

Community Conditions There was consensus that community conditions had improved since the Midtown Community Court opened. The change was noted by residents, community leaders and police. Dramatic decreases in the levels of graffiti, prostitution and unlicensed vending were noted. Observers acknowledged that various parallel efforts to improve community conditions were underway. The very visible efforts made by the BIDs were frequently cited, as were changes in policing. The Midtown Community Court was generally regarded as something positive being done for the community, part of a general commitment to improve conditions in and around Times Square.

Although direct involvement with the Court remained largely confined to the inner circles in Chelsea and Clinton, there was broad-based sentiment that local conditions were improving. Community members were aware that work crews associated with the courts or city agencies were making a tangible contribution by removing graffiti, maintaining tree pits and removing rubbish, although they were hungry for more information and feedback about the Court.

Dialogue with the community was a central factor in the evolution of the Midtown Community Court from an idea to a realized model of community justice. In both its planning and its implementation phase, the Court benefited greatly from a sophisticated and critical audience, located in the criminal justice system and in community-based groups and organizations. Individuals interviewed for this research took a broad view of the Court's effects on the total justice system and on community conditions, rather than emphasizing their own interests and concerns. The effort to promote a deep and resonant dialogue with community leaders and community organizations is a basic, defining element of a community court.

Notes

1. Few residents of her block, which is relatively "upscale," are closely linked to community organizations. She estimated that only two or three households in her 40-unit building would be informed about the Court.
2. As noted in Chapter 8, there is consensus among all Midtown judges that they should not be responsive to local community pressure when imposing sentences. Midtown judges acknowledged that detailed knowledge of the community can provide a context for sentencing—as when the judge notes that an offense occurred on a residential block or near a school. Instead of focusing on the community, judges defined the key differences between the Midtown and Downtown courts as the availability of more sentencing options, expanded information about defendants that judges need to select a sentence, the ability to monitor compliance and the availability of social services.

CHAPTER TEN

CONCLUSION

For an initiative with as many components and agendas as the Midtown Community Court, there is no single answer to the question: Did it work? There are clear answers to some specific questions about measurable project impacts: Did it reduce arrest-to-arraignment time? Did it increase the Court's use of intermediate sanctions or improve compliance rates? There are more complicated, detailed answers to other central research questions: What effect did the Court have on quality-of-life conditions in Midtown? How did community attitudes toward the Court change over the first eighteen months?

Overall, the Midtown Community Court represents a marked departure from "business as usual" in New York City criminal court arraignment parts. Many of the constituent components of the Court transform traditional practice: expanded information about defendants; customized technology; a resource coordinator, linking the courtroom to alternative sanctions programs; the emphasis on immediacy and accountability; on-site services; community service as "pay back" to the neighborhood where crimes took place; community involvement and community feedback; bridges to local police; and a coordinating team to monitor and develop innovation. These elements are key components of the Court's effort to develop a community-focused problem-solving agenda.

SUMMARY OF FINDINGS

The Midtown Community Court represents the nation's most comprehensive model to date of what a community-focused court might be. Designed as a pioneering effort, it has sparked a wide-ranging conversation about community courts and what they can contribute to the neighborhoods they serve. Even in the early stages of project planning, that conversation was heated and lively. Court planners articulated a vision of a community-based misdemeanor court that would expand the use of intermediate sanctions, "pay back" the neighborhoods where crimes took place and provide court-based services to help solve the underlying problems of defendants. As reviewed in Chapter 1, planners anticipated that the Court would produce multiple impacts, including:

- an increased use of intermediate sanctions as an alternative to "walks" and short-term jail sentences;
- improved community service compliance rates;
- improved community conditions; and
- improved community attitudes toward the Court.

During the planning period, there was substantial debate about the proposed Court, which both challenged and enriched project design. Critics of the Court were pessimistic about the expected caseload, depicting the pool of eligible cases as either too small or too large. Some predicted substantial procedural difficulties in routing cases to the new Court and argued that there would be too few cases to justify its existence. Others contended that the flow of information into the Court would be too erratic for the Court to handle its caseload in a single shift. Others questioned whether the project would have any effect at all on "business as usual." Criminal justice professionals contended that large numbers of defendants would adjourn their cases to the Downtown court to avoid sentences to community services and social service. They predicted that widespread "forum shopping" would increase system costs and make it difficult to change "going rates" for low-level offenses. Critical observers predicted low community service compliance rates, little effect on local quality-of-life conditions and little influence on community attitudes toward the courts.

Overall, the debate helped define central issues to be addressed by the research on the implementation and effects of the Court. The project benefited considerably from the active role of community leadership in the planning process and the sophisticated challenges posed by critics of the Court. The following sections summarize the findings of that research.

Process Analysis

Process analysis revealed relatively few barriers to the implementation of the Court. Although procedural problems delayed the transfer of some summary arrests arising in Midtown to the Court, by the end of the research period the daily caseload had not only reached the project's target of 60 arraignments per day, but expanded to include additional matters not generally heard in arraignment parts (updates about treatment participation, violations of conditional discharge, voluntary and involuntary returns on warrants). Other start-up issues concerned inefficiencies related to the Court's developing technology, the confidentiality of assessment information about defendants and the perceived influence of the resource coordinator on judicial decision making.

By the end of the first eighteen months, there was clear evidence that the project had achieved its five operational goals, as described below:

1. As anticipated by planners, "justice was swifter" at the Court. Arrest-to-arraignment time averaged eighteen hours in Midtown, substantially faster than at the Downtown court. This was accomplished in a single shift per day, in contrast to the two-to-three shift arraignment schedule Downtown. In addition, coordinating staff encouraged a "same-day" or "next-day" start for many offenders sentenced to alternative sanctions (40%). Procedures at the Court made it difficult for sentenced offenders to walk out without scheduling community service, a relatively common occurrence Downtown. In some instances, defendants were arraigned, sentenced and done with community service sentences, all on the same day.
2. There were substantial efforts to make "justice more visible to the community." The Court established and convened a Community Advisory Board; assigned community service clean-up crews to problem spots, identified by community members; conducted extensive outreach with community groups; hosted tours; held community meetings at the courthouse; and garnered local, national and international media coverage. Although community leaders recognized the value of these efforts, they pushed for even greater visibility for community service projects and more frequent feedback about Court accomplishments.
3. Project planners also anticipated that the Court would "encourage the enforcement of low-level offenses" by demonstrating a commitment to take quality-of-life crimes seriously. As part of this agenda, coordinating staff met regularly with precinct commanders, made presentations at precinct "roll calls" and provided

feedback about case outcomes to commanders and line officers who generally don't find out what happens to low-level cases. Precinct commanders, community affairs officers and community police staff were particularly receptive to the Court's approach to low-level crime.

Over time, new relationships developed between the Court and local police officers. Word of mouth about the Court's effect on prostitution spread. Local police began to enforce bench warrants on low-level cases, generally accorded low priority, for repeat quality-of-life offenders. They began recommending community service projects and drawing upon court-based social service staff to help solve local problems. These first steps ultimately led to plans for a street outreach service, pairing local police with court-based social service staff, to link community members with serious problems (homelessness, addiction) to needed services.

During the first year, the effort to "encourage enforcement of low-level offenses" was strongly complemented by a citywide focus on quality-of-life offenses. A new mayor and a new police commissioner placed a strong emphasis on quality-of-life enforcement leading to a sharp increase in misdemeanor arrests throughout Manhattan. The increase in arrest volume, however, was most notable in non-Midtown precincts largely because of the substantial reduction in prostitution and unlicensed vending in the Midtown area. As documented by ethnographic observations and interviews with local police, community members and street offenders, the combined influence of police and Court efforts in Midtown reduced the frequency of street-level offending, leading to a reduction in overall arrest volume for some Midtown offenses.

4. The Court was also expected to "marshal the energy of local residents and businesses." Even before opening, the Court demonstrated an unprecedented commitment to building bridges between courts and communities. Court staff worked closely with community groups to identify local quality-of-life problems and develop ways to address these problems through community restitution. Project staff assembled a wide array of community-based partners both to provide a broad range of services

at the courthouse itself and to supervise neighborhood-based community service projects. In addition, the project reached out to community members as central advisors during the planning process; as members of a Community Advisory Board, designed to provide feedback and help guide developing operations; and, more broadly, through a community newsletter, designed to keep the neighborhood abreast of Court activities. In addition, court-based mediation focused on conflicts between community groups that might never come to the attention of a court.

5. The Court's final objective was to promote a recognition that communities are victimized by low-level crime. Community service projects at the Court embody this recognition; projects are explicitly designed as community "restitution," to "pay back" the neighborhoods where crimes took place. In addition, Court staff experimented with new methods of broadening understanding of the effect of low-level crime on the community, including:

    - community impact panels, that bring community residents face-to-face with low-level offenders for facilitated discussions. Modeled after victim-offender reconciliation panels, these discussions are designed to help offenders understand the effect of their actions on the community and to help community members envision more constructive responses to crime; and
    - geo-mapping of offenses, designed to show judges and community members how concentrations of low-level offenses change over time and to help judges review a history of arrest locations for individual offenders.

Conclusions Process analysis provided clear evidence of the project's ability to achieve its operational objectives during the first eighteen months. It also pointed to several key features of the Court that depart markedly from "business as usual" and support the Court's problem-solving agenda. These include:

- customized technology to support judicial decision-making and promote accountability for alternative sanction programs;

- court-based services, to promote immediacy and to establish the courthouse as a gateway to treatment and related services;
- non-traditional funding streams and public-private partnerships to support court innovations; and
- a coordinating team to monitor overall performance; identify and analyze problems; and develop and assess solutions.

The major barriers to project implementation were overcome during the Court's planning period. Before opening, project planners confronted difficulties in gaining approval for the initial site for the Court; the lack of prosecutorial support; and the effort to raise sufficient funds to sustain an ambitious demonstration project. Once these hurdles were overcome, the project had relatively little difficulty in putting the central components of the Court into place.

Impact Analysis

Project planners anticipated that the Court would have impacts in four specific areas: case outcomes, rates of compliance with intermediate sanctions, community conditions and community attitudes. The analysis of preliminary impacts shows that, in its early months, the Court had substantial effects in all four areas, reviewed below.

Case outcomes A central objective of the Court was to move sentencing for low-level offenses into the middle ranges, between "walks" (e.g., sentences of "time served" and conditional discharge, with no condition imposed) and jail. Sentencing at the Court produced significantly more intermediate sanctions than the Downtown court (more than double the frequency of community service and social service sentences for all charges), after controlling for differences in criminal history, arrest type (DAT or summary) and defendant characteristics. This was accomplished by (1) dramatically reducing the frequency of "walks" for all charges and (2) significantly reducing the frequency of jail sentences for petit larceny, prostitution and turnstile jumping. Although the Court handed out fewer jail sentences than the Downtown court, Midtown jail sentences were typically longer than those Downtown, particularly for petit larceny and prostitution cases. This difference in jail sentence length appears to spring from the use of intermediate sanctions as an alternative to *short-term* jail.

"Forum shopping" The research also examined the hypothesis that extensive "forum shopping" would substantially increase the frequency of adjournments at arraignment, thereby escalating system costs. Research shows that there was no significant difference in the frequency of adjournments at the Midtown and Downtown courts, after controlling for differences in charge type, arrest type and precinct of arrest. Although for some charges (unlicensed vending and prostitution), there were significantly more adjournments at the Midtown Community Court than the Downtown court, for other charges (petit larceny, drugs) adjournment rates were lower at Midtown. There was no evidence that the Court encouraged widespread "forum shopping."

Desk Appearance Tickets Research also looked at differences in appearance rates for Desk Appearance Tickets at the two courts. Although aggregate appearance rates (i.e., no warrant ordered) are lower at Midtown, analysis showed that these aggregate differences in appearance rates reflect long-standing differences in charge and the location of arrest.[1] After controlling for these factors, DAT appearance rates at the two courts did not differ significantly, except for one charge: DAT appearance rates for unlicensed vending were significantly *higher* at Midtown than Downtown. Research also found that efforts to improve appearance rates by reducing the time between arrest and scheduled arraignments at the Midtown Community Court had no effect.

Overall, the research on case outcomes demonstrated that the Midtown Community Court achieved its objective of promoting an increased use of community service and social service sentences for low-level offenses, without increasing either adjournment rates or failure-to-appear at arraignment. At the Court, the process of arrest and arraignment for low-level offenses is clearly *not* the punishment.

Intermediate sanction compliance rates Planners anticipated that the Court would produce higher compliance rates for community service sentences than the Downtown court by promoting both immediacy and accountability. In 1993, roughly 20 percent of defendants sentenced to short-term community service Downtown left court without reporting to the scheduling office. At the Midtown Community Court, court officers escort defendants to the scheduling floor, to facilitate the scheduling process. The majority of defendants are scheduled to begin community service within a week of sentencing—substantially faster than at the Downtown court. The Court's technology helps promote strict accountability by helping Court staff maintain computerized daily attendance records and providing immediate feedback to the Court about a defendant's participation status.

The available evidence suggests that the Midtown Community Court had a marked influence on compliance rates for short-term community service sentences. This was partly because the design of the Court made it difficult for some defendants to fail, by providing escorts to the scheduling floor and by scheduling some defendants to carry out their sentence on the day of arraignment. In addition, tight procedures for monitoring compliance and maintaining up-to-date information on the Court's computer network sent a message to defendants that alternative sentences were taken seriously. There is clear evidence that aggregate community service compliance rates are higher at Midtown than at the Downtown court (75% compared to 50%) and that some populations thought to pose a high-risk of non-compliance (e.g., prostitutes) had relatively high rates of compliance at the Midtown Community Court. Yet the data available for the Downtown court were insufficient to control for underlying differences in charge, criminal history and arrest type (summary or DAT), making it difficult to generate precise estimates of the extent of the Court's impact on compliance rates for a matched group of cases.

Community conditions There was substantial evidence that the Court had contributed to improvements in quality-of-life conditions in Midtown. Together, observations of local "hot spots," interviews with offenders, analysis of arrest data, focus group interviews and interviews with local police, community leaders and residents pointed to substantial reductions in concentrations of prostitution and unlicensed vending in Midtown. In addition, community members reported a marked reduction in graffiti along Ninth Avenue, the commercial strip that serves the residential community.

The Court contributed to these improvements in a variety of ways: by assigning community service crews to clean up local eyesores; by imposing lengthy community service sentences on repeat offenders, thereby increasing the costs of "doing business" in Midtown; and by offering help to those defendants who were ready to change their lifestyles. Several factors converged to produce a general improvement in neighborhood conditions—increased police enforcement, clean-up crews provided by Business Improvement Districts, the redevelopment of the Times Square Area and general economic development in Midtown as a whole. The Court's "attentive publics" saw it as one of several, mutually supportive contributors to the marked improvement in quality-of-life conditions in the Midtown area.

Community attitudes Before the Midtown Community Court opened, observers voiced mixed expectations about the project's ability to transform sentence outcomes, promote community service compliance or improve community conditions. Community leaders and residents complained that courts paid insufficient attention to low-level crime and supported the effort to provide more constructive response to low-level offenses. Yet their expectations about what the Court might accomplish were muted by prior experience with failed neighborhood improvement initiatives. Courtroom staff (clerks, court officers, CJA interviewers) started out as skeptical observers, uncertain of the potential of the Court's technology, curious about how judges would use the expanded options available at Midtown and concerned about their role in the new Court. Some groups, including attorneys and local police, were initially skeptical about the Court.

Over time, the initial attitudes of community groups and some, but not all, criminal justice personnel changed substantially. The initial concerns gave way to specific questions about whether aspects of the Court might be adapted to other settings. The evolution of attitudes toward the new Court are described below:

- *Community leaders* Although community leaders were initially supportive of the community court experiment, their expectations about the project's ability to improve community conditions or help offenders change their lives were restrained. By the end of the research period, they were confident that the Court was having a broader influence than expected on individual offenders and on patterns of offending. They saw the Court as a major factor in the reduction in both prostitution and unlicensed vending and credited both the deterrent effect of punishment and the availability of court-based services.
- *Community residents* Community residents, even those involved in community activities, knew less about the

Court than community leaders. Community members who were active in neighborhood organizations were generally aware of its existence and its plans for community service sentencing. They were initially skeptical about the possibility of neighborhood change, based on prior experience with highly publicized improvement efforts. By the end of the first year, they gave the new Court credit for reducing local quality-of-life problems.

- *Police officers* Although police management and precinct supervisors strongly supported the new Court, local police doubted that the Court might improve community conditions. By the end of the first year, many local officers, especially community police officers, had become vocal supporters. They were particularly impressed with the Court's impact on prostitution and associated low-level offenses. Although some local officers remained skeptical about the project's ability to supervise community service crews, precinct managers requested the assistance of community service crews in maintaining the local station house.
- *Judges* Judges reported that they "did things differently at Midtown" because expanded information and strict accountability promoted the use of court-based alternative sanction programs. They were confident that they could find out what happened when they sentenced an offender to court-based programs, including long-term treatment, and were, therefore, more willing to take risks. They also reported that judges at the Downtown court took Midtown sentences seriously, because they recognized that alternative sanctions were monitored more rigorously than they were Downtown.
- *Attorneys* At the outset, the District Attorney's Office and representatives of the Legal Aid Society had publicly opposed the development of the Midtown Community Court. The defense bar raised issues about the confidentiality of new information about defendants and about the possibility of "net widening" through an expansion of intermediate sanctions. Over time, defense attorneys also came to believe that their clients benefitted from the expanded array of social service sanctions and the ready access to court-based services.

  Prosecutors raised issues of cost and equity. They characterized the project as the "rich man's court" and argued that it favored business interests. They questioned the fairness of lavishing additional resources and top-quality court personnel on a single community, rather than working to improve outcomes and procedures at the Downtown court. They also challenged the equity of having sentences outcomes differ according to "geography." These issues persisted throughout the study period. Over time, the District Attorney's criticism focused increasingly on the reduced use of jail sentences at the Midtown Community Court.

- *Courtroom staff* Courtroom employees gradually changed from ambivalent observers to willing participants in the Court and advocates for court-based intermediate sanction programs. Although several were drawn to the project by the opportunity to work with cutting-edge technology, they reported frustration with the inefficiencies associated with its developmental stages.
- *Defendants* Defendants generally perceived the Midtown Community Court as cleaner, faster and tougher than the Downtown court. They were aware that community service sentences were more common at Midtown than Downtown and were aware that the Court monitored compliance closely: as one put it, "they know everything about you." Overall, they reported that sentencing was consistent and fair, even if tougher, and that program staff at Midtown "treat you like a human being."

A central achievement of the Court was the fact that it pulled together staff from different agencies—judges; court clerks and court officers; attorneys; CJA interviewers; police officers in the Court's holding cells; court-based community service and social service staff from non-profit and city agencies; administrative, technology and research staff—to work together as a team. Instead of being overwhelmed by "turf" issues and inter-agency skirmishes, personnel throughout the courthouse took part in the broad-based effort to ensure rigorous monitoring of offenders' compliance with the conditions imposed by the Court and to link troubled defendants to appropriate services. Many roles expanded beyond traditional job descriptions. Together, the project's mission-driven focus and relatively small scale had a palpable effect on the culture of the courthouse.

The Court's early months raised expectations about the likelihood that things might be done differently, both in community courts and in centralized courts, and demonstrated that the status quo can be changed.

Remaining Research Questions Some key questions about the Court can't be answered without a longer period of observation. The research to date has focused on implementation and preliminary impacts. A second phase of research on the Court will explore the longer-term effects of the project on quality-of-life conditions in the community; examine whether early impacts on case outcomes and compliance rates can be sustained in the face of an expanded and changing caseload; and focus on key issues that were not addressed in the first phase of the research. These include:

- the effect of the Court on recidivism rates for defendant sub-groups (e.g., high-rate repeat offenders; defendants who enter long-term treatment; defendants who are new to the criminal justice system);
- the overall effect of the Midtown Community Court on "jail time," compared to the Downtown court, including re-sentences following failure to complete alternative sanctions;
- the extent of community awareness of the Court and of changes in quality-of-life problems in the target area;
- the perceived value of court-based social services to service providers and defendant-participants;
- the overall costs and benefits of the experiment.

The cost-benefit analysis is particularly relevant to the early debate about the project. During the demonstration period, the project was subsidized by a mix of federal, city and private funds which helped support court-based services, technology development, community service supervision, community outreach efforts and project coordination. Critics questioned the cost-effectiveness of the new Court and argued that an infusion of funds and resources might be used effectively at the Downtown court.

Although the first phase of the research identified both cost savings and benefits—reduced arrest-to-arraignment time, community service contributions, reductions in prostitution, vending and graffiti—the dollar value of such benefits, particularly improvements in quality-of-life and community attitudes, is difficult to calculate. Can the impact of the Midtown Community

Court on quality-of-life conditions in Midtown be separated from the complementary influences of expanded enforcement, economic development and Business Improvement Districts? What are the trade-offs between the costs entailed by decentralization and the benefits of local delivery of justice? A final assessment of costs and benefits requires knowing whether early impacts were sustained and whether any additional system costs (e.g., total jail time) were identified.

The second phase of the research will also permit an examination of issues that surfaced during the first phase. These include: "feedback" effects on the court system as a whole; the influence of "start up" energy on preliminary accomplishments; and the relative contribution of the various complementary initiatives that contributed to improved conditions in Midtown Manhattan.

COMMUNITY-FOCUSED COURTS: DEVELOPING MODELS

The National Context

Over the past decade, courts around the nation have become increasingly interested in building bridges to communities and in developing the capacity to address broad community problems. This interest was fed by several factors, including:

- an awareness of widespread community dissatisfaction with court processes and court outcomes;
- a growing recognition of the need to move beyond case-by-case adjudication to develop constructive responses to specific problems (substance abuse, domestic violence);
- an awareness that courts can benefit from community partnerships in developing broader solutions to local problems; and
- a developing interest, fed by the victim's movement, in a "restorative justice" approach to low-level crime, that recognizes that communities are victimized by conditions of disorder.

The Midtown Community Court pulls together two trends, favoring the local adjudication of low-level offenses and new bridges between courts and communities. Some notable examples of these trends are described below.

Dispensing justice locally The first contemporary community court was established by the Los Angeles Municipal Court in 1987, to hear non-traffic misdemeanor cases arising from the Hollywood police precinct. The Hollywood court features locally delivered alternative sanctions, including treatment and education; community restitution; a recognition of the impact of highly concentrated prostitution markets on the neighborhood; and an individual calendaring system that assigns defendants to one of three permanent judges to promote judicial continuity across court appearances.

There are other examples as well. In Wichita, Kansas, Neighborhood Environmental Courts were established in 1995 under the Federal Weed and Seed Program to deal with local code violations (e.g., building, fire and zoning), traffic offenses and other violations. The courts convene in four police substations one evening per week (a time when employed local residents can attend). A judge, prosecutor and clerk travel the "circuit," holding court at each facility. Court hours were recently expanded to include a Drug Court component, with close links to treatment providers.

Improving court-community relations Other jurisdictions around the country have begun to introduce various forms of court-community collaboration within centralized court settings. Many courts began public education programs, including "meet your judge" sessions both at the court-house and in the community. Courts have also developed internship and volunteer programs that bring community members into the courthouse to give tours; staff information booths; serve as advocates for children and elderly individuals appearing before the court; and assist court personnel in their tasks.

Other jurisdictions have developed initiatives that foster dialogue between courts and communities, promote a community role in juvenile justice, or foster broad-based dispute resolution, as described below:[2]

- *Franklin County Futures Lab, Greenfield, Massachusetts* Based on a statewide effort to envision the future of Massachusetts courts, *Reinventing Justice 2022*, Greenfield established a Futures Lab Task Force in 1994 to develop mechanisms for promoting court-community dialogue and partnership. Representing a cross-section of neighborhoods, service providers, citizens and court officials, the 38-member Task Force convened a series of

Town Meetings to review concerns about the justice system, establish long-term goals and begin to develop solutions.

- *Juvenile Conference Committees, Hudson County, New Jersey* In Hudson County, volunteer Juvenile Conference Committees (JCC), first established in 1952 and composed of community representatives, help dispose of one third of all delinquency cases entering Family Court. Court intake workers divert delinquency cases which would not receive a court hearing to local JCCs throughout the county. JCCs review the facts of the case and recommend dispositions to Family Court judges for approval. Although the program is administered centrally, community groups, carefully selected to match the racial and ethnic composition of the area, play a central role in the diversion and sentencing process.
- *Citizen Advisory Council, Norfolk Juvenile and Domestic Relations Court, Norfolk, Virginia* In 1984, a Citizen Advisory Council was established to advise the Director of the Court Services Unit about developing and extending links between courts and service providers; producing annual reports to the Court about local facilities that provide services to local children under court orders; and making recommendations to the Court and the General Assembly about legislation affecting children and domestic relations law.
- *Peacemaking Division, Navajo Nation* A traditional feature of Navajo culture, Peacemakers are selected by clan members for their communication and leadership skills. Peacemakers follow an established ceremonial pattern to foster dispute resolution. In 1992, a Peacemaker division was added to adversarial courts to promote the resolution of community disputes through problem-solving and consensus building.
- *Handgun Intervention Program, 36th District Court, Michigan* A local judge, working with probation officers, police officers, religious leaders and community members, introduced a half-day program for juvenile and adult offenders charged with handgun-related offenses. Attendance is a mandatory condition of pretrial release. A local task force, community organization and volunteers have established a structured curriculum about the risks of handguns and developed procedures for linking defendants to the program.

Defining Community Courts

The court-community collaborations reviewed above represent a growing hunger for community-focused justice. This hunger reflects an even broader trend toward expanding community-focused criminal justice initiatives, including community policing, community prosecution, community courts and community probation. In 1996, an NIJ monograph provided an overview of such initiatives and, more recently, Attorney General Reno embraced a community-focused court agenda (Reno, 1996). These initiatives share a recognition that public safety problems are rooted in neighborhood conditions and often require local solutions.

With the exception of community policing, most forms of "community-focused" justice—courts, prosecution, probation—are in their infancy. In the case of community courts, there are relatively few existing models and no clear definition of what a generic "community court" is.

Identifying core components of a community court The planners of the Midtown Community Court have proposed a preliminary definition of the core components of community courts. In a memo reviewing plans for future community courts in New York City, they defined such courts as "decentralized, problem-solving courts that look to go beyond case processing to improve the quality of life and address local conditions of disorder." This definition touches upon core components of the Midtown model: a decentralized setting in a self-contained target community; a dedication to solving local quality-of-life problems; strict accountability; and the support of a broad array of partnerships with local organizations, providing court-based social services and community service supervision. Three central features—community base, community focus and community partnerships—are key components of the Midtown model, closely linked to the Court's over-arching problem-solving agenda.

Planners contend that community-focused, problem-solving courts work best locally. They point to key accomplishments—the collaborative development of community restitution projects, community dialogue and feedback, partnerships with local police—that flourish in a neighborhood setting. They also acknowledge that community courts require more than a community location. A satellite traffic court, for example, although less remote and more efficient than a centralized court part, is not dedicated to identifying and responding to community problems. Whether or not decentralization is an essential component of community-focused courts, it is clearly not *sufficient* to make a court be community-focused.

Some suggest introducing a community-focused agenda within a centralized setting while others point to community-focused initiatives, begun in centralized settings, that promote a local role in the adjudication process (community panels, peer courts). Still others cite specialty courts (drug courts, domestic violence courts) as an example. Such courts establish partnerships with community-based service providers to help solve problems that cut across individual cases. Yet, specialized court parts do not focus on the specific problems of a designated target area nor do they establish a broader role for community members at the court.

Research on the Midtown Community Court provides an opportunity to begin the process of distinguishing between *core* components of a model and *complementary* components, which support the objectives of the court, but may not be essential to future replication. The following represents a preliminary effort to identify core components of a community court, including:

- *Collaborative problem-solving agenda* A distinguishing feature of community courts is the recognition that courts can take broad responsibility for community problems, rather than focus entirely on individual case adjudication. Community courts practice collaborative problem-solving on several levels. On a case level, they attempt to provide more constructive outcomes for individual cases by responding holistically to the defendant before the court. On a community level, they marshall resources to address broad-based local problems, including conditions of disorder, community-level disputes, substance abuse, domestic violence, environmental issues, and so on. They also address systemic problems, by identifying and responding to inefficiencies and discontinuities in the criminal justice process.
- *Designated target area* Community courts serve self-contained communities with an identifiable set of problems. In some settings, the target area might be a single neighborhood or set of neighborhoods. In small jurisdictions, an entire town or village might constitute the court's target community.
- *Community partnerships* Community courts establish broad-based partnerships with community organizations,

local government agencies and local businesses. These partnerships provide court-based services; supervision for community service projects; community volunteer programs; and guidance for new initiatives, designed to address local problems.

- *Accountability* Community courts require defendants in both civil and criminal cases to be fully accountable for complying with conditions imposed by the court. Community courts establish procedures for ensuring timely and accurate reporting about compliance and hold community partners accountable for transmitting information about defendant participation in external programs to the court.
- *Judicial sponsorship* Community courts rely upon the support of administrative or chief judges and dedicated courtroom judges, who are willing to accept an expanded judicial role. Like judges in specialized drug courts and domestic violence courts, community court judges may engage defendants directly in dialogue as they craft and monitor constructive sentences. Community court judges may also be called upon to participate in community meetings and become direct partners in developing new approaches to address the problems of defendants appearing before the court.
- *Institutionalized dialogue* During the planning stage, community members play an active role in the process of identifying central problems and developing solutions. Once implemented, community courts establish mechanisms for promoting dialogue and disseminating information, including community advisory boards, public meetings, meet-the-judge sessions, town hall conferences, newsletters, outreach campaigns, etc. Court-community dialogue is structured to avoid discussion of individual cases, so that judges can participate without risk to their independence and impartiality.
- *Reflective courthouse* Judges and staff in community courts participate in a reflective organizational style conducive to redefining how the court does business. Community courts monitor their own performance. They rely upon an internal analytic capacity to assess their ability to meet specified objectives, identify emerging problems and assess attempted solutions.
- *Consumer focus* Community courts are designed to permit easy access. They promote a "user friendly"

atmosphere through physical design, signage, information booths, staff training in customer relations and other mechanisms.

Other *complementary* features of community courts are central to their mission and supportive of their objectives. As community courts evolve in other settings it is anticipated that they will include many of the following components:

- *Infrastructure for Assessment and Matching* Community courts take advantage of technology to increase the information available to the court and to support individualized decision-making and judicial monitoring.
- *Restorative justice and community mediation* Community courts recognize that neighborhoods as a whole are victimized by the fear of crime and by quality-of-life offenses. As part of their problem-solving agenda, community courts attempt to "pay back" the communities that are harmed by crime and to resolve local disputes through mediation. They may draw upon community impact panels to demonstrate the cost of offending to defendants.
- *Court-based services* By locating services "under one roof," community courts can re-define the courthouse as a gateway to treatment and related services. Court-based services promote immediacy, permitting service providers to build upon the crisis of arrest to motivate defendants to get help.
- *Non-traditional resources* Community courts draw upon public-private partnerships to leverage support for problem-solving initiatives. They may also draw upon non-traditional funding streams to access community-based services, innovative technology and other resources that support identified objectives.
- *Experimental role* Community courts define themselves as inherently experimental. They serve as platforms for testing new approaches to traditional models. In contrast to traditional courts, they are likely to evolve substantially from year to year as they develop new procedures, partnerships and programs in response to developing problems.

Replication Efforts

The Midtown Community Court has already fostered substantial interest in replication, both locally and nationally. Several

New York City neighborhoods and a number of urban jurisdictions around the country are eager to establish their own community courts. Some are interested in replicating the Midtown model in distressed center cities or adapting the model to other settings, including inner-city neighborhoods. Others are interested in adapting features of the Midtown model—innovative technology, on-site services—to a centralized court setting.

As new models of community courts develop, both locally and nationally, they are likely to differ from the Midtown Community Court. Because community problems vary from place to place, problem-solving courts will vary accordingly. Depending upon the neighborhood, courts might address a variety of civil and criminal matters—domestic violence; widespread delinquency; environmental crimes; landlord-tenant disputes; community-wide patterns of addiction, linked to neighborhood-based drug markets.

The role played by the community is also likely to vary. In some jurisdictions, community distrust of the courts might emerge as a primary problem. Such jurisdictions might focus on developing mechanisms for promoting community involvement in the disposition or diversion of non-felony matters, such as peer courts, community impact panels, victim impact panels and trained community mediators. They might make extensive use of meet-the-judge sessions; town hall conferences, bringing together community members and criminal justice personnel; legal education; adopt-a-school programs; and other community-focused court initiatives.

The partnerships and political coalitions that support community courts are also likely to vary from place to place. In some jurisdictions, the prosecution and defense bars might be active partners. If probation departments are under the Court's supervision, probation officers might play an active role in linking defendants to service programs and promoting accountability for compliance with court orders. Non-profit organizations, a strong component of criminal justice programming in New York City, may have a less prominent role.

Local initiatives Community groups in some Manhattan neighborhoods, intrigued by early reports about community "pay back," court-based services and improved quality-of-life conditions in Midtown, have begun exploring the feasibility of developing their own neighborhood courts. The prospect of developing community courts in other New York City neighborhoods—including the Red Hook area of Brooklyn, Upper Manhattan,

Greenwich Village—has raised issues about how the Midtown model might be adapted to other areas with different populations, different caseloads and different problems.

New York City's second community court, to be located in the Red Hook area of Brooklyn, is slated to open in the fall of 1999, bolstered by recent support from the Bureau of Justice Assistance. Red Hook is a geographically and socially isolated community with very different characteristics than Midtown. Over 70 percent of residents live in public housing. Drug sales and drug use are rampant; domestic violence and juvenile delinquency are far more prevalent than in Midtown.

The Red Hook Community Justice Center is a collaborative project of the New York State Unified Court System, the City of New York, the Kings County District Attorney and the Fund for the City of New York. It will adjudicate defendants arrested for selected offenses in two target precincts and other defendants, who live in the neighborhood and commit offenses in other parts of Brooklyn. Court operations will be multi-jurisdictional, hearing criminal, civil and family court matters, including landlord-tenant disputes, small claims, delinquency cases and domestic violence cases.

The Justice Center will adapt key features of the Midtown model—community restitution; court-based services; and aggressive problem-solving—to a different type of setting: a low-income inner-city neighborhood. In contrast to Midtown, where the defendant population is drawn from the city as a whole, in Red Hook many defendants will be community residents. Both residents and defendants might benefit equally from an infusion of neighborhood-based services. Therefore, the Red Hook project will offer job training, drug treatment, domestic violence counseling and other services to the entire community—victims, family members and defendants alike.

Brooklyn Treatment Court In June 1996, the Brooklyn Treatment Court, jointly developed by the UCS/FCNY planning team responsible for the Midtown Community Court, began introducing key components of the Midtown model to a specialized drug court, within the centralized Brooklyn Supreme Court. Like Midtown, a central intake and case management unit connected to the Court serves as the hub of a criminal justice/service continuum for substance-abusing offenders. Other features include an infrastructure for assessing and matching defendants to appropriate programs; customized technology to support judicial decision-making and promote strict accountability; and a court-based service center staffed by project case managers, representatives of the Department of Health, nurse practitioners and other court-based service providers.

A grant from the State Justice Institute has permitted the Brooklyn Treatment Court to explore further possibilities for court-community collaboration in a centralized drug court setting. The grant will support a variety of efforts to build bridges between the treatment court and selected neighborhoods, including community-offender dialogues; community newsletters; volunteer programs; Adopt-a-School projects; and other community-focused initiatives.

Other forms of replication Several cities, including Baltimore, Atlanta and Philadelphia, have begun the process of planning community-based courts, built on the Midtown model, to promote constructive responses to low-level offenses in central cities. In these jurisdictions, there is strong support from business groups, based on a belief that addressing quality-of-life issues in central cities can help stabilize distressed "Downtown" neighborhoods and spur economic development. Other jurisdictions, including Hartford, Chicago, Boston and Portland, have also expressed interest in building community-focused courts. The list of interested jurisdictions is growing. Some jurisdictions have also expressed interest in adapting individual features of the Midtown model—innovative technology, on-site services—to a centralized court.

Early efforts to develop new community courts led to a recognition that the shape and functions of a community court must be adapted to the particular set of problems that a given neighborhood presents. Even among communities presenting radically different problems, there is one clear common element across jurisdictions: community courts require a comprehensive, collaborative planning effort to identify the central problems to be addressed, define how courts might intervene and recruit community resources to help solve those problems.

Emerging Issues

Potential replications of the Midtown model raise challenging questions about whether it's possible to define with precision what a generic community court is. Must a community-focused court be community-based? Does it require a stand-alone facility? Court-based services? Dedicated alternative sanction staff? Customized technology? Must it focus on quality-of-life crime?

What types of civil jurisdictions might work in a community court setting? Could smaller jurisdictions build strong community partnerships in a centralized setting?

The prospect of replicating community courts in other jurisdictions raises other questions as well. Do community courts require the full "weight" of formal court processing? Could they be staffed by lay magistrates or enhanced by creating designated community panels, charged with resolving relatively minor court matters? Do they require staff continuity and a shared sense of "mission" among staff?

Decentralization Several components of the Midtown Community Court are relevant for jurisdictions considering establishing decentralized problem-solving courts and for jurisdictions seeking to improve "business as usual" within a centralized setting—an expanded array of constructive sentence alternatives, court-based services, community service projects and innovative uses of technology. In the coming months there is likely to be increasing interest in identifying which features of the community court model might be adapted to centralized settings and which work best locally.

Some features of the Court might prove difficult to adapt to large-scale centralized settings. These include mechanisms for designing and administering neighborhood-specific restitution projects; broad-scale community collaboration and planning; neighborhood advisory groups; community-focused problem-solving; partnerships with local police; and mediation focused on community-level disputes. Other features of community courts are also linked to decentralization and the smaller scale of decentralized courts, as described below:

- reducing police travel time transporting defendants to central booking helps cut arrest-to-arraignment time and return police to the streets rapidly;
- working on a smaller scale helps clerks stay on top of the daily caseload, speeding case processing;
- fostering an integrated "team" approach can encourage productivity, help link defendants to appropriate services and help promote rigorous monitoring of court-imposed conditions.

At the Midtown Community Court, decentralization and manageable scale helped mitigate potential "turf" battles that arise all too frequently in centralized settings.

Evolving models: community-focused courts Decentralized community courts have re-emerged at the same moment as a variety of community-focused court initiatives. A review of these initiatives indicates four emerging models:

- *System-wide change: community-focused agenda* As in Franklin County, Massachusetts, entire communities may be enlisted in the effort to re-think how courts operate, how they relate to the communities they serve and how they might transform "business as usual." Such efforts are likely to focus on broad community concerns, rather than the problems of particular neighborhoods.
- *Fostering community dialogue* Some communities are seeking ways to improve court-community relations through institutionalized dialogue, such as town hall meetings, "meet the judge" sessions and other mechanisms. These initiatives are likely to develop in both centralized and decentralized settings.
- *Specialized courts* Drug courts, domestic violence courts and other specialized courts rely on community partnerships to develop solutions to specific sets of problems. To date, these courts have been introduced primarily in centralized settings. Specialized courts have generally not focused on the problems of specific neighborhoods or communities.
- *Community-based problem-solving courts* As exemplified by the Midtown Community Court and the Kansas City neighborhood courts, community-based courts can bring a variety of strategies to bear on the multiple problems of their designated target communities. Such courts work closely with community partners—leaders, residents, service organizations, businesses, local police—to develop constructive responses to criminal and civil matters before the court.

Future hurdles Reforms in criminal justice are notoriously susceptible to phases of early enthusiasm followed by retrenchment and reassessment. As the Midtown Community Court and other community courts move toward maturity, there are several hurdles ahead. Innovative projects can be difficult to sustain. Court projects that depend on a single charismatic leader may suffer when key personnel depart. The energy of the "start-up" period can dissipate as operations become institutionalized into a new form of "business as usual." In addition, community support that coalesces around a group of "hot" neighborhood problems may dwindle if there is either too little progress, discouraging further enthusiasm, or too much, reducing the perceived need for further collaboration.

Community courts, however, appear to have a more secure foundation than many other criminal justice experiments. By establishing broad-based partnerships among court officials, other criminal justice agencies, non-profits and community organizations, community courts will be well positioned to withstand key changes in personnel and community conditions. In addition, by maintaining a capacity for self-assessment, problem identification, response and analysis, problem-solving community-focused courts should be able to regenerate the energy of their "start-up" period as they address developing problems in their target communities.

There is still much to be learned about what happens to community courts as they mature. The time is ripe for this exploration. There is currently a groundswell of interest in both community-based and community-focused justice. In contrast to many previous experiments in court reform, which were stimulated by either external criticism (e.g., bail reform, speedy disposition initiatives) or federal funding opportunities (e.g., case processing reform), the current enthusiasm is largely driven by local initiative. The coming expansion of community-focused justice stems largely from courts' growing interest in improving how they do business, how they relate to the public, how they assess their own performance and how they contribute to the solution of the nation's serious problems.

Notes

1. Even before the Court opened, DATs issued in Midtown had higher rates of non-appearance than DATs issued elsewhere in Manhattan, after controlling for differences in charge. One possible explanation for this difference is that the population receiving DATs in Midtown is more transient—i.e., more often drawn from other boroughs and other cities—than the population receiving DATs in other locations.
2. Descriptions are based on material collected by the Community-Focused Courts Development Initiative, a project of the National Center for State Courts, funded by the Bureau of Justice Assistance. Other information about court-community collaboration is drawn from National Townhall Video Conference, jointly sponsored by the State Justice Institute, the American Judicature Society and the National Center for State Courts.

Appendix

COMMUNITY DEMOGRAPHICS

Surrounding Areas

	MCC Catchment	Community Board 2 (Greenwich Village)	Community Board 6 (East Side)	Community Board 8 (Upper East Side)	Manhattan overall	NYC
Race/ethnicity						
White	66%	78%	81%	87%	49%	43%
Latino	20%	6%	7%	6%	26%	24%
Black	8%	3%	4%	3%	18%	25%
Other	6%	13%	8%	4%	7%	8%
Unemployment Rate	7.1%	4.9%	4.5%	3.9%	8.0%	9.0%
Percent persons 25 and over						
with High School Diploma	84%	86%	93%	92%	75%	68%
with Bachelor's Degree	47%	59%	59%	65%	42%	23%
Percent Homeless	3.9%	1.4%	1.2%	0.1%	1.2%	0.5%
Percent Households with Below Poverty Incomes	16%	5%	8%	3%	21%	19%

GLOSSARY OF TERMS

ACD

Adjournment in Contemplation of Dismissal. ACDs specify that the case will be dismissed and sealed unless the defendant is rearrested within the next six months. Defendants whose cases are disposed through an ACD in New York City generally have little prior involvement with the criminal justice system. In recent years, judges have increasingly imposed intermediate sanctions (e.g., one day of community service) with ACDs. If the defendant is rearrested or fails to comply with the conditions imposed by the court, the case can be restored to the calendar.

The ACD is a disposition, not a sentence. It is comparable to the disposition of "Continued without a Finding" in some jurisdictions.

Adjournment

In New York City, misdemeanor cases that are not disposed at arraignment are "adjourned" or "continued" to an all-purpose part. Because the Midtown Community Court is designated as an arraignment part, cases that are not disposed at arraignment are adjourned to an all-purpose part at the Downtown court.

CD

Conditional Discharge. Sentences of conditional discharge in New York State can specify participation in alternative sanctions, such as community service, treatment readiness programs, long-term drug treatment, etc.

CPL

New York State Criminal Procedure Law.

CJA

The Criminal Justice Agency, New York City's pretrial services agency.

DAT

Desk Appearance Tickets (DATs) in New York City schedule individuals arrested on misdemeanor charges to appear at a specified future arraignment date. According to police policy, DATs cannot be issued to arrestees who lack identifications; are under the influence of drugs or alcohol; or have been arrested for photographable offenses (prostitution, soliciting prostitution, and trademark counter- feiting) or marijuana sales. DATs are similar to citations in many jurisdictions.

FCNY

The Fund for the City of New York.

"Forum shopping"

Defendants who adjourn their cases at arraignment in an effort to get a better offer from a judge sitting in an all-purpose part are "forum shopping," also known as "judge shopping."

NCSC
: The National Center for State Courts.

NYPD
: The New York City Police Department.

Part
: Courtroom.

"Stroll"
: Location where street prostitution takes place. Also known as "track."

Time served
: Sentences of time served are issued to defendants who have been detained before their case is disposed. Although these sentences are incarcerative, they do not impose additional jail time beyond the time served in detention before disposition.

"Walk"
: Criminal justice professionals in New York City frequently characterize court outcomes in which no punishments are imposed as "walks." In this report, walks include ACDs in which no conditions are imposed, sentences of time served and CDs in which no conditions are imposed.

REFERENCES

Abrams, R. 1993 "Prostitution and the Midtown Community Court: A New Look at the World's Oldest Profession." New Haven: Yale Law School (unpublished paper).

Adams, E. 1992 "Misdemeanor Court Set for Midtown Site." *New York Law Journal,* July 16:1.

Anderson, D. 1997 "Crime Stoppers." *The New York Times Magazine,* February 9:47–52.

Bazemore, G. and Umbreit, M. 1994 *Balanced and Restorative Justice.* Washington, DC: Office of Juvenile Justice and Delinquency Prevention.

Bennet, J. 1992 "A New Court for Midtown to Combat Area Crime." *The New York Times,* July 16:B1.

Carter Goble Associates 1985 *Palm Beach County Judicial Master Plan.*

Clear, T. and Hardyman, P. 1990 "The New Intensive Supervision Movement." *Crime and Delinquency,* 36:42–60.

Crosson, M. 1990 "When Court is Just Around the Corner." *Newsday,* November 12:45.

Daly, W. 1995 "Law Enforcement in Times Square, 1970s–1990s." In, Robert McNamara (Ed.), *Sex Scams and Street Life*, pp. 99–106. Westport: Praeger.

Deschenes, E., Turner, S. and Greenwood, P. 1994 "Drug Court or Probation?: An Experimental Evaluation of Maricopa County's Drug Court." *Justice System Journal* 18(1):55.

DeStefano, A. 1990 " 'Lay Judges' Eyed for Class B Crime." *Newsday,* February 20:3.

Dykstra, G. 1995 "The Times Square Business Improvement District and Its Role in Changing the Face of Times Square." In, Robert McNamara (Ed.), *Sex Scams and Street Life,* pp. 75–83. Westport: Praeger.

Eckstein, B. 1993 *Perspectives on Quality of Life Offenses and the Midtown Community Court: A Qualitative Study.* New York: National Center for State Courts.

Eckstein, B. 1995 *Perspectives on the Midtown Community Court One Year Later: The Second Phase of Qualitative Study.* New York: National Council for State Courts.

Feeley, M. 1979 *The Process is the Punishment.* New York: Russell Sage Foundation.

General Accounting Office 1995 *Drug Courts: Information on a New Approach to Address Drug-Related Crime.* Washington, DC: GAO.

Glaberson, W. 1990 "New Community Courts Urged in New York City," *The New York Times,* September 27:B1.

Goldkamp, J. and Weiland, D. 1993 *Assessing the Impact of Dade County's Felony Drug Court, Final Report.* Philadelphia: Crime and Justice Research Institute.

Goldstein, H. 1990 *Problem-Oriented Policing.* New York: McGraw-Hill.

Greene, J. and Mastrofski, S. (Eds.) 1988 *Community Policing: Rhetoric or Reality.* New York: Praeger.

Hardenbergh, D. 1991 *The Courthouse: A Planning and Design Guide for Court Facilities.* Williamsburg, VA: National Center for State Courts.

Horowitz, C. 1993 "How Bad is It?" *New York Magazine*, October 18:58–64.

Johnson, E. 1978 *Courts and the Community.* Williamsburg, VA: National Center for State Courts.

Kelling, G. and Coles, C. 1996 *Fixing Broken Windows.* New York: The Free Press.

Levitt, L. 1992 "Community Courthouse Set to Open in Midtown." *New York Newsday,* July 15:33.

MacKenzie, D. 1990 "Boot Camps: Components, Evaluation and Empirical Issues." *Federal Probation,* September.

Mahoney, B. 1994 "Drug Courts: What Have We Learned So Far?" *Justice System Journal* 17(1):127.

Mastrofski S. 1988 "Community Policing as Reform: A Cautionary Tale." In, J. Greene and S. Mastrofski (Eds.), *Community Policing: Rhetoric or Reality,* pp. 47–67. Westport: Praeger.

McDonald, D. 1982 *Punishment Without Walls.* New Brunswick, NJ: Rutgers University Press.

McElroy, J., Cosgrove, C., and Sadd, S. 1992 *Community Policing: The CPOP in New York.* Beverly Hills, CA: Sage.

Midtown Community Court 1994 *The Midtown Community Court Experience: A Progress Report.* New York: Midtown Community Court.

Moore M. and Kelling G. 1983 "To Serve and Protect: Learning from Police History." *The Public Interest*, Winter:7.

Morris, N. and Tonry, M. 1990 *Between Prison and Probation: Intermediate Punishments in a Rational Sentencing System.* New York: Oxford University Press.

National Clearinghouse for Criminal Justice Planning and Architecture 1976 *Statewide Court Planning.* Champaign, IL: University of Illinois.

New York Newsday 1990 "Junior Judges to the Rescue." February 28:30.

Newmark S. 1995 "The 42nd Street Development Project." In, Robert McNamara (Ed.), *Sex Scams and Street Life,* pp. 67–75. Westport: Praeger.

Pate A. et al. 1986 *Reducing Fear of Crime in Newark and Houston.* Washington, DC: Police Foundation.

Petersilia, J. 1987 *Expanding Options for Criminal Sentencing.* Santa Monica, CA: The Rand Corporation.

Reno J. 1996 "Keynote Address." The National Conference on the Future of the Judiciary. Willamsburg, VA, March 24.

Skogan, W. 1990 *Disorder and Decline: Crime and the Spiral of Decay in American Neighborhoods.* New York: Free Press.

Sontag, Deborah 1993 "Unlicensed Peddlers, Unfettered Dreams." *The New York Times*, June 14:A1.

Supreme Judicial Court, Commonwealth of Massachusetts 1992 *Reinventing Justice.* Boston.

Trojanowicz, R. and Carter, D. 1988 *The Philosophy and Role of Community Policing.* Community Policing Series No. 13. East

Lansing, MI: National Neighborhood Foot Patrol Center, Michigan State University.

von Hirsch, A. and Ashworth, A. (Eds.) 1992 *Principled Sentencing.* Boston: Northeastern University Press.

Wilson, J. and Kelling, G. 1982 "Broken Windows: The Police and Neighborhood Safety." *The Atlantic Monthly,* March:29–38.

Yankelovich, Skelly et al. 1978 *The Public Image of the Courts: A National Survey of the General Public, Judges, Lawyers and Community Leaders.* Yankelovich, Skelly and White, Inc.

Young, M. 1995 *Restorative Community Justice: A Call to Action.* Washington, DC: National Organization for Victim Assistance.

INDEX